IMO Workbook

Part IV

IMO Level I and II Grade IV

CBSE, IGCSE, State Boards, Olympiads, Talent Search

Combination of 100 Worksheets and Self-Assessment Modules

Chandan Sukumar Sengupta

 We learn many things and also come across many experiences in our daily life. Some of such experiences strike our mind to a greater extent and some of the gained experiences remain as an off-sided thing because of the ignorance of our mind. Learning, as one can go through in life, is not any forceful effort of the mind. It should have a support of mind, body and intellect. Then only it can bring variations in our thought process. There are so many faculties through which the learning of a student might move on. It may be a hybrid faculty combining some of the inter-related streams of study; such as Astronomy and Physics will jointly make the faculty of Astro-Physics; Geology and Information Technology will make the faculty of Geo-Informatics and many more. Parents often claim that their ward is proficient in some of the selected faculties and work with limitations in some other. Actually the trend of the study of a learner is a non-identifiable trend because of the chance of its alterations in relation to time. One cannot guess about the affinity of the brain before the age of 13 of a student. Learning affinity and allied success largely depends upon the combination of parenting and related service linings. Only parenting and any service lining without parenting may not bring any desired result in time. Combination of both the factor can link up the milestones leading ultimately towards success.

India Government has decided to centralise the process of admissions to various Graduate level Medical Colleges. This admission process will be accomplished by the entrance examinations taken up by National Testing Agency (or NTA). Aspirants having a willingness to attain the Entrance Examination conducted by NTA or other such testing agency should have access to the knowledge system duly prescribed for the prevalent knowledge drilling and information delivery pattern. Preparation for such kind of testing is also a job which requires prolonged involvement of the fellow learner. The learner with such willingness should have a strong base of knowledge which will ensure the smooth and swift propagation of mind and intellect through the definite path of success.

We restrict our discussion to the limit of the content areas for which the present workbook is having some inputs. Students of class six should have a proper understanding of basic shapes, number system, daily life problems and ecological concerns. Most of the problems are related to daily experiences and normal operational concerns.

It is expected that students should go on facing day to day problems from science, mathematics and humanities. They should also address problems related to high order thinking skills. They also participate in online digital classes and social media platforms for exploring relevant information on certain topic. Hunting merely for information may not fulfil the purpose in particular. Information duly collected should have adequate alignment with facts and figures for ensuring the process of remembering and recollecting such kinds of learning during need.

Arabinda Nagar, Bankura - 722101 WB , India

This book is prepared for fellow aspirants of Grade 4 and 5 of National and International Curriculum.

Contents

Foreword

The curriculum recommended by CBSE and ICSE are on the same format like those developed and implemented by different state level educational organisations. After integrating all such streams a common core of the curriculum is duly obtained for making the book a widely applicable one. Some of the mathematical problems are from past test papers. In some papers there may remain some questions of identical format. All such questions will be addressed only after proper understanding of the relevant theories.

Some of inter related areas are converged to bring compactness in the representation of the content areas. There may exist some types of questions in more than two places with an aspiration of exhibiting its composite nature.

Before moving through the collection of worksheets and related fields of activities it is recommended for all the students that one should go through the content areas duly provided by the authority of examinations.

After such thorough practices one can opt for the composite worksheets with some easiness.

Major areas of the curriculum are as follows:

1. The number system and its application in our day to day life.
2. Representing a whole number in the number line.
3. Factors and multiples.
4. Measurements of length, mass temperature and time.
5. Basic shapes of two dimensions and three dimensions.
6. Mean, median and mode.

Numbers may be divisible by 2 (Even Numbers) or may not be divisible by 2 (Odd Numbers). Numbers having only 2 factors ; 1 and the number itself are called prime numbers.

A list of prime numbers between 1 and 200 :

2, 3, 5, 7, 11, 13, 17, 19, 23, 29, 31, 37, 41, 43, 47, 53, 59, 61, 67, 71, 73, 79, 83, 89, 97, 101, 103, 107, 109, 113, 127, 131, 137, 139, 149, 151, 157, 163, 167, 173, 179, 181, 191, 193, 197, and 199.

2 and 3 are a pair of consecutive prime numbers.

A prime number 2 less or 2 more than another prime are called twin prime numbers. You can find more than a pair of twin primes from the list of primes provided.

For example: 11 and 13; 17 and 19; 29 and 31; and so on.

We are also incorporating few words from the faculty of mathematics. Most of the part of publication is based on the pattern of questions people select for Olympiads, Talent Search Examinations and other competitive examinations of similar nature. This publication also introduces a learner with some apprehensions of Critical thinking.

Mathematics deals with some fundamental aspects related to time and space. We all learn different rules and related operations starting from our elementary stage of schooling. Different students take the subject differently as per their interest and willingness. Some students calculate values with adequate speed and some other students do the same with lot of difficulties. We also point out the development of fear related to Mathematics in the mind of some of the fellow students. We cannot analyse the possible reasons of the development of such fear in the mind of students. This development cannot be generalised. It is not developed in the minds of all the fellow students. Things often become difficult when our fellow ward fail to correlate the linkages of real life problems with that of mathematical ones. It is the main reason of the lack of proper orientation in the process of the development of mathematical skills. A skilful student can correlate both the aspects of mathematics and real life problems with much efficiency. A skilful student of mathematics should be a good observer, a perfect planner, optimum analyser and abled calculator. Some students can take much time in solving any individual mathematical problem that compared to the time taken by the other fellow from the same peer group. This book is designed to expose a student to different types of mathematical problems from the allied fields of the curriculum specified for the middle school. It is expected that this workbook can equip a student in different ways and enable them to acquire mathematical skills with a long lasting impression in mind.

Preface

This book is for aspirants looking for some more practices to enhance their mathematical skills and competence. It can be used only after completing the text books and reference books recommended by the school of the fellow learner. This book accommodates all possible streams of curriculum prescribed for the students belonging to the age group of 09 to 13 years. It can even help them in gaining skills of tackling composite mathematical problems duly coined for addressing more than three and more basic skills.

Answers of individual problems are not included in this booklet. There exists a separate collection for fulfilling such purposes. Due to this reason this handbook can be used by teachers and fellow parents for assessing achievement levels of their aspirants.

For all students it would be better if they acquire such skills in advance before moving through the composite worksheets.

A book can provide timely relevant support to students. It can even equip a student differently for making oneself fit for accepting challenges of some broad spectrum. This collection is exclusively meant for students aspiring for examinations of Standard 4th. It can also provide adequate references to students aspiring for various competitive examinations. The collection of this series is coming in accord to the subject areas.

Basic Mathematics is the field of study which is common for most of the competitive examinations. The general understanding on the theories and their applications is the general expectation of examiners from a student of school education. One should understand the application of scientific temperaments for solving day to day problems. Ecology and environment is the common core of content areas for all possible levels of discussions related to science and scientific observations.

We expect a kind of understanding from students of Grade IV of the National Curriculum. The fellow student should understand the number system and related operations. There are some relationships exist in between number systems of various types. We often come across four different number systems in computer Science. For the class works and mathematical operations as mentioned in their respective workbooks meant for school students we restrict our discussion to decimal system only.

I hope the kind of effort and combination of problems might enhance the knowledge base of our fellow students.

Questions are there without respective answers. It can be obtained from the source. There exists a plan of fulfilling dual purpose of the effort. These sets can be utilized to engage a student for working out the possible outputs without being inflicted primarily with answers. If answers are provided alongside the questions then the material will fulfill half of the purpose. It cannot contingent for overcoming the problems and also cannot facilitate in skill enhancement efforts. Set of questions can be used for the purpose of assessing skill acquisition process and also can be assigned to the ward by parents and guides.

This workbook contains some activity sheets and reference worksheets suitable for the students of Grade 4. It is also suitable for aspirants preparing for Olympiads and other such enrichment activities. Answer sheets with explanations are there in a separate sheet. It will enable parents and teachers for organizing the task in a better way. I am confident enough about the competence of fellow students having willingness to move up to the final stage of the Mathematics Enrichment Activities of various stages. There are different worksheets in accord to the time of studies that can be assigned to the fellow student. Answers are in a separate sheet paper that can be kept at different place. Parents and teachers use this book of activities to develop interest of students on mathematical as well as analytical skills.

For Students

We expect a kind of understanding from students of Grade 4 of the National Curriculum. The fellow student should understand the number system and related operations. There are some relationships exist in between number systems of various types. For the class works and mathematical operations of Grade 4 we restrict our discussion to decimal system only.

I hope the kind of effort and combination of problems might enhance the knowledge base of our fellow students.

To Parents

Questions are there without respective answers. It can be obtained from the source. There exists a plan of fulfilling dual purpose of the effort. These sets can be utilized to engage a student for working out the possible outputs without being inflicted primarily with answers. If answers are provided alongside the questions then the material will fulfil half of the purpose. It cannot contingent for overcoming the problems and also cannot facilitate in skill enhancement efforts. Set of questions can be used for the purpose of assessing skill acquisition process and also can be assigned to the ward by parents and guide.

Whenever we come across any new events then our mind start recollecting different ideas related to our knowledge base. We also start correlating the reported events for assuring applicability of such knowledge base. Some of the events from our daily life often strike our mind differently. Why tooth pastes are basic in nature? Why room cleaners are acidic? Why metallic copper cannot react with salt solution of iron, zinc or sodium? Other such questions of particular types can be advanced to ascertain the need of intensive studies of the related areas of science for making oneself adequately equipped for accepting some higher challenges. This handbook provides ample scope of skill enhancement through offering series of test materials in which aspirants have to use more than one skill at a time. It will also improve the ability to think and work out own strategies of resolving mathematical problems.

There are mathematical problems which require knowledge of more than one thematic area. Such problems are incorporated in the collections of Composite worksheets. In this workbook such composite worksheets are more in number.

This activity book can provide an ample scope of learning to the fellow learners which are needed for improving their skills and competences related to science and technology. Extended worksheets and self-evaluation modules can be used for assessing the progress of the individual learner. Chapters are grouped on the basis of their inter-relations. These are also grouped on the basis of their subject areas.

It is not mandatory to go through all sets of problems, but not to skip any of the problems is recommended for assuring the perfect skill acquisition. Mathematics is the ever-growing field of knowledge. Most of the human activities depend directly or indirectly on the proposals of science. It also increases the basic understanding of a person regarding the day to day events and related concerns. We can even describe most of the daily events on the basis of our scientific observations.

Other books in this series are as follows:

1. Handbook of Mathematics
2. Creative Mathematics Book 4 Part 1
3. Olympiad and Talent
4. Aspirations of Mathematics
5. My Own Book of School Mathematics.
6. Everyday Mathematics Part I, II and III
7. My Mathematics Companion Part I to V
8. IMO Mathematics Workbook Part I to Part VIII

All these books are suitable for students of School stage having age group 09 to 13 years.

Chandan Sukumar Sengupta

Things to Remember

1. We can construct 6 different three digit numbers by using digits 2, 4 and 8 only once.

   Six such numbers constructed by using digits 3, 6 and 9 are:

   369, 396, 639, 693, 963 and 936

2. There are two different types of numeration, one is Indo-Arabic system of numeration and the another one is International system of numeration. All numbers can be expressed in any of the given system of numeration.

   The given number : 125894534

   Indo- Arabic Numeration : 12,58,94,534

   Twelve crore, fifty-eight lakh ninety four thousand five hundred and thirty four

   The given number : 125,894,534

   One hundred twenty five million, eight hundred ninety –four thousand five hundred and thirty four.

3. Sum total of all the interior angles of a triangle is 180^0 .

4. Hour hand, minute hand and second hand of a clock complete one rotation by forming a complete angle at the center (360^0).

5. The greatest five digit number without repeating any digit twice is 98,765.

6. The smallest five digit number without repeating any digit twice is 10,234.

7. 3 must be subtracted from the greatest five digit number to make the value divisible by 4.

[99,999 – 3 = 99,996 ; $\frac{99,996}{4}$ = 24,999 ;]

8. Numbers having only 2 factors, 1 and the number itself, are called prime numbers. 1 is not a prime number. 2 is the smallest and only even prime number.
9. Any natural number and whole number can be represented in a number line.
10. All basic shapes having length and breadth are called 2 dimensional shapes.
11. All basic shapes having length breadth and height are called 3 dimensional shapes.
12. All basic shapes occupy a definite space.
13. All 2 dimensional shapes lie on a definite plane.
14. Two planes meet through a straight line.
15. Decimals are special types of fractions having denominators in the form of a multiple of 10.
16. Percentage is a special type of fraction having denominator 100.
17. All decimal numbers (continuing repeating types and terminating types) can be placed on the number line. Continuing non-repeating types of decimals cannot be placed on number line.
18. Clinical thermometer is graduated by using Fahrenheit (^{0}F) scale, but laboratory thermometers are graduated by using ^{0}C (Celsius) scale.
19. We can accommodate three non-overlapping triangles inside a pentagon.
20. Sum of all the interior angles of a quadrilateral is equal to two straight angles.
21. Sum of first 50 natural numbers is equal to (50 +1) X $\frac{50}{2}$.
22. We can draw three lines passing through two out of three non-collinear points.

A Model Paper

I: Write in scientific notation.

1. Tilottama bought 16 cakes by paying Rs sixteen hundred ninetysix. She wanted to collect another four cakes at the same rate. The total amount payable by her at the cash counter will be Rs. ______________.

2. A supermarket receives 625 cases of oranges. Each case holds 135 oranges. How many oranges in all does the supermarket receive?

3. Mr Bandarnayake got an assignment which can be finished by employing 13 workers for 12 days. New work order came for finishing the similar assignment in 13 days. Number of workers to be appointed at the new site will be _________.

4. 12% of 12% of $\frac{1}{144}$ X 13,013 = ___________.

5. Bandarnayake observed that a Goods Train covered a distance of 100 m in ten seconds. Another Mail train covers 72 km in one hour. Compare speed of both the train.

6. Mr. Bandarnayake finishes his journey of 120 km in 2 and half hours. While moving with same speed he has visited his native place and it took him 45 minutes to drive to and fro his native place from his home of countryside. Find the distance of his native place from the countryside.

7. What least number must be subtracted from a seven digit greatest number to make the number divisible by 11?

8. Convert the following:

   4 m 55 cm = _____ cm   7 m 6 cm = _____ cm   8 m 89 cm = _____ cm

   7 m 45 cm = _____ cm   3 m 16 cm = ______ cm   18 m 8 cm = _____ cm

   8 km 45 m = ____ km   5 km 520 m = _____ km   44 km 660 m = ____ km

   18 km 425 m = ____ km   5 km 50 m = _____ km   23 km 166 m = ____ km

9. Make 3 different 3 digit numbers using 1, 9 and 8, where each digit can be used only once.

   Check which of these numbers are divisible by 9.

10. Which numbers among 2, 3, 5, 6, 9 divides 12345 exactly? Write 12345 in reverse order and test now which numbers divide it exactly?

11. Write different 2 digit numbers using digits 3, 4 and 5. Check whether these numbers are divisible by 2, 3, 5, 6 and 9?

12. Write the smallest digit and the greatest possible digit in the blank space of each of the following numbers so that the numbers formed are divisible by 3.

   i. __ 6724   ii. 4765__ 2   iii. 7221__ 5

   Find the smallest number that must be added to 123, so that it becomes exactly divisible by 5?

II. Write in standard form.

13. 23×10^2 14. 9×10^3 15. 3.6×10^4 16. 3.09×10^5

17. 4.014×10^5 18. 1.01×10^5 19. 4.015×10^6 20. 6×10^7

21. 2.001×10^9 22. 4.090×10^7 23. 5.908×10^9 24. 1.2×1.004

III. Find out measure of missing angles in each of the following:

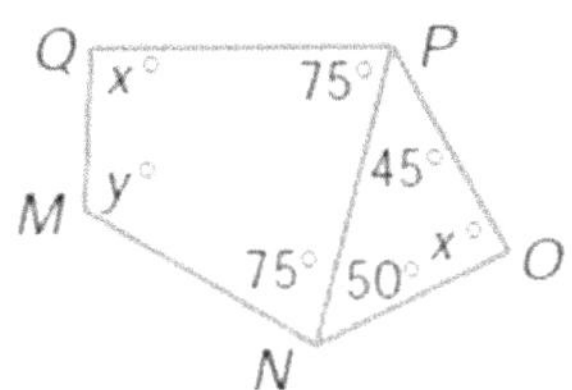

Figure P

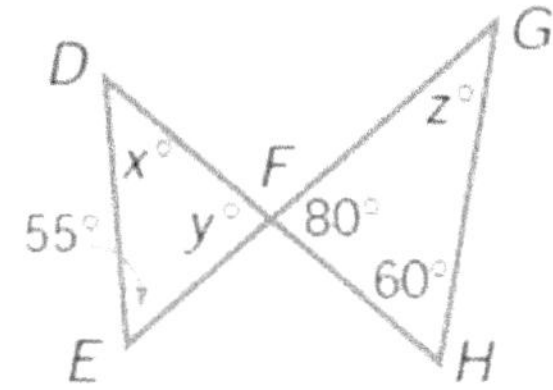

Figure Q

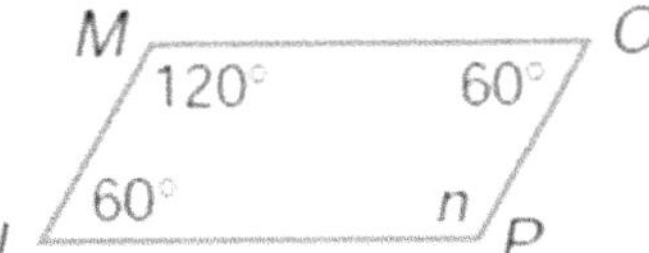

Figure R

Figure S

IV. If $x + 1/x = 2$, then $x^{2010} + x^{2009} =$ ____.

V: Find out value of variables in each of the following.

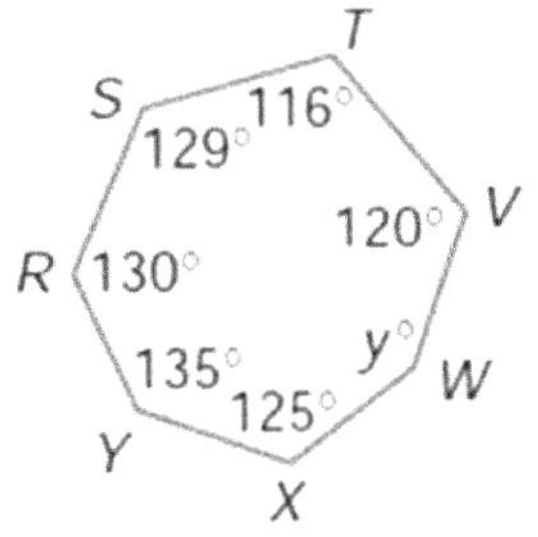

P

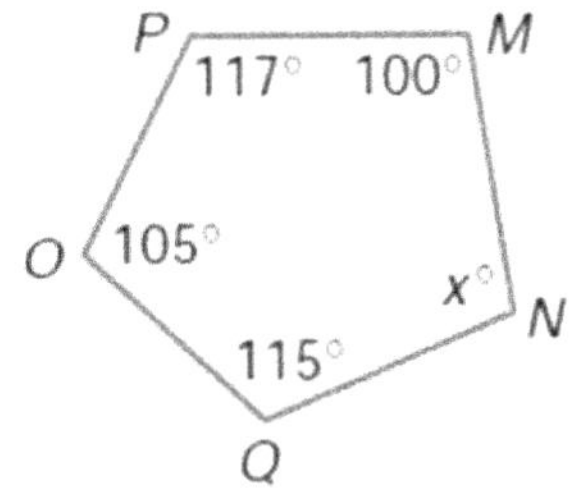

Q

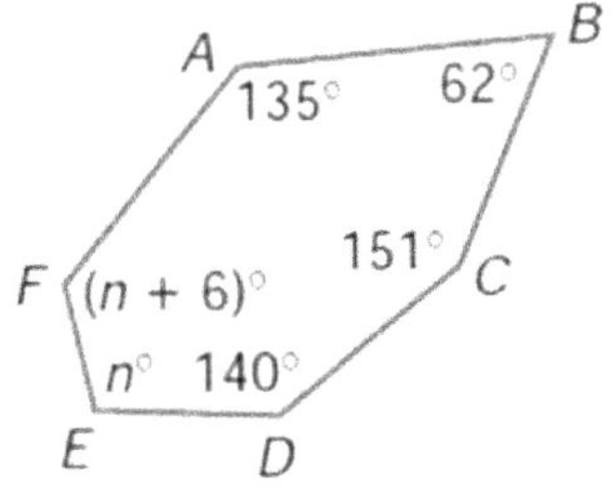

R

VI. How many non-overlapping triangles can be accommodated in each of the following?

1. heptagon
2. nonagon
3. quadrilateral
4. decagon
5. hexagon
6. octagon
7. 15-gon
8. 17-gon

VII. Calculate area of the following.

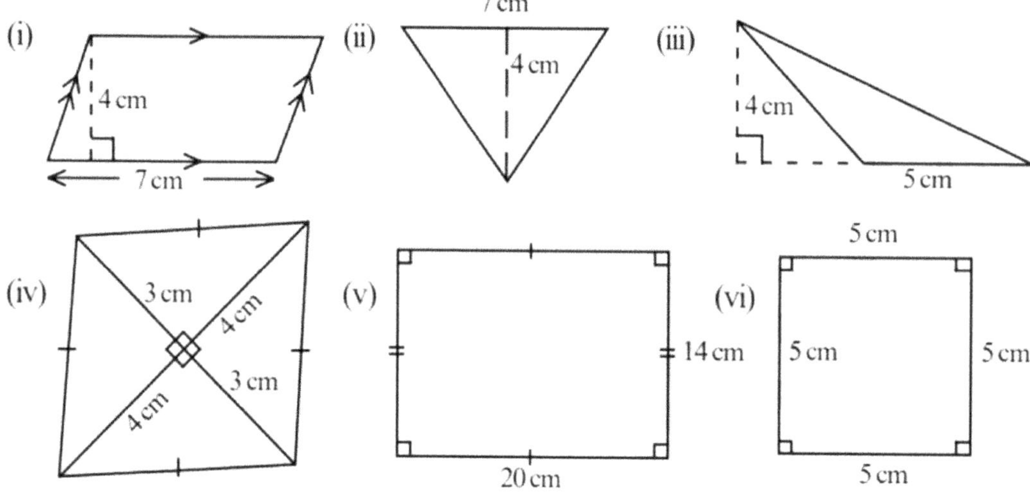

Important Questions

1. Temperature of a city increased by 5 ^{0} C last week. If a corresponding increase of temperature in ^{0} F is 1.8 times more than that of the value in ^{0} C , then find the value of such increase of temperature in ^{0} F

   A: 18^{0} F B: 9^{0} F C: 8.9^{0} F D: 6 ^{0} F

2. A racing car covers 100 km in 2 hours and another 400 km 4 hours. The speed of the car during second time is ____ times more than that of the first time.

   A: 1 B: 2 C: 3 D: 4

3. The product of the place values of 5 in the following number is ______________

   32,435

   A: 9,000 B: 90,000 C: 9,00,000 D: 900

4. What must be added to 10932 to make it exactly divisible by 9?

5. $\frac{3}{6}, \frac{7}{6}, \frac{1}{6}, \frac{5}{6}, \frac{11}{6}$

   If we arrange these fractions in ascending order, then denominator of the product of 2nd and 3rd fraction in simplest form will be __________

   A: 12 B: 24 C: 36 D: 48

6. Half of one sixth of 72 is the _______ multiple of three.
7. A wire of a square sized shape of side 32 cm is reshaped to form a circle. Find the circumference of that circle. [Circumference of a circle is the outer boundary of a circle].
8. A solid cylinder has ____ flat faces and ____ curved faces.

9. The product of all the factors of 121 is _______ less than its greatest factor.
   A: 1 B: 11 C: 1,452 D: 1331
10. Two bells toll at an interval of 6 seconds and 8 seconds respectively. They toll together at 11:55 a.m. When do they toll together again for the second time?
    A: 12:19 pm B: 12:19 am C: 12: 24 pm
11. Ruchika observed that a 300 m long goods train is taking 45 seconds to cross a light-post. Find the average speed of that train. Also find the time taken by that train to cross a 1500 m long railway platform.
12. Compare the place value of 5 in 235,934 and 54,435. Find difference of both the place values.
13. A milk-dairy produces 25,545 liters of milk every day. It supplies 15,625 liters of milk to a milk-depot and the rest to the market. How much milk is supplied to the market?
14. The sum of two numbers is 94506. One of the numbers is 49605. Find the other number.
15. The sum of two numbers is 45650. One of the numbers is 22587. Find the other number. Which part of the sum is the given number?

16. There are 35,278 students in Class III, 32,184 students in Class IV and 25,375 students in Class V in the schools of a city. Find the total number of students reading in Classes III, IV and V. Among these students 60,324 are girls. Find the number of students who are boys.
17. A person had $ 197,865. He gave $ 50,753 to his wife and $ 75,928 to his son. The rest of the money he gave to his daughter. How much did the daughter get?
18. What should be added to the sum of 3,46,068 and 3,24,263 to get the sum of 8,05,400?

19. There are 4021 students in a school. Each section can accommodate a maximum number of 25 students. There are equal number of students in each section, find their number in each section. Is there any section having less than 25 students? How many such sections are there?

20. Write in standard form:

    32 tens + 54 hundreds + 121 ones + 1001 ten thousandths = __________.

21. Points located on same line are called ________________ points.

22. A line has no ____________________ but a line segment has ___ such ______ _____________.

23. A _______ can be extended endlessly in both the directions.

24. 32 hundreds + 302 hundredths + 1008 thousandths = ________.

25. Instead of writing 321 thousands Rita has written 3 lakhs 12 thousands. Find the difference between the original and the derived answer.

26. Total cost of 5 pens and 6 pencils is Rs. 145. Total cost of 6 pens and 5 pencils is Rs. 251. Find individual cost of a pen and a pencil. Also find the total cost of 5 pens and 3 pencils.

27. 5 km 5 m + 102 km 102 m + 32 km 32 m = __________________ m

28. Sam has a collection of 963 comic books. What are the five different ways Sam could divide his comic books into equal groups?

29. A study table is 3 m long and 1.5 m wide. Another large table is thrice as long and twice as wide as the study table. What is the area of both the table?

30. Cost of fencing a square shaped garden at the rate of Rs. 120.00 per m was Rs. 48,000.00. Find the length of a side of that garden.

31. At the end of the party, the kids broke open the gift packs. When they assembled all the candy, Bill got 9 pieces. Sara got 3 times as many pieces as Bill. Nitin got one third of the number of candies gathered by Bill. Which of the statements depicted below are true?

I. They have collected total number of candies which is also equal to third multiple of 3.

II: Sara got 4 times more than Nitin.

III: Share of Nitin and Bill was 15 less than that of Sara.

IV: Sara got 9 times more candy than that of Nitin.

32. A wall mount clock takes 2 seconds to toll 2 bells at 2 a.m. Find the time by that clock to toll 11 bells at 11 a.m.
33. Simplify:

$$\left(1+\frac{1}{9}\right)\left(1+\frac{1}{10}\right)\left(1+\frac{1}{11}\right)\dots\left(1+\frac{1}{1{,}007}\right)\left(1+\frac{1}{1{,}008}\right)=$$

34. How many five digit numbers are there in all?
35. What least number should be subtracted from five digit greatest number to obtain a common multiple of 2, 4, 6 and 8?
36. Product of 9099, 1089, 203899 and 10879 is represented in standard form. The digit at ones lace in that product will be ….
37. Mohan wants to distribute 129 sweets and 321 almonds amongst his 63 friends equally. Calculate the number of sweets and almonds that remain to Mohan after the distribution.
38. The product of two numbers is 41310. If one of them is 270, find the other.
39. In certain division algorithm the quotient is 57, the divisor is 45 and the remainder is 29, find the dividend.
40. The annual income of Sam is Rs. 98,364. What is his monthly income if he earns an equal amount every month?
41. A number was divided by 97; the quotient was 3806 and the remainder 76. Find the number.
42. When 650 is multiplied by a number, the product is 5590. Find the number.

43. 49,000 fruits were distributed among 1,000 clubs equally. How many fruits did each club get?

44. There are 2,983 boys and 2,175 girls in a school. Find the total enrolment of the school. Find also the number of more boys than girls on the rolls of the school.

]

45. What least number must be added to make the six digit smallest number a multiple of 11?

46. What should be added to 79,415 to make it the greatest five-digit number?

47. By how much is 89283 is greater than 79382?

48. What should be subtracted from 98989 to get 88888?

49. There are _____ vertices, _____ faces and ______ edges in a cuboid.

50. Two cubical block of edge 30 cm each joined side by side to form a cuboidal block. Find the surface area of the top and bottom part of that cuboid.

51. Malavika prepared a 25 m long rope by joining different segments of 200 cm each. Find the number of segments she used for making that rope.

52. _______ is the predecessor of smallest four digit multiple of 9.

53. How many times do 7 appear if we write all the natural numbers from 1 to 100?

[Ans: 1]

Olympiad Corner

I: Find area of the following.

1. Area of a rectangle having length 2 m 2 cm and breadth 1 m 1 cm.

2. Area of an isosceles triangle having base 12 cm and one of the equal sides 10 cm.

3. 64 identical squares having area 100 sq. cm. are used to prepare a rectangular design by arranging smaller squares in 6 rows. Find outer boundary of that rectangle.

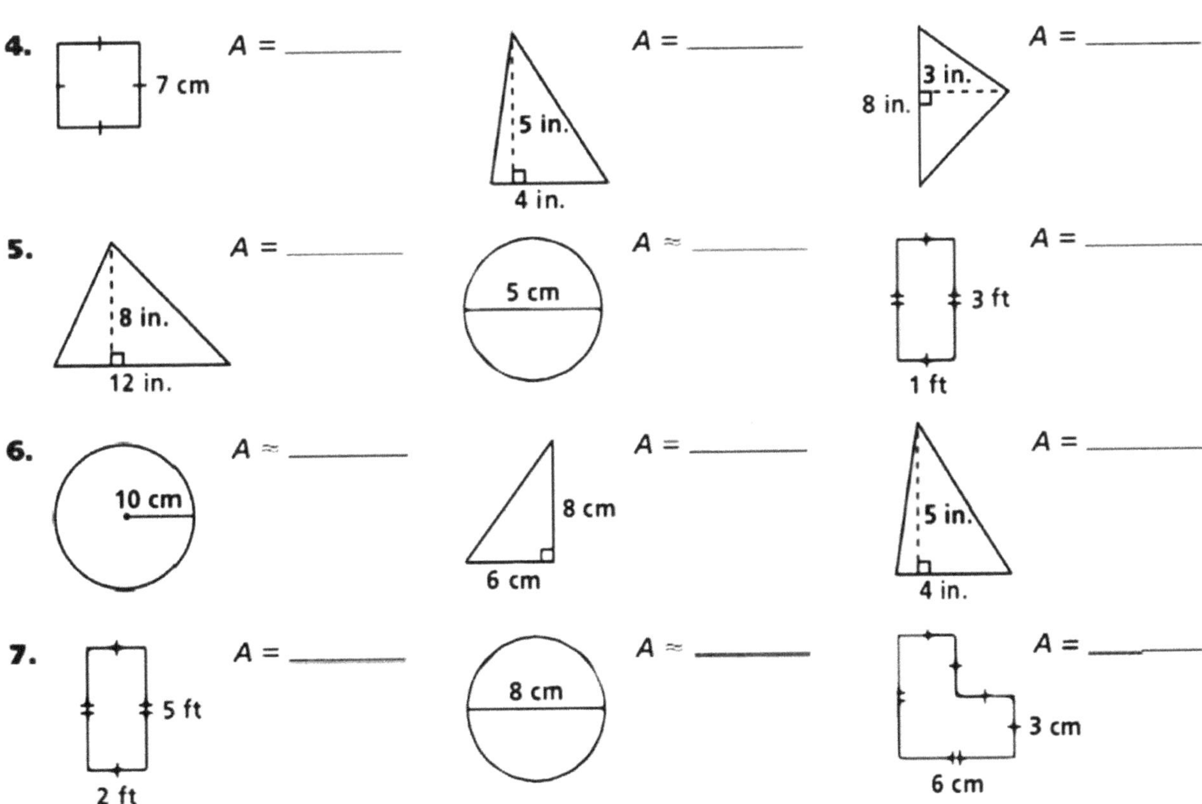

Compare.

II. Complete the following:

1. 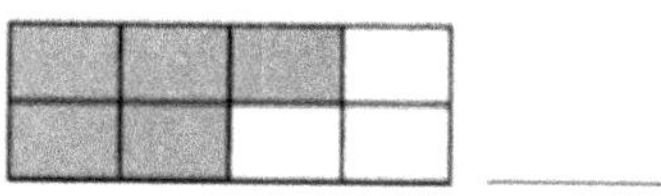 ____ ____ 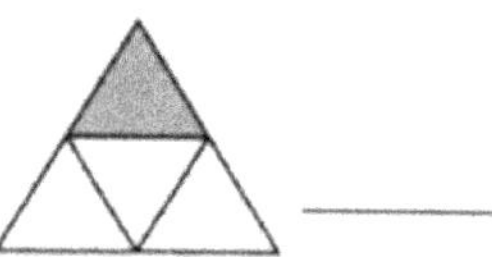 ____

2. 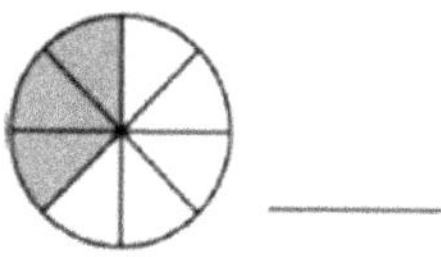 ____ ____ 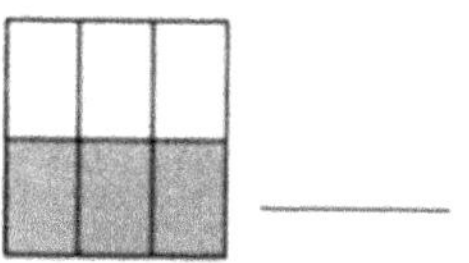 ____

Find the missing numerator.

3.	$\frac{4}{5} = \frac{\_\_}{15}$	$\frac{5}{6} = \frac{\_\_}{42}$	$\frac{2}{3} = \frac{\_\_}{51}$	$\frac{11}{12} = \frac{\_\_}{60}$
4.	$\frac{6}{7} = \frac{\_\_}{14}$	$\frac{3}{4} = \frac{\_\_}{40}$	$\frac{1}{5} = \frac{\_\_}{50}$	$\frac{4}{15} = \frac{\_\_}{45}$
5.	$\frac{1}{3} = \frac{\_\_}{21}$	$\frac{3}{5} = \frac{\_\_}{45}$	$\frac{7}{8} = \frac{\_\_}{32}$	$\frac{2}{17} = \frac{\_\_}{51}$
6.	$\frac{7}{8} = \frac{\_\_}{64}$	$\frac{7}{10} = \frac{\_\_}{20}$	$\frac{4}{6} = \frac{\_\_}{72}$	$\frac{7}{12} = \frac{\_\_}{48}$

III. Find outer boundary of a regular heptagon of side 21 cm.

IV. Quarterly earnings of Vipasha are Rs 121,980. Find her annual income. Also find her savings after 2 years at the rate of 20% of her earning.

V. Rounak observed that a goods train crosses a light post in 45 seconds. It was moving with a uniform velocity of 36 km/h. It that train continues moving with same velocity then the time taken by the train to cross a 1 km 40 m long platform is _______________.

VI. If we add all the consecutive odd numbers then the product obtained will be the square of the number of values added. For example, 1 + 3 = 2 X 2 = 4. During one such computation a square value 12321 is obtained. How many consecutive odd numbers were added?

VII. Complete the following:

1. (1.001 + 10.002 + 1.003 + 1.004) – 0.009) km = ... m
2. 12 m 12 cm + 102 m 2 cm + 21 m 8 cm = ... m ,,,,,,, cm.

9. 12 km 12 m + 13 km 13 m + 14 km 14 m + 15 km 15 m = ... km .... m.

10. Light travels 3 X 10^{0} m per second. Light travels .... km in 8 minutes.

11. The following cards with digits 0,7,9,4 and 5 are given. 0 7 9 4 5
The students are asked to form the smallest and greatest 5 digit number using all the cards. Find difference of these two numbers duly formed by students.

12. Form the biggest 6 digits number using all the digits given below: 6 , 4 , 0, 2, 5 and 9;

13. Complete the following:

___,494	fifty eight thousand four hundred ninety four
327,067	___ thousand sixty seven
908,_____	908 thousand six hundred seventy four
_,743,475	5 million, 743 thousand four hundred seventy five
36,207,650	36 million, ___ thousand six hundred fifty
247,384,812	___ million 384 thousand eight hundred twelve
5,490,000,500	5 billion 490 million five hundred

6,742,165,000 6 billion 742 million 165 thousand.

14. Complete the following:
    a. One complete circle covers _______ degrees
    b. 60 minutes =_______ degrees.
    c. Angle between two consecutive numbers in clock = _______ degrees
    d. _______________lakhs = 1 crore
    e. Right angle = ________ degrees
    f. An obtuse angle is more than a _______ angle but less than _____ angle.
    g. 2 x Right angle = _____ degrees.
    h. ______ thousand makes 2 lakhs.

15. Write in standard form: 13 thousandth + 13 thousand + 13 ones = ____________________.

16. A ____________ has no definite length and no end points.

17. 5% of 5% of one fifth of 10^6 = ___________.

18. Write in standard form: 13 thousandth + 13 thousand + 13 ones = ____________________.

19. A ____________ has no definite length and no end points.

20. 5% of 5% of one fifth of 10^6 = ___________.

21. Rijuana completed typing a letter in 25 minutes. She shared typing 20 such letters with her fellow partner working in the same office. They can finish typing all the letters in ____ hours.

22. 20 % of 20 % of 1000.001 = _____________.

Achievers

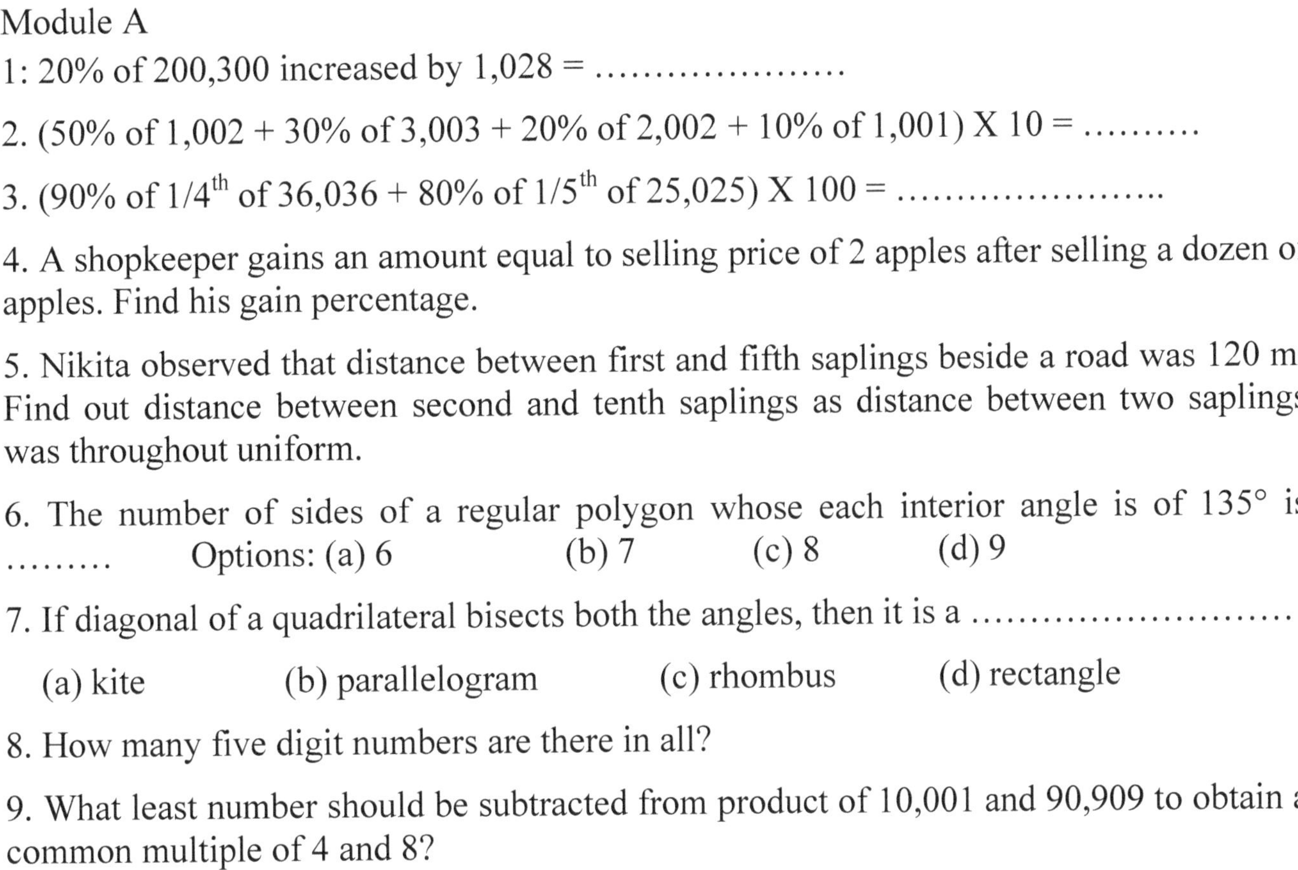

Module A

1: 20% of 200,300 increased by 1,028 = ...

2. (50% of 1,002 + 30% of 3,003 + 20% of 2,002 + 10% of 1,001) X 10 = ...

3. (90% of $1/4^{th}$ of 36,036 + 80% of $1/5^{th}$ of 25,025) X 100 = ...

4. A shopkeeper gains an amount equal to selling price of 2 apples after selling a dozen of apples. Find his gain percentage.

5. Nikita observed that distance between first and fifth saplings beside a road was 120 m. Find out distance between second and tenth saplings as distance between two saplings was throughout uniform.

6. The number of sides of a regular polygon whose each interior angle is of 135° is .... Options: (a) 6 (b) 7 (c) 8 (d) 9

7. If diagonal of a quadrilateral bisects both the angles, then it is a ....

(a) kite (b) parallelogram (c) rhombus (d) rectangle

8. How many five digit numbers are there in all?

9. What least number should be subtracted from product of 10,001 and 90,909 to obtain a common multiple of 4 and 8?

10. Three bells toll at uniform intervals of 4 minutes, 10 minutes and 12 minutes respectively. After what time interval all these three bells toll together?

11. Interior angle of a regular polygon is equal to 135^0. How many vertices are there in this polygon?

Module B

I. Complete the following.

1. Find Square root: $(30 + 2\sqrt[2]{90} + \sqrt{440} + \sqrt[3]{792\sqrt{99}}$

2. How many times do 7 occur if we start writing all the natural numbers starting from 1 to 200?

3. How many even multiples of 3 are there in between 1 and 1,999?

4. Few saplings were planted beside a highway at a uniform interval of 16 $\sqrt{3}$ m to cover up a length of 2 km 560 m. How many saplings were used for this work?

5. (1.001 X 10.01 X 100.1 X 0.1001 X 0.001001) = ... X 1,001

6: How many times do digits 3 occur if we write all the numbers from 1 to 100?

7. (2.005 X 20.05 X 200.5 X 2,005 X 0.02005) X 2005^{-1} X 10^{-3} = ...

8. Three fifth of ten eleventh of 33,077 =...............; 9. Half of a quarter of x = 16,096. X = ...

10. $\frac{1}{2}X\frac{2}{3}X\frac{3}{4}\ldots\ldots X\left(1-\frac{1}{1000}\right) = \ldots\ldots$ 11. $\left(1+\frac{1}{10}\right)\left(1+\frac{1}{11}\right)\ldots\left(1+\frac{1}{10{,}001}\right) = \ldots$

12. 20% of 60% of 100,400,600 = ... 13. (2.345 + 23.45 + 234.5 + 2345) =

14. (1 + 2 + 3 + 4 + ... + 10,000) X $(10{,}001)^{-1}$ X (25,000) = 5^p X 10^q; p = ... ; q =

15. 201 thousands + 201 hundreds + 201 tens + 201 thousandths + 201 tenths = 201 X ..;

16. What least number should be subtracted from the greatest number of seven digits to make the number divisible by 11?

17. A seven digit number is formed by using different digits without using any of them for two times. Find difference of such greatest and smallest numbers.

18. $(\frac{1}{\sqrt{801}} + \frac{1}{\sqrt{801}} + \frac{1}{\sqrt{801}}\ldots\ldots\ldots.800\ times\ X\left(\frac{1}{\sqrt{801}}\right)\ X\ 400\ X\ 3{,}200$ = 2^p X 10^q ; p = ...; q = ...;

19. 20% of x = 30% of y = 60% of z ; $\frac{\left(\frac{1}{x}+\frac{1}{y}+\frac{1}{z}\right)(x+y+z)}{xy+yx+zx}\left(\frac{x}{yz}\right)$ = ...

20: What percentage of all the natural numbers from 1 to 2,000 are multiples of 400?

21. What percentage of 230,230 is equal to 230?

22. What will be the digit at unit place if we multiply 9, 99, 999 and 1009?

23. Sonalika subtracted a smallest possible three digit number from 34,98,098 to obtain a number divisible by 3. Find out the number which was subtracted.

24. Three interior angles of a triangle are in the ratio of 2: 3: 4. Find out the greatest angle. Also find out its supplementary angle.

25. How many three digit numbers are there in all?

26. Mr John travelled half of a distance by bus, half of the remaining by car, half of the remaining distance by auto and remaining 1.25 km by CAB. Calculate total distance travelled by him collectively by bus and car.

27. A passenger train takes 29 seconds to cross a light post while travelling at an average speed of 72 km/h. Calculate total length of the train.

28. (1 + 2 + ……. + 20,000) X 10,000 X 1.0987 ÷ $\left(1+\frac{1}{20{,}000}\right) X\ 10^{-6}$ =

29. Rijuana observed that half of a number exceeds sixth multiple of six digit smallest number by 606. Find out the number.

Module C

1. Third multiple of 3,009 + fourth multiple of 4,012 + fifth multiple of 5,015 = ... X 1,003.

2. What least number should be subtracted from four digit greatest even number to obtain a common multiple of 2, 4 and 8?

3. $(x^2 + 4)(x^2 - 4)(x^4 - 16) =$ .... 4. $\left(\sqrt{36 + \sqrt{36 + \sqrt{36 \ldots\ldots..\propto}}}\right)$

= ....

5. x+ y = 2 and xy = 4; $(x^4 - y^4)(x^3 - y^3) =$ ..... 6. Factorise: $P^2 + q^2 - r^2 - 2pq$

7. $\left(\frac{\sqrt{3}+\sqrt{2}}{\sqrt{3}-\sqrt{2}}\right)\left(\frac{\sqrt{(5-2\sqrt{6})}}{\sqrt{5+2\sqrt{6}}}\right)\left(\frac{1}{1001}+\frac{1}{1001}+\cdots \ldots 1{,}000\ times\right) X \left(1-\frac{1}{2000}\right) X\ 1{,}999 =$ ....

8. $\left(\frac{1}{x}+\frac{1}{y}+\frac{1}{z}\right) = 55,\ (x+y+z) = 5,\ xy+yz+zx =$ ....

9. $(x - 1)(x^2 + 1)(1 + x)(x^4 - 1) = 255$; Find the value of $\frac{x^2+x+1}{x+1}\ X \left(\frac{1}{\sqrt{x}}+\frac{2}{\sqrt{x}}+\cdots \ldots..+\frac{100}{\sqrt{x}}\right) X\ \sqrt[3]{6+x}$

10. (pq + rs + st) = 256; p + q + r = 625; $p^2 + r^2 + q^2 =$ ....

11. $\left(x+\frac{1}{x}\right) = 11\sqrt{11}$; $x^3 + \frac{1}{x^3} =$ .... ; $x^6 - \frac{1}{x^6} =$ ..... ; $x^9 + x^4 - x^{-3} - x^{-9} =$ ....;

12. Factorization of the polynomial $(x - y)^2 a^2 + 2(x - y)(x + y) ab + b^2 (x + y)^2$ gives ___

13. The polynomial $a^2 - b + ab - a$, on factorization, reduces to _________.

14. $\left(\sqrt{16+\sqrt{16+\sqrt{16+\cdots \ldots .\propto}}}\right)\left(\sqrt{81+\sqrt{81+\sqrt{81+\cdots \ldots .\propto}}}\right)=\ldots\ldots$

15. $\left(x^3+\frac{1}{x^3}\right)=62;\ \sqrt{x^3}+\frac{1}{\sqrt{x^3}}=\ldots\ldots\ldots\ldots\ldots\ldots\ldots;\ \sqrt{x}^{-3}+\frac{1}{\sqrt{x}^{-3}}=\ldots\ldots\ldots\ldots\ldots\ldots\ldots$

16. $\left(\frac{1}{356}+\frac{1}{356}+\frac{1}{356}+\cdots\ldots+1{,}000\ times\right)\ X\ \left(1+\frac{1}{1000}\right)X\ 1{,}780\ =\ldots\ldots\ldots\ldots\ldots\ldots$

17. Simplify:

$$\left(\sqrt{30+2\sqrt{90}+2\sqrt{110}+2\sqrt{99}}\right)\ X\left(\sqrt{33+2\sqrt{120}+2\sqrt{110}+2\sqrt{132}}\right)$$

18. $(1a^0+2a^1+3a^2\ldots+1000\ a^{999})=1001\ X\ 500;$
Find the value of $(a^3+3\ a^2+3a+1)(a-1)^3$

19. What least number should be added to six digit greatest number to make the value a perfect square number?

20. $(\sqrt{3}+\sqrt{3}+\sqrt{3}+\sqrt{3}+\cdots.\ 2{,}000\ times\ )\ X\ \frac{1}{\sqrt[3]{14+3\sqrt{3}+)}}\ X(1-\frac{1}{\sqrt{3}}\ )\ =\ldots\ldots$

21: Find x.

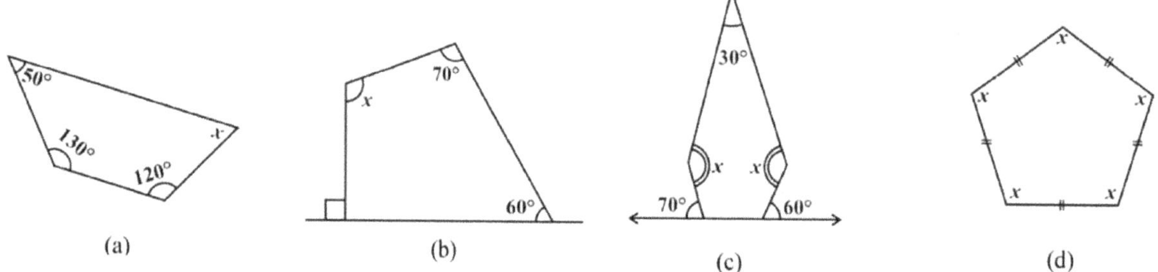

22. Find exterior angles.

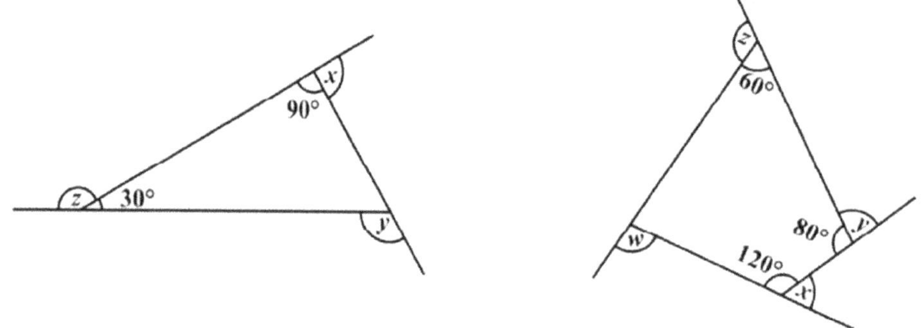

23. Anum's family purchased 5 packets of cooking oil at the rate of Rs 121.80 per packet, 3 bags of rice at the rate of Rs 235.50 per bag and 40 kg flour at the rate of Rs 42.70 per kg. Find the total amount paid by her.

24. Sonalika purchased the following items for her home.

i. Two electric bulbs at the rate of Rs 80.95 each.
ii. Four small stools at the rate of Rs 105.50 each.
iii. Three tables at the rate of Rs 530.95 each.
iv. Six chairs at the rate of Rs 458.30 each.

Find the total amount paid by her.

25. Bamboo is so low in nutrients that a giant panda eats as much as 175 kg of it in 20 hours. About how many pounds can it eat in a couple of hour?

26. A book covers 2370 pages with 24 lines on every page. If we make the same book of 2000 pages with increasing number of lines in each page then how many lines would be there on each page?

27. 513 + 299 = 812. 513 and 299 are not compatible for addition. Justify.

28. What percent of a day is equal to 4 hours?

29. A tank containing 336 gallons of fuel can be emptied in 12 minutes. How many gallons of fuel can be emptied in one minute?

30. There are 540 children enrolled in Valley School. If there are 18 classrooms in the school, what is the average number of students in each classroom?

31. How many times do 8 occur if we write all the numbers from 1 to 200?

32. What least number should be subtracted from product of 20,002 and 999 to obtain a common multiple of 2, 4 and 8?

33. Three interior angles of a quadrilateral are in the ratio of 4: 5: 8. Fourth angle is a right angle. Find out magnitude of all the interior angles f that quadrilateral.

34. How many seven digit numbers are there in all?

35. $11/13^{th}$ of a natural number is equal to 121,121,055. Find out the number.

36. How many digits will be there in the product of 101, 1000, 10000 and 200?

Module D

1. Find measure of the following angles.

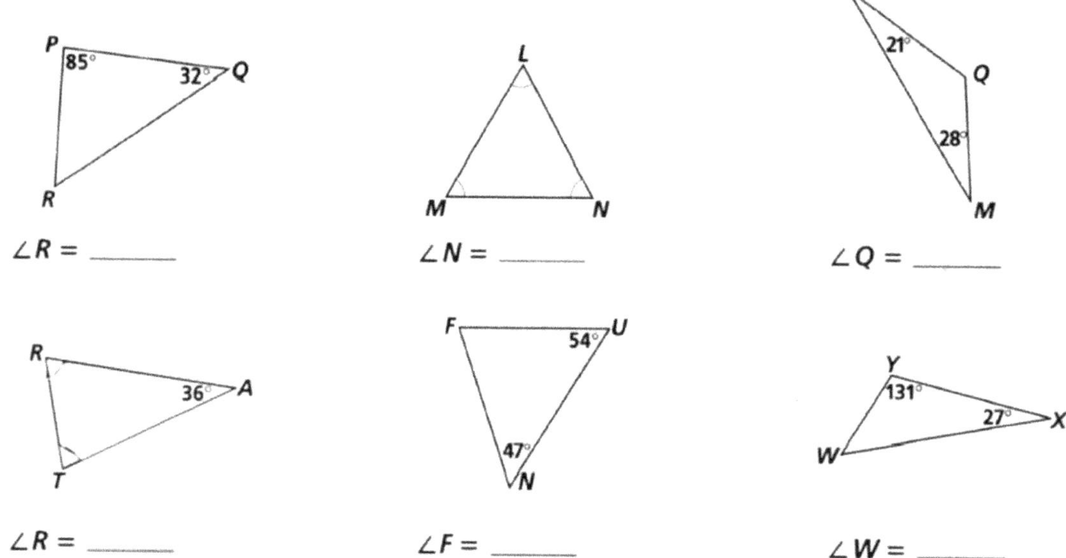

2. Three angles of a triangle are in the ratio of 4: 5: 9. Find measure of all the three angles.

3. Complementary and supplementary angles of a given angle are $(x + 9)^0$ and $(3x - 63)^0$ respectively. Find measure of the angle.

4. $\left(\frac{1}{\sqrt{10001}} + \frac{2}{\sqrt{10001}} + \frac{2}{\sqrt{10001}} + \dots\dots\dots\dots + \frac{10{,}000}{\sqrt{10001}}\right) X \left(25{,}000 X \frac{12}{\sqrt{10001}}\right) =$ ....

5. Nandanwar finished a work in 66 days while working 10 hours per day. She wanted to finish her work earlier by increasing her daily engagement by 1 hour. Find the number of days saved by Nandanwar.

6. A passenger train crosses a person standing on 1.5 km long platform in 45 seconds while moving at an average speed of 36 km/h. This train will cross the platform in ....m ....s while moving with same average speed of 36 km/h.

7. A wall mount clock strikes 6 bells at 6 O'Clock in 12 seconds. Find the time taken by this clock to strike 11 bells at 11 a.m.

8. $\left(1-\frac{1}{2}\right) X \left(1-\frac{1}{3}\right) X \left(1-\frac{1}{4}\right) X \ldots\ldots\left(1-\frac{1}{10{,}000}\right) X\ 500{,}000\ X\ 200 =$ ....

9. A goods train takes 1 m 34 s to cross a 880 m long tunnel while running at an average speed of 36 km/h. Calculate total length of the train.

10. What least number should be subtracted from 43,54,609 to make the number exactly divisible by 9?

11. What least number should be added to 43,65,609 to make the number divisible by 3 and 2 leaving remainder 1 in each case?

12. How many three digit numbers will be formed by using digits 2, 4 and 8 only once ?

13. Namrata five digit greatest and four digit smallest numbers by using different digits only once in each case. Calculate sum of both the numbers.

14. Seven eleventh of a number exceeds 22,055 by 3,300. Find out the number.

Module E

I: Complete the following.

1. 20% of 30% of 100,200,300 = ………….. 2. 40% of 50% of 200,200,200 = ………………

3. 50% 0f 102 + 60% of 1,003 + 70% of 2,003 + 80% of 2,001 = …………………

II. Identify the following.

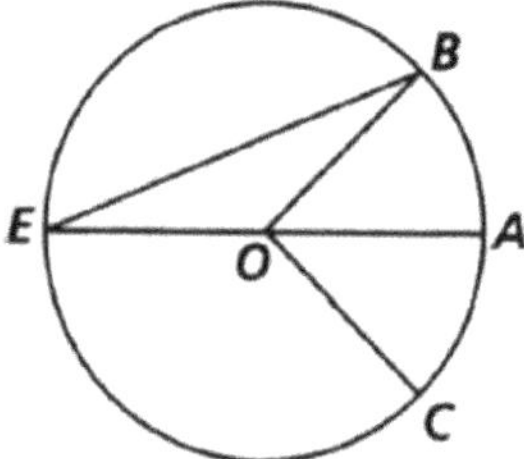

1. $\overline{AE}$: ____________
2. $\overline{OB}$: ____________
3. $\overline{BE}$: ____________
4. $\angle BOA$: ____________
5. $\overset{\frown}{EBA}$: ____________
6. $\overset{\frown}{BC}$: ____________

O: ____________

$\overset{\frown}{CEB}$: ____________

Write the measure of the arc or the angle.

7.

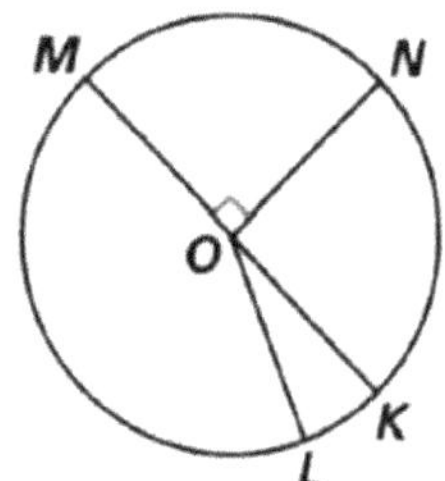

center at **O**
diameter $\overline{MK}$
$\angle LOK = 23°$
$\angle MON = 90°$

$\angle LOM$ = ______ $\overset{\frown}{LK}$ = ______

$\overset{\frown}{LNM}$ = ______ $\overset{\frown}{MNK}$ = ______

$\angle KON$ = ______ $\overset{\frown}{LM}$ = ______

8. ……………… non-overlapping triangles can be accommodated inside a heptagon.

9. There are ……………. diagonals radiating out from a definite vertex of a hexagon.

10. (1 + 2 + ……. + 10,000) ÷ 10,001 X 25,000 = 5^x 10^y; find the value of $\left(\frac{x+y}{x-y}\right) - 4xy$

11. Speed of a boat while moving against river stream is 2 m/s. That boat moves along stream at an average speed of 18 m/s. Speed of stream is less than the stream of the boat. Calculate the actual seed of that boat.

12. Is there any pair of number having LCM 1331 and HCF 169?

13. Is there any pair of natural having HCF 121 and LCM 1331?

14. Sum total of five consecutive multiple of 5 is equal to 250. Find product of second and fourth multiple of the numbers included in this series.

15. $(\frac{1}{\sqrt{3}+\sqrt{2}} X \frac{1}{\sqrt{3}-\sqrt{2}}$ = p; find the value of (p – 1) (p^2 + p + 1)

16. One of the interior angle of a regular polygon is equal to 108^0. How many sides are there in that polygon? How many diagonals can be drawn in that polygon?

17. $\left(\frac{1}{139} + \frac{2}{139} + \cdots \ldots \ldots \ldots + \frac{138}{139}\right) X \frac{1}{69} X\ 125\ X\ 8$ = 10^p ; find the value of (p^2 + 1)(p^2 – 1) -4pq.

18. (x – 2)(x + 2)(x^2 + 4) (x^4 + 16) = 0; find the value of (x – 1)(x^2 + x + 1) = ……………..

19. Somalwar's father is 44 years old. If he is 5 years older than thrice Somalwar's age, which of these equations gives, the age of his father?
(A) $3x + 5 = 44$ (B) $44 + 5x = 3x$ (C) $44-3y = 5+3y$ (D) $3x-5 = 44$

20. The present age of A is twice that of B. 30 years from now, age of A will be 1 ½ times that of B. Find the present ages (in years) of A and B respectively.

21. Ramesh got 15 marks more than Sonu in a test. If the total marks secured by them are 645, how many marks did Ramesh get?

22. In a math test, the highest marks obtained by a student in the class is 7 added to twice the lowest marks. If the highest score is 87, what is the lowest score?

23. Three angles of a triangle are in the ratio of 5: 6: 7. Find out the greatest angle.

24. $(1 + 2 + 3 + \ldots\ldots + 50{,}000) \text{ X } 5{,}000 \text{ X } 400 \div \left(1 + \frac{1}{50{,}000}\right) X\ 10^{-9} = \ldots\ldots\ldots$

25. Four non-overlapping triangles are joined side by side to construct a polygon. Find out total number of sides of that polygon if all the triangles get adjusted inside the polygon.

24. Total number of sides of a polygon is 9. How many non-overlapping triangles can be adjusted in it?

1. Worksheets Level 1

Worksheet 1

1: Convert the following expression into an equivalent fraction.

a: 20 tenths + 203 hundredths + 2,005 thousandths + 12 tenths

b: 15/19th of 19,019 + 11/13th of 13,013 + 16/33rd of 33,033 = ...

c: Half of 500 multiplied by 625 and again multiplied by 1,000

2: Sum total of a number and its reciprocal is equal to 8.125. Find the number.

3: Somalia converted six digit greatest multiple of 4 into a common multiple of 5, 10 and 15 by subtracting .... from it. (Consider it as a smallest possible number.).

4: Is there any pair of number having LCM 12321 and HCF 1690?

5: What least number can be subtracted from the greatest even number of six digits to obtain a multiple of 6?

6: Sum total of five consecutive numbers is equal to third multiple 150,005. Find sum total of smallest and greatest numbers of this number series.

7: Rohit can finish half of a wall painting in 12 days and Mohan can finish quarter of the same painting in 4 days. They started working jointly to finish 7 such wall paintings. They can finish their works in .... days.

8: A train can cross a light post in 1 m 4 seconds while moving with a uniform speed of 72 km/h. Find time to be taken by this train to cross a tunnel of length 5 km 60 m.

9: Sneha reduced her consumption of fuel by 20% to balance price rise of fuel. Calculate the percentage increase of cost of fuel by using the above data.

10: After incorporating Joseph in a team of 11 students of average height 1 m 6 cm the average age is increased by 12 cm. Find height of John.

11: Half of a quarter of 16,064 + one seventh of 14,056 + 1/11th of 22,088 = ……………………

12: Simplify: $\left(1+\frac{1}{11}\right)\left(1+\frac{1}{12}\right)\ldots\left(1+\frac{1}{1{,}000}\right) \div 2{,}002\ X\ 121 - 101$ = …………..

13: Fifty times 5,050 divided by one fifth of 175 = ……………………

14: Half of one seventh of 560,070 – 400,005 = ……………..

15. What least number should be subtracted from five digit smallest multiple of 18 to obtain a common multiple of 3 and 9?

16. (n + 2 n + 3 n + ……. 50,000 n) X 5,000 X 8 = 50,001 X 10^{12} X 12.009 ; here n = ……….

17. A train takes 400 seconds to cross a light post while moving at an average speed of 72 km/h. Find out length of that train.

18. What least number should be subtracted from greatest six digit number to obtain a common multiple of 2, 4 and 8?

19. Two interior angles of a triangle are 54^0 and 43^0. Find supplementary angle of the third interior angle.

20. Quarter of 144 + half of 3,408 + one third of 3,939 = ………..

21. [(1 + 2 + .. +10) ÷ 11] X 1,001 = ………………

Worksheet 2

1: What fraction of all the numbers starting from 1 to 1,000 are multiples of 25?

2: Write three fractions which can be placed in between 1/3 and ¼ on a number line.

3. Half of a quarter of a number exceeds eighth multiple of 300,003 by 72. Find the number.

4: Radius of a square sized playground is equal to 21 m. Mohini completes her daily practice of jogging by encircling around it for four times. Find total distance covered by Mohini during her daily jogging.

5: A cistern can fill up a water tank in 45 minutes another cistern takes 1 h 30 m to fill up the same water tank. Both the tanks kept open to fill up the water tank. Time taken by both the cisterns jointly to fill up the water tank will be ....

6: Simplify: [(5.5 + 5.05 + 5.005 + 5.0005 + 5.00005 + 5.000005) – 25] ÷ 5 = ...

7: Cost of half a dozen banana is equal to Rs 40. Cost of 50 bananas will be Rs. ....

8: Rijuana travels 20 m in a couple of seconds by using her car. Mohini travels by using her car with an average speed of 76 km/h. They started jointly from the origin and a gap developed in between them after half an hour. Calculate the gap developed in between them as they were travelling in the same direction.

9: Calculate the least possible time interval after which three bells toll together. These bells toll at an interval of 10 seconds, 15 seconds and 20 seconds respectively.

Worksheet 3

1: What least number should be added to a six digit smallest multiple of 3 to obtain a common multiple of 4, 6, 8 and 12?

2: Simplify: (1.111…+2.222… + 3.33…..+ 4.444…) 10 = ……….

3: Anthony emptied his coin bank and made a bar graph of the numbers of each type of coin. The interval he chose was 5 coins. If the graph showed 5 intervals of quarters, 2 intervals of dimes, 3 intervals of nickels, and 10 intervals of pennies, what was the total amount of money in his bank?

4: The floor of a room a hotel is 12 m long and 10 m wide. 45 tiles of 1 m square was in stock. Tiles come in market in pack of ten tiles. How many more 1m square tiles does the manager need to completely cover the floors of three such rooms?

I: 15 tiles more than 30 full pack

II: 5 tiles more than 31 full pack

III: 25 tiles more than 29 full pack

IV: 50 tiles more than 25 full pack

Select your answers

A: Only I B: Only II C: I, II and III D: Only IV

5: Average of ten consecutive even numbers is 20. Is it possible to work out values of all the numbers? Find the average of first six such numbers.

6. Instead of adding 108, Ravi subtracted 100.81 from a collection of 50 find the difference of the desired result and wrong result.

Worksheet 4

1: Arrange the following shapes as per their increasing number of faces.

Cylinder, Sphere, Cuboid, Triangular Prism, Rectangular Pyramid.

2. A train is running at an average speed of 80 km per hour. It is covering up 4 km 4 m more in every interval of 10 minutes than that of a car. Find the average speed of the car.

3. A half filled oil container is used to store residue oil of capacity 125 liters. After filling the residue three eighth of the container remained empty. Find the capacity of the container.

4. One tenth of a container is equal to 16 cans of capacity 8 liters each. The entire container can hold __________ liters of oil.

5. What least number must be subtracted from 219.376 to make the result exactly divisible by 219? [Ans: 0.157]

6. A train, moving at the speed of 15 m per second, is taking 20 seconds to cross a telephone post. This train can take _______ seconds to cross a 1.5 km long platform. [Ans : 2 minutes]

7. Roshanlal can finish a work in 16 days while working 5 hours a day. He can finish the same work in ……….. days while working 4 hours a day.

8. Rani is buying light bulbs for her Christmas decorations. She buys 1020 but when she gets to the cash, she has to put back 3 hundred 13 because they are broken. How many light bulbs does Marie buy?

Worksheet 5

1. P = 515.15 –15.51–1.51–5.11– 1.11.
   Find the value of 2P + 1

2. If a = (7.5 × 7.5 + 37.5 + 2.5 × 2.5), then find the value of $\frac{a^2+1}{a^2-1} - \frac{a^2-1}{a^2+1}$

3. A began a business with Rs 45000 and B joined after wards with Rs 30000. At the end of a year, the profit is divided in the ratio 2:1. When did B join ?

4. An employer reduces the number of his employees in the ratio 7: 5 and increases their wages in the ratio 15 : 28. State whether his bill of total wages increase or decrease and in what ratio.

5. In three vessels, the ratio of water and milk is 6 : 7, 5 : 9 and 8 : 7 respectively. If the mixtures of the three vessels are mixed together, then what will be the ratio of water and milk ?

6. A drum contains 20 liters of a paint. From this, 2 liters of paint is taken out and replaced by 2 liters of oil. Again 2 liters of this mixture is taken out and replaced by 2 liters of oil. If this operation is performed once again, then what would be the final ratio of paint and oil in the drum ?

7. If a : (b + c) = 1 : 3 and c : (a + b) = 5 : 7, then b : (a + c) = __.

8. 15 men, 18 women and 12 boys working together earned Rs 2070. If the daily wages of a man, a woman and a boy are in the ratio 4 : 3 : 2, the daily wages (in Rs) of 1 man, 2 women and 3 boys are ______________.

9. Ratio of the incomes of A, B and C last year was 3 : 4 : 5. The ratio of their individual incomes during the last year and this year are 4 : 5, 2 : 3 and 3 : 4 respectively. If the sum of their present incomes is Rs 78800, then find the present individual income of A, B and C.

10. 10% of A = 20% of B = 30% of C. Find the value $\frac{AB+BC+AC}{ABC}$.

11. $\frac{1}{10}$ of a number x exceeds $\frac{1}{15}$ of another number y by 5. Find the value of P.

$$P = \frac{3x-2y}{3x+2y} + \frac{3x+2y}{3x-2y}.$$

12. Tap A can fill a tank in 30 minutes and tap B can fill the same tank in 40 minutes. Both the tap can fill the tank jointly in ____ mins.

13: In two alloys, copper and zinc are related in the ratio of 4 : 1 and 1 : 3. 10 kg of 1st alloy, 16 kg of 2nd alloy and some of pure copper are melted together. An alloy was obtained in which the ratio of copper to zinc was 3 : 2. Find the weight of the new alloy ?

14: Railway fares of 1st, 2nd and 3rd classes between two stations were in the ratio 8 : 6 : 3. The fares of 1st and 2nd class were subsequently reduced by $\frac{1}{6}$ and $\frac{1}{12}$ respectively. If during a year, the ratio between the passengers of 1st, 2nd and 3rd classes was 9 : 12 : 26 and the total amount collected by the sale of tickets was Rs 1088, the collection from the passengers of 1st class was ____________.

Worksheet 6

1. How many different possible solutions can satisfy the following equation?
$$(x^2 - 5x + 5)^{(x^2-12x+45)} = 1$$
2. A three digit number is such that the number N = 100a + 10b + c. Again the number is a product of two factors b and 10c + b. Find the number.
3. An integer is a palindrome when the same number is obtained when digits are reversed. 121,253, 132 etc. are all palindromes. Find a number in such that n^2 will be a palindrome with 6 digits.

4. Sum of the digits of a smallest possible number N is 18. Sum total of all the digits of 2N is 27. Find out the value of N.

5. What least number must be added to a six digit smallest number to make the number 1210214 divisible by 74.

6. Evaluate the following.
$$(\sqrt{2}+\sqrt{11}+\sqrt{13})(\sqrt{2}+\sqrt{11}-\sqrt{13})(\sqrt{2}-\sqrt{11}+\sqrt{13})\ (-\sqrt{2}+\sqrt{11}-\sqrt{13})$$
7. Each interior angles of a heptagon is obtuse. Angles are multiples of 9. Find the degrees of sums of the two largest angles.

8. A three digit number is multiplied by 3 and 1 added to it, then the result is a reverse of the original number. Find the original number.
[Hints: (100 a+ 10b + c)X3 +1 = 100c + 10b + a 100 a+ 10b + c = ?]

9. If ab = a^b and $\frac{a}{b} = a^{3b}$, find b^{-a}

10. $0.33 < \frac{m}{n} < \frac{1}{3}$. Find the smallest possible value of n to satisfy the above mentioned relationship.

11. Find the smallest seven digit number which is divisible by 11. What are the two digits will be there in tens and ones place of that number?

12. Mark deposited \$ 23,500 in his savings bank account which was offering 4% simple interest per year. Find the amount that Mark will obtain after a tenure of 4 years and 5 months.

13. -4.5 + 5.64 + ______ = 0. Make this equation true.

14. Solve the following

    a. $7 \text{ X } 20 - 2 \text{ X } 4 + 3^2 + 12 \div 4$

    b. $\frac{\left(\sqrt[3]{0.125} + \sqrt[2]{.0064}\right)}{\sqrt[3]{1.331} - \sqrt[2]{0.0081}}$

    c. If $x + \frac{1}{x} = 9$ then find the value of

    d. $(2x - 9)^2$

15. A shopkeeper purchased 16 dozen bananas at the rate of Rs 24 per dozen and found that 5% of his stock became non sellable. Rest of his stock was sold at the

rate of Rs 30 per dozen. Find out the rate percent of his gain or loss incurred in this business.

16. Simplify the following: $7[120 - 2(4 + 3)^2 + 12] \div 2$

17. What fraction of all the natural numbers from 1 to 200 are multiples of 25?

18. Write a smallest five digit number which is a common multiple of 2, 4, 6 and 8.

19. Ratio of 5 m 5 cm and 2 m 2 cm = ...

20. 11th multiple of 1,001 + 9th multiple of 2,002 = ...

21. Salary of Mark is increased by 16%. His previous salary was ____ % less than that of the increased salary.

22. Solve the following equation : $\frac{11}{144} X \frac{12}{169} X \frac{13}{121} X \frac{132}{341} X \frac{682}{1001} X \frac{13}{19} =$

23. There are two combinations of packs containing pens and pencils. Packet one containing 6 pens and 5 pencils costs Rs 128. Packet B containing 5 pens and 6 pencils costs Rs 103. Calculate the cost of a new pack containing 10 pens and 10 pencils of such type?

    A: Rs. 250 B: Rs. 120 C: Rs. 135 D: Rs. 210

24. Sum total of all the even numbers starting from 2 to 10,000 is ______

25. half of 2,626 + quarter of 3,636 + $1/7^{th}$ of 1,414 = ...

26. Ratio of three interior angles of a triangle is 2: 3: 5. Find out supplementary angle of the greatest angle.

Worksheet 7

1. X = 0.3333… + 0.4444 + 0.9999.. Find the value of $\frac{x+1}{x-1} + \frac{x-1}{x+1}$

2. Shweta joined a Yoga Centre and her body weight was reduced from 76 kg to 65.6 kg. Find the percentage weight loss that she made during the tenure of her exercises.

3. Base of a triangle is reduced by 5% and its height is increased by 5%. Find the total percentage increase or decrease in the area of the triangle.

4. All the five sides of a regular pentagon is 12 cm each and apothem is 8 cm. find the area of this pentagon.

   [Hints: The apothem of a regular polygon is a line segment from the center of the polygon perpendicular to a side.]

5. A __________ angle is an angle with its vertex at the center of a circle whose sides are radii.

6. Calculate the total surface area of a cuboidal room of dimension 8mX6mX5m.

7. Arrange the following values in ascending and descending order:

8. What is the next number in the following sequence: 2, 4, 8, 16, _____, ______?

9. Write 3/7 and 5/9 in their corresponding decimal form. What are the common things in both the decimal form?

10. The cost of a camera is reduced by 10% to make it equivalent to another camera having a selling price calculated on the basis of 10% profit on the cost price of 21,850. Find the original cost price of the first camera.

11. 3% of 600 is ________ less than 5% of 500.

12. A college offers 25% of all seats of the Graduate programme to local candidates. Last year 125 local candidates got admission in that college. Find the total seat capacity available in that college for Graduate programmes.

13. A shopkeeper offers two discounts of value 5% and 8% on an item. Calculate the equivalent discount of two such consecutive discounts.

14. Population of a city increases at the rate of 10% of previous year's population. Calculate the population of a city in which population before two years was 125,000. Also calculate the population of that city after two year.

15. Parking lot of a school is represented by an expression: $\frac{3}{4}\left(2(2+4k)+2\left(3+\frac{5}{6}k\right)\right)$

    Convert this expression in simplest form.

16. 30% of a number is equal to 40% of another number. Calculate the ratio of both the number.

Worksheet 8

1. A 500 m long train crosses a telephone post in 20 seconds. The same train crosses a platform in 90 seconds. Find the length of that platform.

   [Ans: 1 km 750 m]

2. Two trains of length 200 m and 400 m respectively. They cross each other in 15 seconds while moving in opposite direction and 75 seconds while moving in the same direction. Find speed of both the train. [Ans: 24 m/sec. and 16m/sec]
3. Normally Nikita performs her morning walk at an average speed of 12 km/h. Today her speed was 5/6th of the average. Because of this reason she was late by 10 minutes. Find the normal time that she spends daily for morning walk. [Ans: 50 minutes]
4. Speed of a train was reduced from 65 km/h to 50 km/h. Earlier this train was taking 1.5 hours to cover certain distance. Now it will take ________ minutes more to cover the same distance. [Ans : 27]
5. In a kilometer race A beats B by 100 meters, B beats C by 100 meters. A beats C by ____ meters. [Ans : 190 meters]
6. A bus moves a distance without stoppage at an average speed of 420 km/h. With stoppages the same distance is covered by that bus at an average speed of 28 km/h. find the hourly stoppage time of that bus.

   [Ans: 20 minutes]

7. A 300 m long car is running at an average speed of 90 km/h. another car of length 200 m is running in the same direction at an average speed of 60 km/h. Find the time taken by the first car to overtake the second one.

[Ans: 50 seconds]

8. Length of a train is half that of a km long bridge. A train clears this bridge in 2 minutes. Find the speed of that train.

[Ans: 45 km/h]

9. A train of length 110 m passes a man, who is walking against it at an average speed of 6 km/h, in 6 seconds. The speed of this train is ____________.

[Ans: 60 km/h]

10. A boat running upstream takes hours 48 minutes to cover certain distance. It takes 4 hours to cover the same distance running downstream. Find the ratio between the speed of the boat and speed of the stream. [Ans: 8:3]
11. What fraction of numbers in between 1 and 50 are prime numbers?
12. What least number must be added to 1029.1016 to make it exactly divisible by 1029?
13. Third multiple of a prime number which is greater than 90 and less than 100 = _____.

14. Find the value of $\frac{m^2+1}{m^2-1} - \frac{m^2-1}{m^2+1}$,

if $\sqrt[3]{m} = \left(1-\frac{1}{2}\right)\left(1-\frac{1}{3}\right)....\left(1-\frac{1}{1000}\right)$

15. If $\frac{2}{1+\frac{1}{1+\frac{x}{1-x}}} = 1$, then find the value of

$\left(\frac{x+1}{x-1}\right)^2 + \left(\frac{x-1}{x+1}\right)^2$.

16. Find the value of x if $x^2 + x + 1 = 0$.

17. Capacity of three cans is in the ratio of 1:2:3. Smallest can holds 200 ml less than a liter of any liquid. Find capacity of all the cans.

18. Find the two largest numbers of four digits having 531 as their HCF.

19. Quarter of a natural number exceeds five digit smallest number by 201. Find the number.
20. Three seventh of 14,084 added to fourth multiple of 10,001. Find out the number.
21. 30% of 1,010 + 40% of 2,020 + 50% of 1,010 = ……………
22. Ratio of two interior angles other than right angle of a right triangle is 3:5. Find out magnitude of both the angles.

23: $P = \sqrt{20} - \sqrt{20} + \sqrt{20} - \sqrt{20} \ldots\ldots\ldots \infty$. Find the value of $P^2 + 3P - 20$.

$\sqrt{15} = 3.88$. Find the value of $\sqrt{\frac{5}{3}}$.

24: A person moved on towards countryside at 6 O'Clock. He travelled certain distance at an average speed of 4 km/h, and then another distance at 3 km/h and again a distance at an average speed of 6 km/h. After reaching he turned back and reached the place from where he had started. That time it was 12 noon in his wrist watch. Find the distance travelled by him. [Ans: 24 km]

Worksheet 9

1. 15 men, 18 women and 12 boys working together earned Rs 2070. If the daily wages of a man, a woman and a boy are in the ratio 4 : 3 : 2, the daily wages (in Rs) of 1 man, 2 women and 3 boys are __________.

2. Bolton started business investing Rs 8000. Three months later John joined him investing Rs 6000. If they make a profit of Rs 5100 at the end of the year, how much should be John's share ?

3. The employer reduces the number of employees in the ratio 9 : 8 and increases their wages in the ratio 14 : 15. If the previous wage bill was Rs 189000, what is the amount by which the new wage bill will increase or decrease ?

4. Rs 2010 are to be divided among A, B and C in such a way that if A gets Rs 5, than B must get Rs 12 and if B gets Rs 4, then C must get Rs 5.50. The share of C will exceed that of B by _________.

5. Find the ratio of 12% 0f 12 and 15% of 15.

6. What least number must be added to 1968 to make it divisible by 11?

7. A bottle is full of spirit. One-third of it is taken out and then an equal amount of water is poured into the bottle to fill it. This operation is done four times. Find the final ratio of spirit and water in the bottle.

8. The students in three classes are in the ratio 2 : 3 : 5. If 40 students are increased in each class, the ratio changes to 4 : 5 : 7. Originally the total number of students was ___________.

9. Find the least number which when divided by 12, 24, 36 and 40 leaves a remainder 1, but when divided by 7 leaves no remainder.

10. A drum contains 20 l of a paint. From this, 2 l of paint is taken out and replaced by 2 l of oil. Again 2 l of this mixture is taken out and replaced by 2 l of oil. If this operation is performed once again, then what would be the final ratio of paint and oil in the drum ?

11. 100 ml 80% alcohol and 150 ml 90% alcohol mixed up properly to make a new combination having strength ______ %.

12. Concentrations of three solutions A, B and C are 20%, 30% and 40% respectively. They are mixed in the ratio 3 : 5 : x resulting in a solution of 30% concentration. Find x.

13. Ratio of incomes of A, B and C last year was 3 : 4 : 5. The ratios of their individual incomes of last year and this year are 4 : 5, 2 : 3 and 3 : 4 respectively. If the sum of their present incomes is Rs 78800. Find the present individual income of B.

14.Ravi earns 25% more than Nisha, gut his earning is 18% less than that of Faquir. Find the ratio of their earnings.

15.The cost of manufacturing a TV set is made up of material costs, labour costs and overhead costs. These costs are in the ratio 4 : 3 : 2. If materials costs and labour costs rise by 10% and 8% respectively, while the overhead costs reduce by 5%, what is the percentage increase in the total cost of the TV set ?

16.A number is increased by 20% and then again by 20%. By what per cent should the increased number be reduced so as to get back the original number ?

17.The number of employees working in a farm is increased by 25% and the wages per head are decreased by 25%. If it results in x% decrease in total wages, then the value of x is __________.

18. A candidate who gets 20% marks in an examination fails by 30 marks but another candidate who gets 32%, gets 42 marks more than the pass marks. The percentage of pass marks is _________.

19.In the expression xy2 , the values of both variables x and y are decreased by 20%. By this the value of the expression will be decreased by

_______________________.

20.In an examination Nancy obtained 20% more marks than Hary but are 10% less than Della. If the marks obtained by Hary are 1080, find the percentage of marks obtained by Nancy, if the full marks are 2000.

21. A student took five papers in an examination, where the full marks were the same for each papers, this marks in these papers were in the proportion 6 : 7 : 8 : 9 : 10. In all the papers together, the candidate obtained 60% of the total marks. Then, the number of papers in which he got more than 50% marks is equal to __________________.

22. A tax payer is exempted of income tax for the first Rs 100000 of his annual income but for the rest of the income, he has to pay a tax at the rate of 20%. If he paid Rs 3160 as income tax for a year, his monthly income is ________________

23. A house-owner was having his house painted. He was advised that he would require 25 kg of paint. Allowing for 15% wastage and assuming that the paint is available in 2 kg cans, what would be the cost of paint purchased, if one can costs \$ 2 ?

24. By receiving 5% less vote than the winner of a by-election a candidate received only 12% of the total vote. Find the ration of votes received by both the candidate.

25. In an election, 10% of the people in the voter's list did not participate. 60 votes were declared invalid. There are only two candidates A and B. A defeated B by 308 votes. It has found that 47% of the people listed in the voters' list voted for A. Find the total number of votes polled.

26. Prices register an increase of 10% on food grains and 15% on other items of expenditure. If the ratio of an employee's expenditure on food grains and other items be 2 : 5, by how much should his salary be increased in order that he may maintain the same level of consumption as before, his present salary being Rs 2590.

27. What per cent is the least rational number of the greatest rational number, if $\frac{11}{12}, \frac{2}{3}, \frac{3}{4}, \frac{5}{9}$ $and \frac{17}{18}$ are arranged in ascending order ?

28. If $\frac{1}{891} = 0.00112233445566778899...$ Then what is the value of $\frac{198}{891}$?

29. If $\frac{p}{q} = 2.525252525 \ldots\ldots$ then find the value of $\frac{p^2+q^2}{pq}$.

30. A flower garden is 22.50 m long. Sheela wants to make a border along one side using bricks that are 0.25 m long. How many bricks will be needed?

31. The time taken by Rohan in five different races to run a distance of 500 m was 3.20 minutes, 3.37 minutes, 3.29 minutes, 3.17 minutes and 3.32 minutes. Find the average time taken by him in the races.

32. What will be the digit at unit place of the product of 99, 909, 9009 and 990099?

33. What least number should be subtracted from six digit greatest number to obtain a common multiple of 2. 4 and 8?

Worksheet 10

1. Anuradha can do a piece of work in 6 hours. What part of the work can she do in 1 hour, in 5 hours, in 6 hours?

2. Ravi can do half of a work alone in 12 days, Munish can do quarter of the same work in 18 days and Roushan can complete one tenth of the work in 2 days. If they all join hands to complete the same work then by what time the entire work will be finished?
3. What is the ratio of two numbers whose difference is 45, and the quotient of the greater number by the lesser number is 4 ?

4. Raj travels 360 km on three fifths of his petrol tank. How far would he travel at the same rate with a full tank of petrol?

5. It takes 17 full specific type of trees to make one ton of paper. If there are 221 such trees in a forest, then what fraction of forest will be used to make; (a) 5 tonnes of paper. (b) 10 tonnes of paper? To save $7/13^{th}$ part of the forest how much of paper we have to save?
6. 23% of a number is equal to the thousandth multiple of 92. Find three fifth of that number.

7. All the multiples of 9 are also multiples of ______, but all the multiples of _____ are not necessarily a multiple of 9.

8. Sum total of digits of ones and hundreds place is equal to the digit located at tens place. Number formed by last two digits is a greatest possible multiple of 4. Find the reciprocal of that number.

9. Municipal Corporation of a city has decided to organize plantation works beside a 25 km long road by placing trees beside both the sides of the road at an interval of 50 m. find the total number of trees that can be planted. Also find the cost of maintaining those plants at a rate of $ 2 for every 5 plants.

10. Half of a quarter of 98 = _____.

11. Three bells toll at an interval of 12 seconds, 36 seconds and 45 seconds. After what time interval do they toll together? How many times do they toll together in a gap of three hours?

12. A train moving with a uniform speed of 72 km/h took 2.5 minutes to cross a light post. Find the time taken by it to cross a 1.8 km long platform.

13. Find the value of $\sqrt{272^2 - 128^2}$

14. The square root of 0.4444.... is __________.

15. 4320 X p is a perfect cube value. Find the value of $p^2 + 3p + 9$

16. $\sqrt[3]{4\frac{12}{125}} = x$. Find the value of $3x^2 + 4x + 5$

Worksheet 11

1. Three athletes completed their rounds in 18 seconds, 24 seconds and 44 seconds, respectively. After how many seconds will they be together at the starting point?
2. Arrange in ascending and descending order .
   12.12, 28.7%, 121 hundredths, (21 + 0.21 + 1.012), 21% of 60
3. What least number must be added to 132.98 to make it divisible by 8?
4. Simplify: $6\frac{2}{9} + 2\frac{7}{9} - 4\frac{3}{11} + 1\frac{3}{11}$
5. 25% of 80 =
6. Simplify : 78 – [5 + 3 of (25 – 2 × 10)]
7. Simplify :78–[24–16–{5–(4–1)}]
8. $\sqrt{a} = 9$; *Find the value of* $\frac{a+1}{a-1} - \frac{a-1}{a+1}$
9. $\frac{21}{39} X \frac{78}{63} X \frac{39}{49} X \frac{63}{13} X \frac{121}{270} =$
10. Mohan reached his office by 15 minutes late. It was 11:28 A.M. What was his office time?
11. While calculating perimeter of her garden Ratna calculated the length and breadth of the garden. It was 1500 m long and 600 m wide. ____ times the sum total of length and ________ will be the perimeter of the garden. Find the perimeter in km.
12. For a punch bowl, Carin needs a block of ice with a volume of at least 125 cubic inches. She has a cube of ice that is five inches on each side. Write the volume of the cube using a base and exponents. Then write it in standard form. Is the block of ice big enough? Remember that volume is calculated by multiplying length times width times height.

13. Tickets to the school play cost Rs 300 for adults and Rs 200 for students. If 235 adults and 322 students attended the play, write an expression that shows the total amount of money made on ticket sales. Then simplify the expression.

14. During vacation you spent Rs 127 out of Rs 250. There was another 500 rupees note with you. Find the money left with you.

15. The Akshi Kaikyo suspension bridge in Japan has a span of 6,570 feet. The Humber suspension bridge in England has a span of 4,626 feet. How much longer is the Humber suspension bridge than the Akshi Kaikyo suspension bridge?

16. Julio increases the laps he runs by three laps each day. If he begins on Monday running 4 laps, how many laps will he run on Wednesday at his current rate?

17. Adam is starting a business to take people on hot-air balloon rides. He knows that to carry 2 people, the balloon must have a volume of about 60,000 cubic feet. For his business, he wants a balloon that will carry 4 people. He calculates that the balloon must have a volume of 120,000 cubic feet. Is his answer reasonable? Explain.

18. ________ is the only natural number having only one factor.

19. A __________ has no end point, a _____ has only one end point and a __________________ has two endpoints.

20. A circular wire is reshaped to form a square of 20 cm side. What was the circumference of that circle?

21. Find the difference of areas of two squares having sides 30 cm and 40 cm respectively.

22. A swimming pool measures 50 m by 20 m. The manager plans to construct a cemented road around the pool, which should measure 4 m wide. What is the area of the cemented road?

23. A triangle having more than one _______ angle or more than one _______ angle is not possible.

24. A regular heptagon has ____ lines of symmetry.

25. A hexagon having only one lines of ______ is possible.

26. $5 \times 39 = 5 \times (\_\_\_\_\_\_\_\_\_ + \_\_\_\_\_\_)$

27. $x^3 - 2mx\ 2 + 16$ is divisible by $x + 2$. Find the value of m.

28. $2x^4 - px^3 + 3x^2 + 3x - 2$ is exactly divisible by $x^2 - 3x + 2$.

    Find the value of $p^2 + 3p + 17$.

29. The smallest five digit multiple of 9 exceeds greatest four digit number by ......

30. How many four digit numbers are there in all?

31. How many times do 7 occur if we start writing all the natural numbers from 1 to 100?

32. What least number should be added to 54,54,609 to obtain a common multiple of 3 and 9?

33. First angle of a triangle is three times greater than the third angle and again it is equal to half of the second angle. By using angle sum property of triangles find out measure of all the interior angles.

Worksheet 12

1: Find the digit present in the thousands place in the product

a. $(11011 \div 11)\ X\ 0.7 = P;$
b. $(29029 \div 1001)\ X\ 0.11 = Q;$
c. $(1010101 \div 101)\ X\ 0.005 = R;$
d. $(3090 \div 103)\ X\ 0.08 = S;$

P = 700.7 Q = 3.29 R = 50.005 S= 2.4

Statements:

I. They have values up to thousandths place in their like decimal from.
II. If arranged in ascending order, then Q comes at last.
III. All the results of P, Q, R and S are in decimal form.
IV. Sum total of the greatest and the smallest value is equal to a number which is 3.1 more than the seventh multiple of three digit smallest number.

Which of the above statements are not correct?

Options: A: Only I, III and IV B: Only II, III and IV

C: Only II D: Only IV

2: 20% of 30% of 1,00,100 + 30% of 50% of 2,00,200 = …………

3. Half of a quarter of 8,008 + one third of one fifth of 15,015 = ………

4. Sum of five consecutive natural numbers is equal to 5,00,015. Find out the smallest number.

5. A pair of water tanks of capacity 300 l and 500 l respectively are filled up by a cistern in half of an hour. Three such cisterns are used to fill up three pairs of such water tanks. Calculate total time taken up jointly by cisterns.

6. After adding 0.125 to a decimal number the sum total becomes a decimal number having a position in the middle of 14 and 17. Find the place of that original number on the number line.

Statements:

I. There are more than two options possible for solving the same problem.
II. Sum total of both the numbers to be subtracted respectively from thousands place and thousandths place will be always same.
III. We must go for adding all the digits of the number before verifying it by using divisibility rule.
IV. This problem can be solved without doing the actual division.

Which of the following statements are true?

A: Only II and IV B: Only I and III

C: Only III D: All

7: What must be subtracted from the thousands place and tens place of the following number to make it a multiple of 9?

168,213

Options: _____ from thousandths place and ___ from tenths place.

Worksheet 13

1. Points located on same line are called _____________ points.
2. A line has no _________________ but a line segment has ___ such ______ ____________.
3. A ________ can be extended endlessly in any one direction.
4. A ______ can be extended endlessly in both the directions.
5. 32 hundreds + 32 hundredths = ____________.
6. Instead of writing 321 thousands Rita has written 3 lakhs 12 thousands. Find the difference between the original and the derived answer.
7. Which natural number is having only one factor?
8. 21 tenths = ______________ hundredths.
9. Half of a gross = _________ dozens.
10. Total cost of 5 pens and 6 pencils is Rs. 145. Total cost of 6 pens and 5 pencils is Rs. 251. Find individual cost of a pen and a pencil. Also find the total cost of 5 pens and 3 pencils.
11. List all the factors of 16. Find the sum total of all these factors.
12. 5 km 5 m = ________________ m
13. Sam has a collection of 963 comic books. What are the five different ways Sam could divide his comic books into equal groups?
14. Sum total of all the factors of 6 = ________. This sum total is ____ times greater than the number itself.
15. A study table is 2 m long and 1.5 m wide. Another large table is thrice as long and twice as wide as the study table. What is the area of both the table?
16. Cost of fencing a square shaped garden at the rate of Rs. 120.00 per m was Rs. 48,000.00. Find the length of a side of that garden.

17. At the end of the party, the kids broke open the gift packs. When they assembled all the candy, Bill got 9 pieces. Sara got 3 times as many pieces as Bill. Nitin got one third of the number of candies gathered by Bill. Which of the statements depicted below are true?

I. They have collected total number of candies which is also equal to third multiple of 3.
II. Sara got 4 times more than Nitin.
III. Share of Nitin and Bill was 15 less than that of Sara.
IV. Sara got 9 times more candy than that of Nitin.

18. A wall mount clock takes 2 seconds to toll 2 bells at 2 a.m. Find the time by that clock to toll 11 bells at 11 a.m.
19. What least number must be subtracted from 129.013 to make it a multiple of 129?
20. Which value can repeat itself even after multiplying it by itself?
21. Romanika counted a bundle of sheets, excluding that of top 15 ones, as 132. She has placed 21 sheets in to the printer. How many sheets were there in all?
22. Monika calculated 15th multiple of 5 added to 5th multiple of 15. Find the digit that she might have in the one's place of the product.
23. Compare areas of two circles of 21 cm and 28 cm respectively.
24. Two concentric circles of radius 28 cm and 35 cm will enclose a ring like area of ______ sq. cm.
25. ________ non overlapping triangles can be fitted inside a hexagon.
26. How is 106.076 written in word form?

____

27. Write 16 tenths and 16 thousandths in standard form?

____

Worksheet 14

1. What least number must be subtracted from a three digit greatest number to make it a common multiple of 2, 4 and 8?

2. Find the arithmetic mean of 21, 32 , -74 and 1029.
3. Find the arithmetic mean of first 100 natural numbers.
4. Arithmetic mean of three consecutive odd numbers is 27. Find all the three odd numbers.
5. Submit your answer
6. The average of 199 numbers is 1050. From these numbers average of first 99 members is 900. Find the average of the remaining numbers.
7. A 132 m long train takes 20 seconds to cross a light post. Find its average speed in km/h. If the same train moves continuously for 45 minutes then the distance covered by it will be ………… Km.
8. Fractions like ½, 1/3, ¼, 1/8, 1/12, are also called ______________ fractions.
9. Difference between 0.005 and 0.05 = _____

10. Expand: 1232.4054 =

11. Expand: 1043,546 =

12. $\frac{21}{100} + \frac{132}{1000} + \frac{4321}{10000} =$ __________

13. $\frac{11}{144} X \frac{12}{121} X \frac{11}{139} X \frac{13}{125} X \frac{12}{25} =$

14. 10,000 + 32 hundreds + 29 tens = ___________.

15. An ice cream truck began its daily route with 95 gallons of ice cream. The truck driver sold 78% of the ice cream. How many gallons of ice cream were sold?

16. In a survey of 22,000 people, 14,300 responded that salary was the most important consideration in their ideal career. What percent of the people felt that salary was not the most important consideration?
17. Forty-nine percent of all people who buy running shoes don't run at all. Assuming 340,000 people buy running shoes, how many will use them to run in?
18. In a month Mark makes a 22% down payment on a home in Mumbai . What was the purchase price of the home if her down payment is Rs. 35,200?

19. A family wants to keep the expenditure on sugar intact in the condition of a 20% increase in the cost of sugar. The family will curtail the consumption of sugar by ____ % for doing the same.

20. What percent of hour is equal to 76 seconds?

21. Niharika wanted to give half of a quarter of Choco bar to her friend and half of the remaining Choco bar to her younger sister. Her younger sister will receive ____% of the entire Choco bar.

22. Angles having a common arm and a common vertex are called adjacent angles.

23. Every 2nd, 5th and 10th visitor of a shopping complex receives gifts. How often do three visitors at a time will receive gifts?
24. Before last Saturday there was a rain. Weather station speculated advent of another rain after a couple of fortnight. Which of the forthcoming day would be a rainy day?
25. A circular ring was reshaped to design a square of side 39 cm. what was the circumference of the ring?

26. Sum total of five consecutive natural numbers is equal to 250,750,515. Find out the smallest number.
27. Half of a quarter of a natural number is equal to 100,200,302. Find out the number.
28. Maximum and minimum temperature of a city duly recorded in a day were 21^0 C and 39^0 C. Find out the corresponding increase of temperature in ^{0} F.
29. Pallavi prepared a sweet - dish by using 29 g sugar. She used 5 kg 800 g sugar for preparing similar types of sweet dishes for a kitty party. Find out number of sweet dishes she prepared for the party.
30. (p + 2 p + ….. 1,200 p) – 600 X 123,432 = 1,200 X 300 X 246,864.
31. Rikin covered 14 km 14 m in two hours while jogging around a circular track. Find out total time taken by him to cross the playground by following diameter of the playground.
32. 21st multiple of 100,200,300 = ……….. + 21 X 10^8.
33. Richimon can finish a work in 7 days while working 8 hours a day. He preferred working seven hours a day to finish the same work in …. Days.
34. Sum of seven consecutive natural numbers is equal to 7,028. Find out the smallest number.
35. Half of a quarter of a natural number is equal to 10,001. Find out the number.
36. A 906 m long passenger train takes 1 m 36 s to cross a light post installed beside the track. Find out average speed of that train.
37. Seven times a number exceeds 14th multiple of 10,001 by 707. Find out the number.

Worksheet 15

1. In an assignment 45 mathematical problems were given to all the students. Bandana can solve 30 mathematical problems in an hour. Her brother Rachit can solve 4/5th of all problems in 40 minutes. Rohini can solve 8/9th of these assignments in 50 minutes. Arrange these students in accord to their speed of calculations.

2. Bhavini covered 8/15th of the entire track of a race in 80 minutes. She has another 1.5 km to go. Find the additional time that she need to finish her race without changing her speed. Also find her speed.

3. Marina added 20% of 120 and 40 % of 140 to obtain a number. If 30% of 30 is added to it, it will become a prime number having only two factors, 1 and the number itself. Find out that prime number.
4. Rohini prepared a cup of 200 ml, which can hold water equal to 1/11th of a bowl, 1/25th of a can and 1/100th of a bucket. Calculate the total capacity of all the containers.
5. The difference of the length of the geometry box and scale of Andrea is 6.2 cm. sum total of both the length is 30 cm. find the length of both the object.
6. Mohan and Ravi prepared a Robotic toy which can cover a distance of 173 cm in 20 stepping. Calculate the distance covered by that robot in 180 stepping.
7. The predecessor of a five digit smallest number is the _________ digit greatest number.
8. Four electric lights are turned on at the same time. First one blinks every 4 seconds, second one blinks every 6 seconds, third one blinks every 8 seconds and the fourth one blinks every 12 seconds. In 60 seconds, how many times will they blink at the same time?

Worksheet 16

1. (a + 2 a + 3 a + …… 900 a) = 901 X 450 X 21,098,123. Find out the value of a.
2. A chimp is taking a multiple-choice test. Of course the chimp can't read and is guessing for every question. If there are 4 choices for each question, and there are 84 questions on the test, how many questions can we expect the chimp to answer correctly?

   (hint: There is a 25% chance that the chimp will guess correctly.)

3. First tap can fill a water tank in 30 minutes and second tap can empty the half filled tank in 1.5 hours. By what time the empty tank will be filled up if both the tap kept open?
4. After increasing the selling price of an item by 10% the profit percent on that item is increased from 12% to 15%. Find the ratio of Cost Price and Selling Price of that item.

5. A merchant paid $500 for a table. He then marked it $820. If he then allowed the buyer a 25% discount, how much was the selling price?
6. A sofa cost a merchant $500. He priced the sofa so that he could allow a customer a 25% reduction from the marked price and still make a 23% profit.

7. Certain bank offers a deposit scheme at a simple rate of interest under which any principal doubles itself in ten years of time. Find the rate of interest.

Worksheet 17

1. Kavita had a piece of rope of length 9.5 m. She needed some small pieces of rope of length 1.9 m each. How many pieces of the required length will she get out of this rope?
2. In a survey of 22,000 people, 14,300 responded that watching T.V. was the most important consideration in their daily life. What percent of the people felt that watching T.V. was not the most important consideration?
3. Three boys earned a total of Rs 64.54 less than Rs. 300. What was the average amount earned per boy?
4. 45% of a number is 10 less than a hundred. Find the number.
5. Ravi earned $ 90 in a week. Calculate his annual income.
6. Interior angles of a triangle are in the ratio of 1:2:3. Find all the angles.
7. What least number must be added to the 7 digit greatest number to make it divisible by 11?
8. A shopkeeper issued three consecutive discounts of 10% on certain purchase. Find the single equivalent discount.
9. This number is the reciprocal of itself. It is also the only factor of itself. Find the number.
10. Find a natural number which is also a multiplicative inverse of 0.125.
11. 7 tenths is _____________ more than 17 hundredths.

12. One third of a number exceeds the three digit greatest number by 18. Find one fourth of that number.

13. Selling Price of 6 apples is equal to Cost Price of 8 apples. Find the gain percentage.

14. What least number must be added to the sex digit greatest number to make it divisible by 8?

15. Cost of a pen and a pencil is $ 6. Cost of 3 pens and 5 pencils is $ 22. Find the cost of 5 pens and 7 pencils. Also find the cost of a pencil.

16. Reshma uses ¾ m of cloth to stitch a shirt. How many shirts can she make with 12 m cloth?

17. 20% of a natural number exceeds 400,600,800 by 60. Find out the number.

18. Tamanna prepared a model by using 45% of clay she had in stock. 39% of clay is used by her to prepare another model. Rest of 28 g clay she had with her in stock. Calculate total clay she had earlier?

19. Complete the following:

    a. A number that consists of a whole number and a fraction is called a/an ___________?

    b. An______________________ is a number that represents a part of a whole.

    c. A fraction whose numerical (absolute) value is greater than 1 is called a/an ________________,

d. A fraction whose numerical value is between 0 and 1 is called a/an ______________

20. Pallavi attended a birthday party at 9:35 P.M. She stayed there for 1 and half hours. By what time she will be returning back?

21. Ten metal cubes of volume 10 cu.cm each melted and casted again to form a larger cube of edge _______ cm.

22. What percentage of all the numbers from 1 to 500 are multiples of 20?

23. If $\frac{1}{x} = \frac{1}{y} = \frac{1}{z} = \sqrt[3]{81}$, $p = \frac{xy+yz+zx}{xyz}$, then $p^3 - 1 =$ _.

24. Sum of four consecutive natural number exceeds fourth multiple of six digit smallest number by 22.

25. 30% of 40% 0f 50% of 100,200,300 = ……………..

26. Seventh multiple of a number exceeds 14,009 by 40. Find out the number.

27. How many diagonals can be drawn in a quadrilateral?

28. Two out of three non- collinear points are used to construct a line. How many such lines could be constructed? What will be nature of that polygon?

29. Smallest five digit multiple of 99 is added to 90,0919 to obtain a number. Find out the number. Also find out smallest number which can be subtracted from that number to make the value a multiple of 9.

30. A flask holds 1 L 29 ml water. What will be total capacity of 100 such flasks?

Worksheet 18

1. Julia stores 3,535 cans of juice on 7 shelves in a stockroom. Each shelf has the same number of cans of juice stored on it. How many cans of juice are stored on each shelf?

2. What least number should be subtracted from seven digit greatest number to obtain a multiple of 18?

3. Provide representative fraction. (13 thousandth + 103 hundredth + 1003 hundredth + 12 tens)

4. What fraction of 12.012 is equal to 3.003?

5. 20% of 30% of 2,009 + 30% of 50% of 3,012 = ...

6. One sixth of two seventh of 21,063 = ...

7. A beaker can measure 600 ml of liquid. Another beaker can measure 200 ml of liquid. Both the beakers were used for twenty times each to fill up 90% of a container. Find total capacity of that container.

8. (5,009 + 5,009 + ...3,000 times) X $\left(5+\frac{9}{1,000}\right)X\left(1-\frac{9}{5,009}\right)X\left(1--\frac{9}{5,009}\right)$ = ...

. Length and breadth of a rectangle is 40 cm and 20 cm respectively. 16 such rectangles are arranged in such a way that longer sides remained side by side to form a row of all the 16 shapes. Find outer boundary of that shape.

10. Is there any pair of number having a common multiple 1,009 and a common factor 79?

11. 20% of 20,000 + 30% of 30,000 + 40% of 40,000 = ... X 1,000;

Worksheet 19

1: What fractions of the following are shaded?

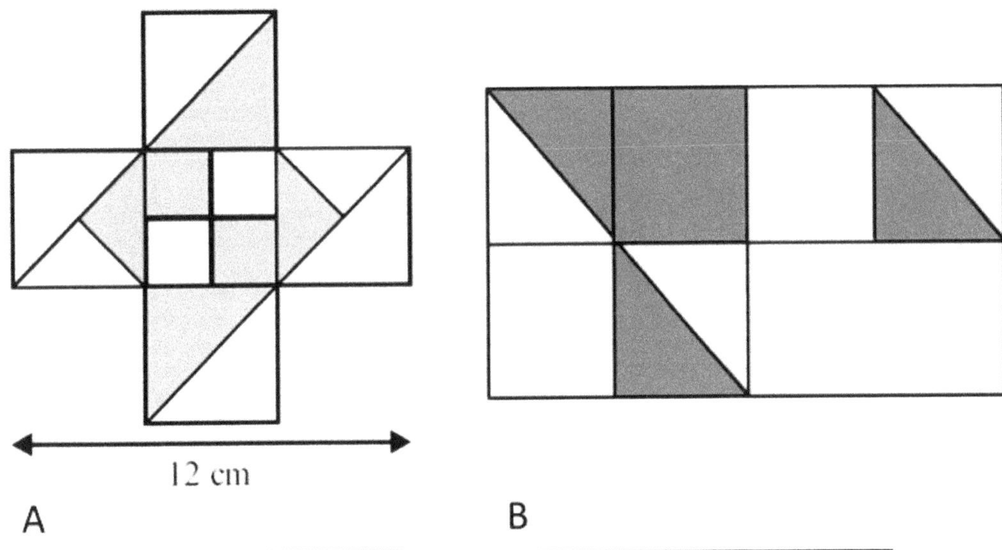

2. Find out area and outer boundary.

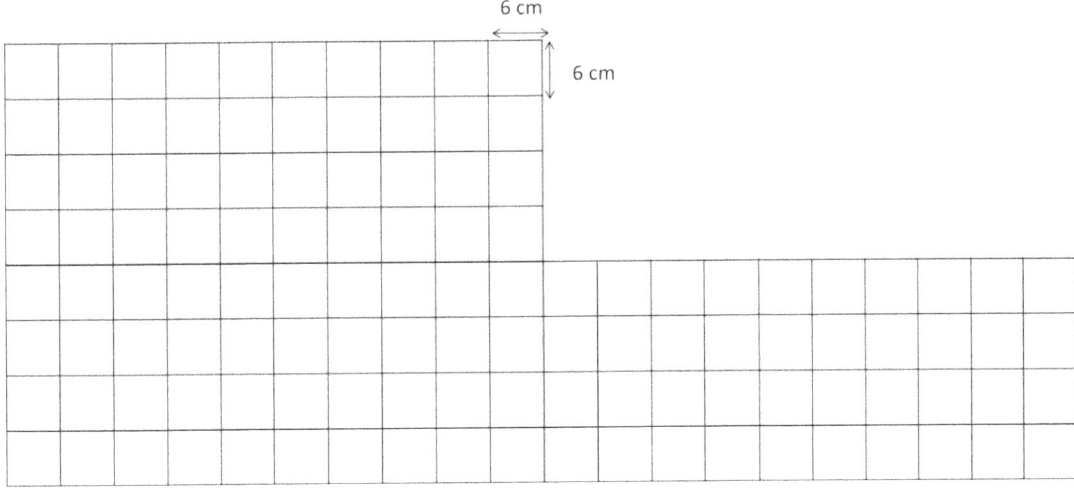

3. Represent shaded parts in decimals and fractions.

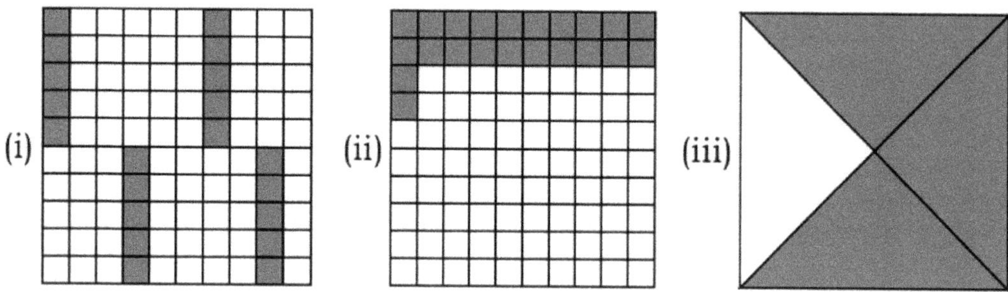

4. A train spends 45 seconds to cross a milestone while moving with an average speed of 36 km/h. find out length of the train.

5. Find out values of x.

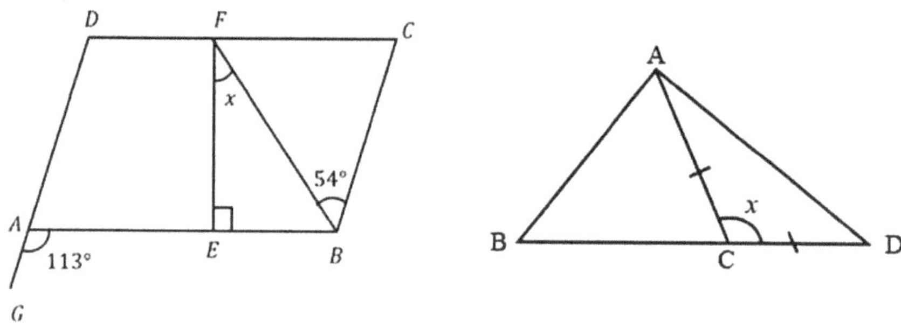

6. What fraction of the following is shaded?

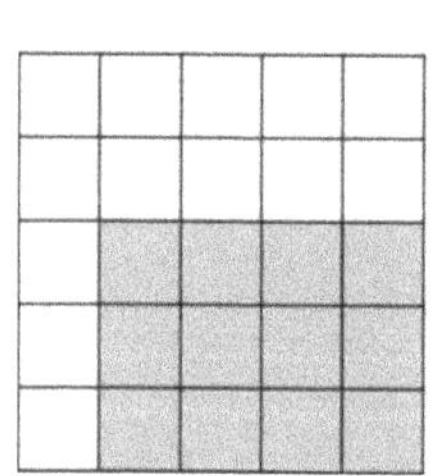

Shape P

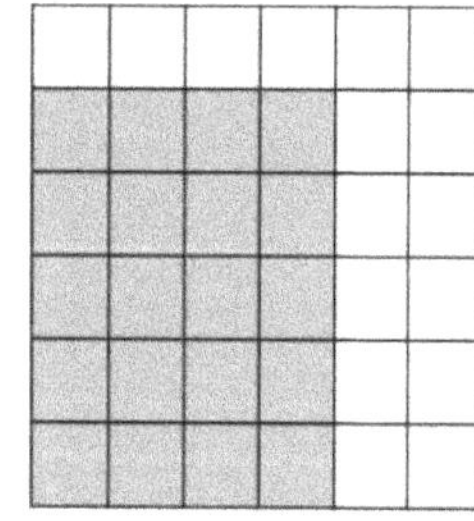

Shape Q

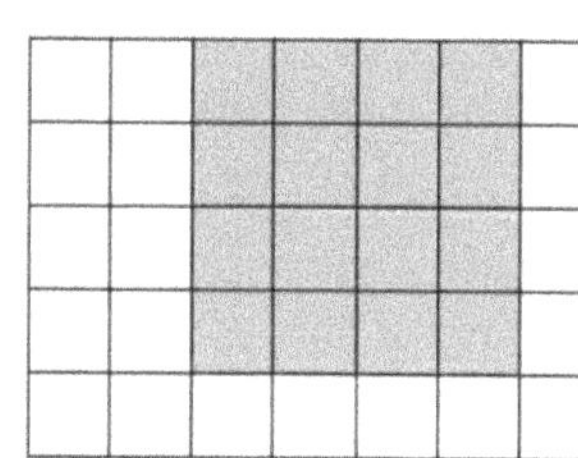

Shape R

7. Area of individual unit squares is 36 sq.cm. Find outer boundary of the following grid.

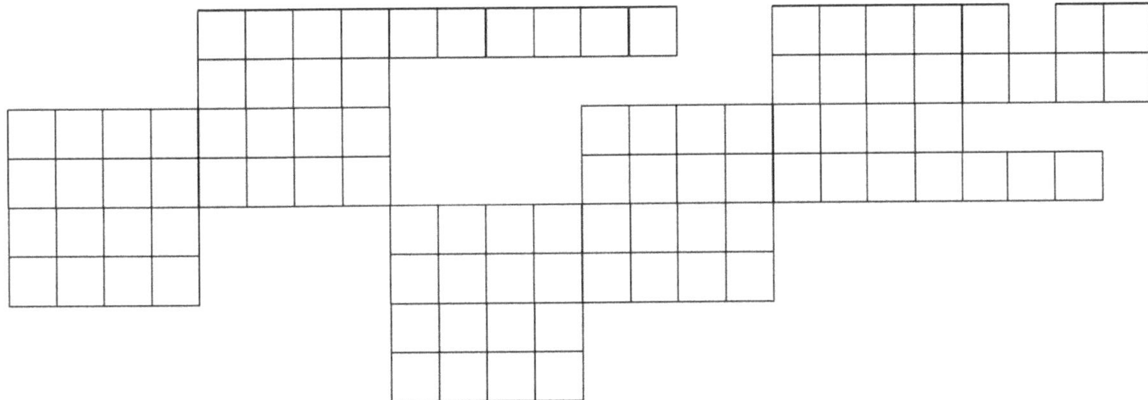

8. Ratio of three interior angles of a triangle is 2: 3: 5. Find out magnitude of the greatest angle.

9. Sum of five consecutive natural number is equal to 15,00,050. Find out the smallest number.

12. Half of a quarter of 80,016,072 = ...

13. Two third of a number exceeds 20,0016 by 308. Find out the number.

14. $\frac{11}{25} + \frac{7}{125} + \frac{81}{50} + 11.001 + \frac{121}{625}$ = ... [in decimal form]

15. How many five digit numbers are there in all?

16. Four interior angles of a quadrilateral are in the ratio of 2: 3: 4: 5. Find out magnitude of the greatest angle of that polygon.

17. Find out sum of three digit smallest and four digit greatest numbers which were formed by using different digits. None of the digits were repeated in each case.

Worksheet 20

1: What fraction of the following is shaded?

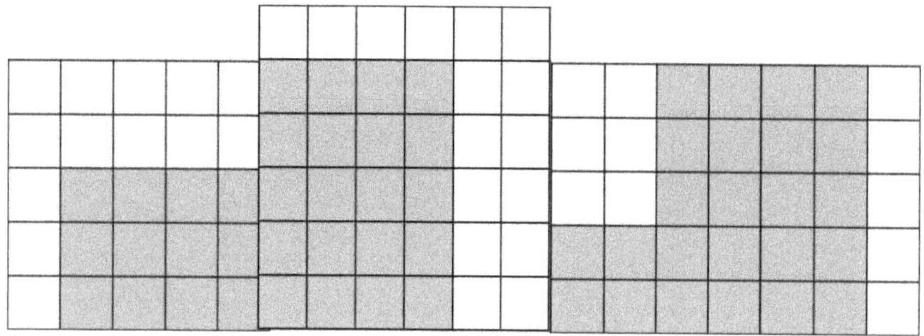

2. Arrange the following shapes on the basis of increasing area.

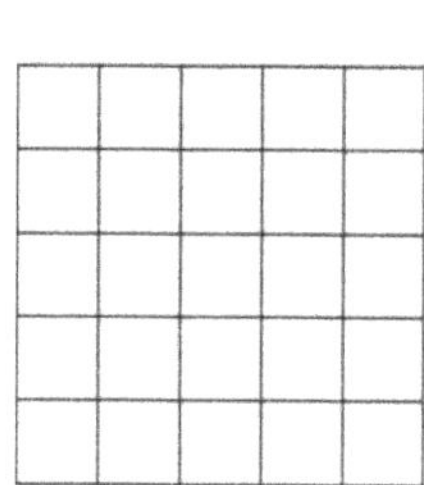

Shape P

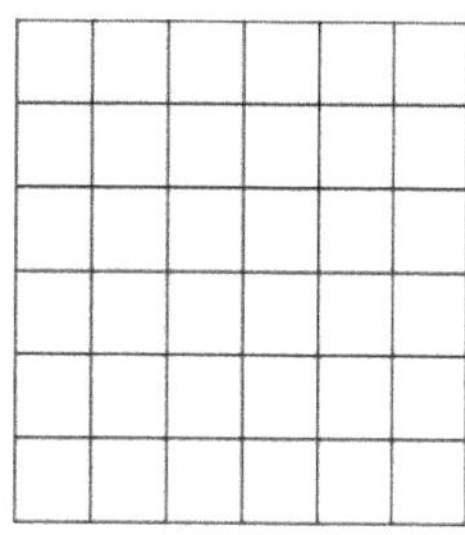

Shape Q

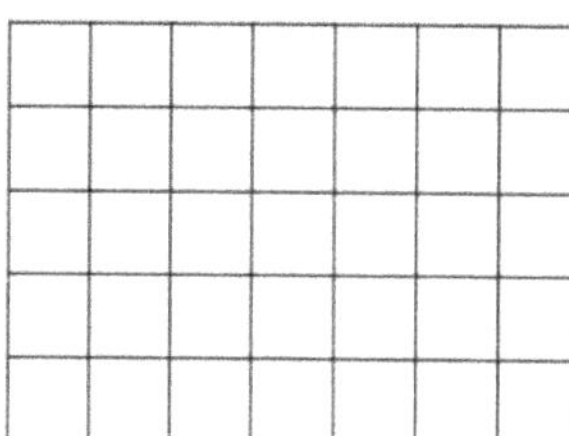

Shape R

3. Complete the following:

☆ + △ = 2789, 6 ✡ = 36.054 and ✡ + △ = 7,013

5 ☆ + 2 △ = ...

4: Half of a water tank is filled up by cistern A in half on an hour and Quarter of the same tank is filled up by cistern B in 40 minutes. Both the cisterns kept open to fill up three such water tanks. Calculate total time taken by both the cisterns jointly.

5: $(x - 1)(x^2 - 1) \ldots\ldots (x^{100} - 1) = 0$; value of $(x^{99} + 10x^{101} - 199\, x^{23}) = ..$

6: Complete the following.

a. 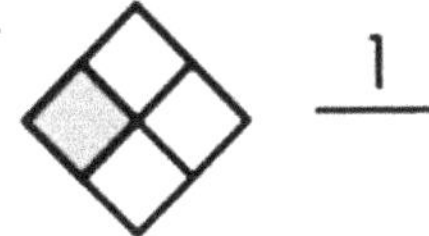

b. 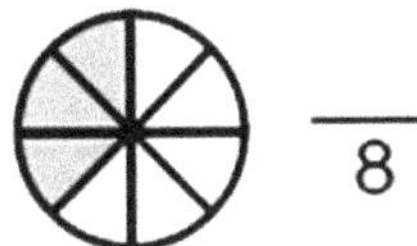

c. 

d. 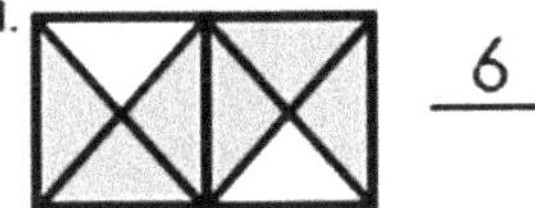

e. 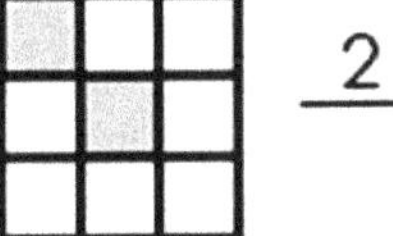

f. 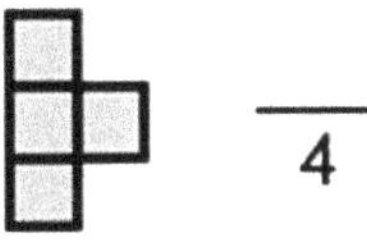

g. 

h. 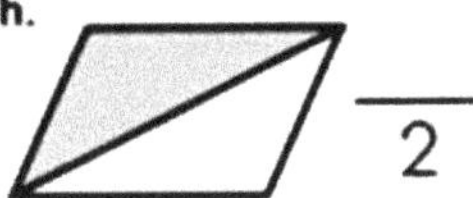

i. 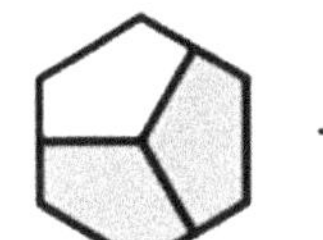

j. 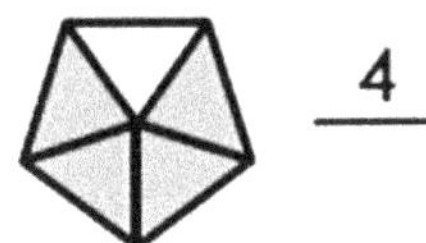

k. 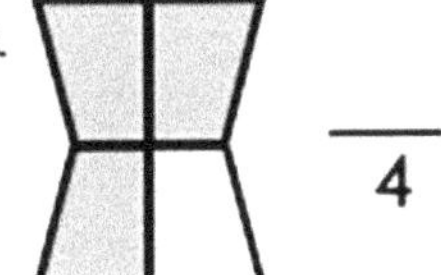

l. 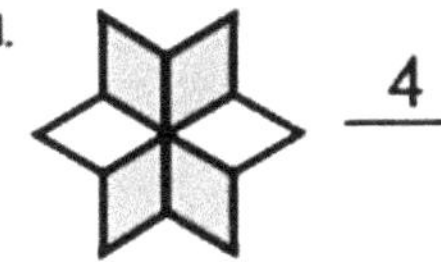

m. 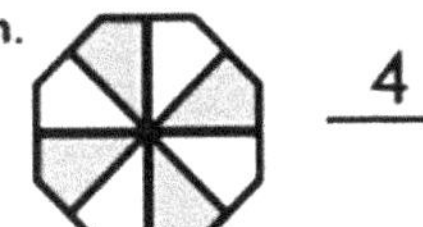

n. 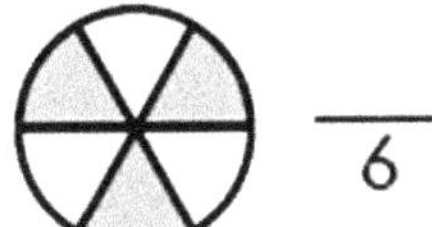

o. 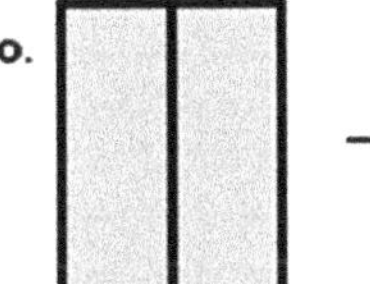

Worksheet 21

1: Find out area of the following.

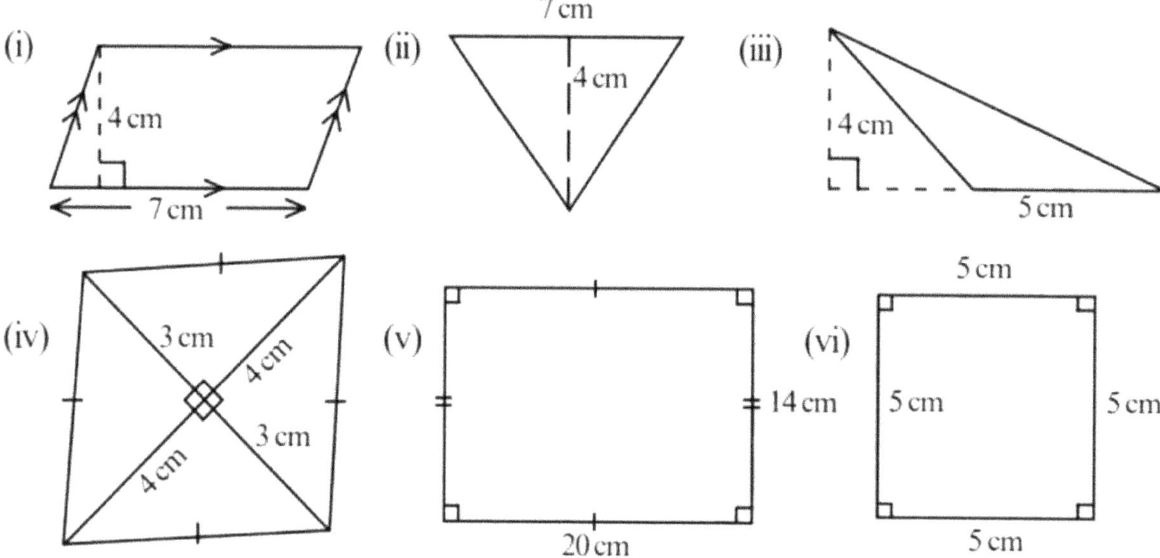

2: Find out area of the shaded portion.

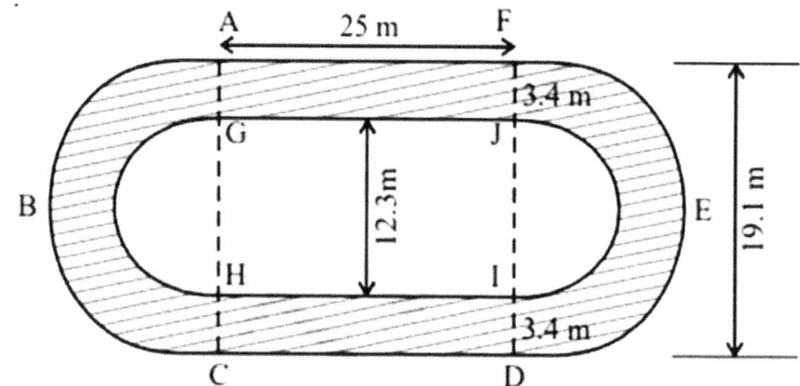

3: Interior angles of a quadrilateral are in the ratio of 2: 3: 4: 6. Find out magnitude of the greatest angle.

4: How many reflex angles can be used to construct a quadrilateral?

5. A triangle can have .... right angle(s), not more than that.

6. Compare area and outer boundary of the following.

1. 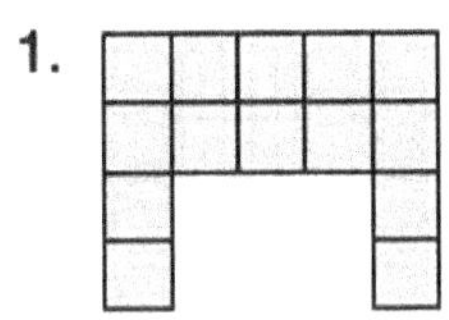

2. 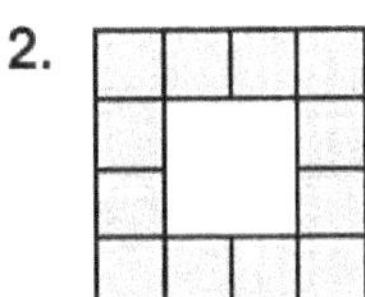

3. 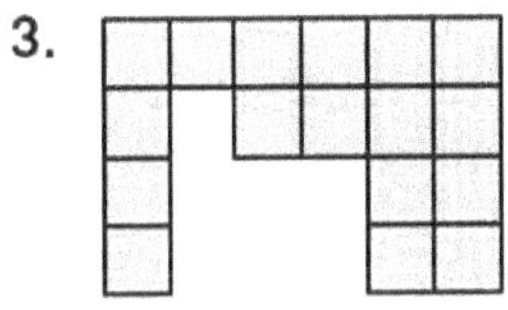

4. 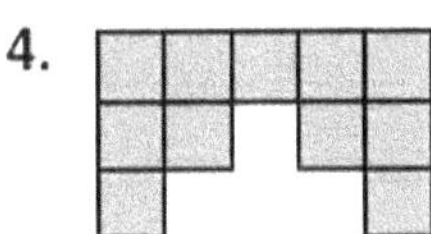

5. 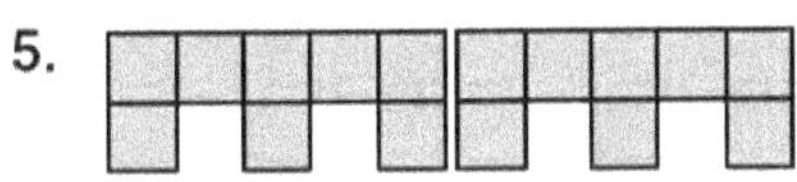

6. 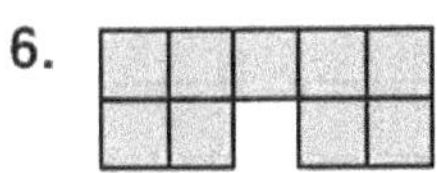

7. 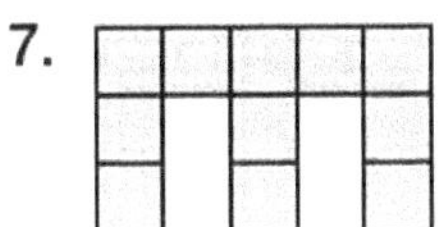

8. 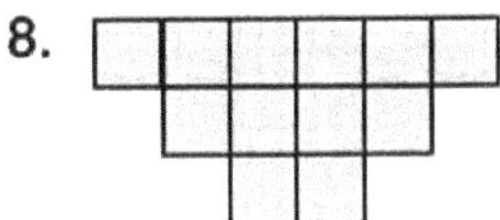

9. 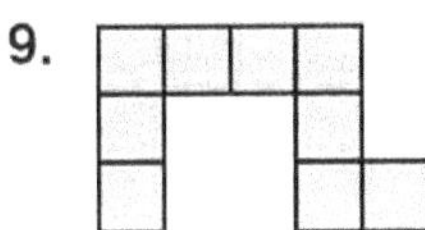

7. Which of the following represents a pair of parallel line?

1. 

2. 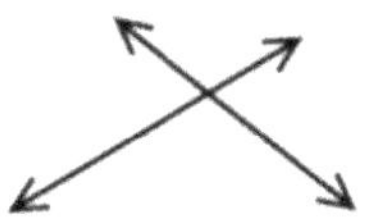

3. 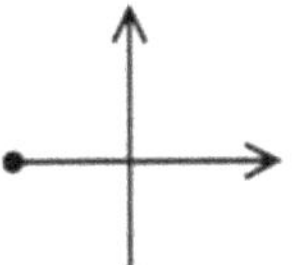

4. 

8. Area of a triangle = ½ of height X base. A parallelogram can have two identical non-overlapping triangles.

Worksheet 22

Find area of the following

1.

6 cm

8 cm

2.

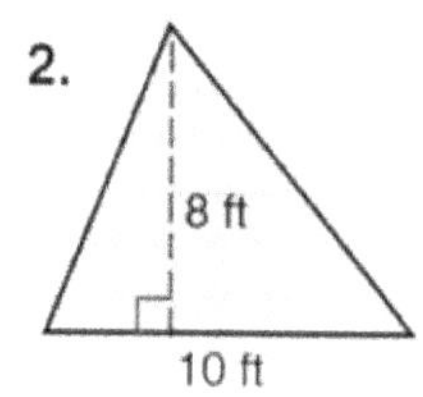

3.

30 cm

12 cm

4.

2 yd

5 yd

5.

3 cm

4 cm

6.

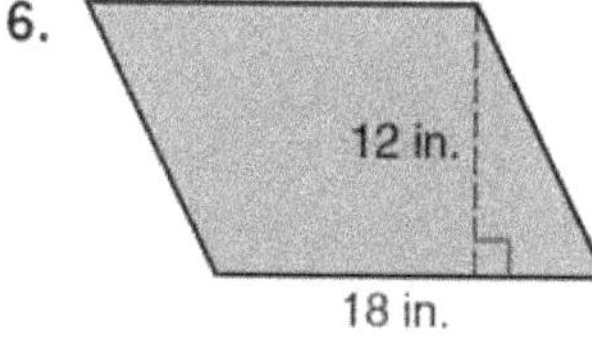

7.

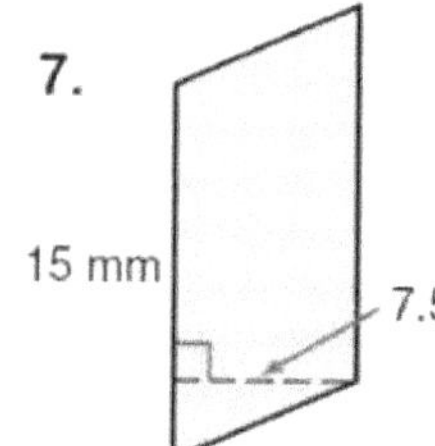

8.

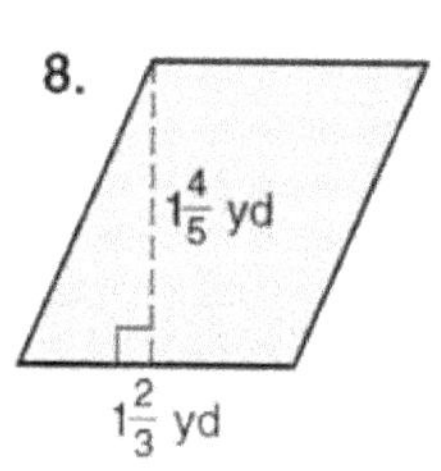

9. Which of the following represents a straight angle?

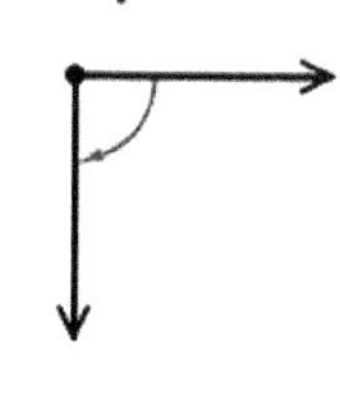

P

Q

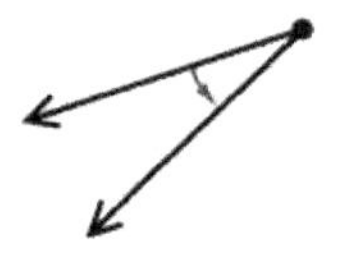

R

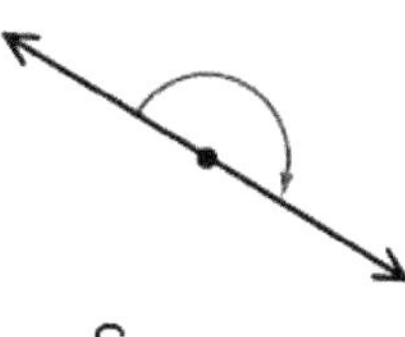

S

10: Find out values of x in the following.

a.

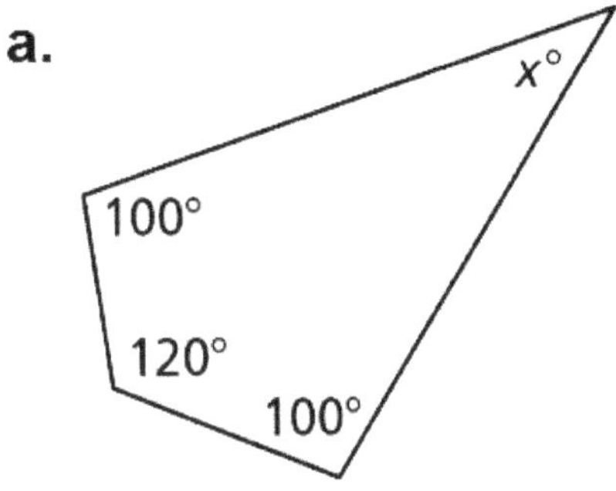

b.

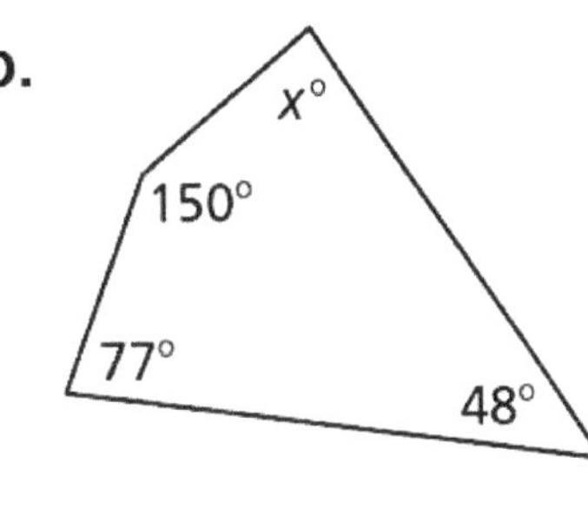

c.

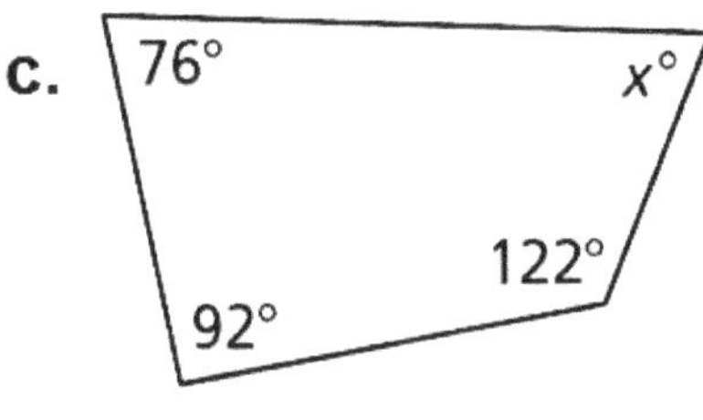

d.

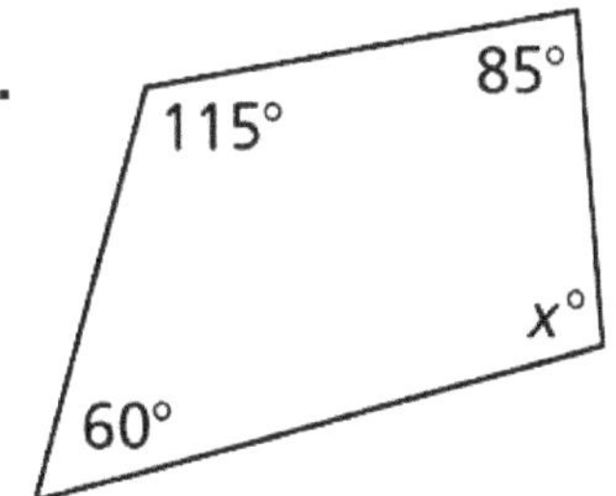

11: Side of a regular hexagon is 4 cm. Several such hexagons are used to form the following grid. Find outer boundary of the grid.

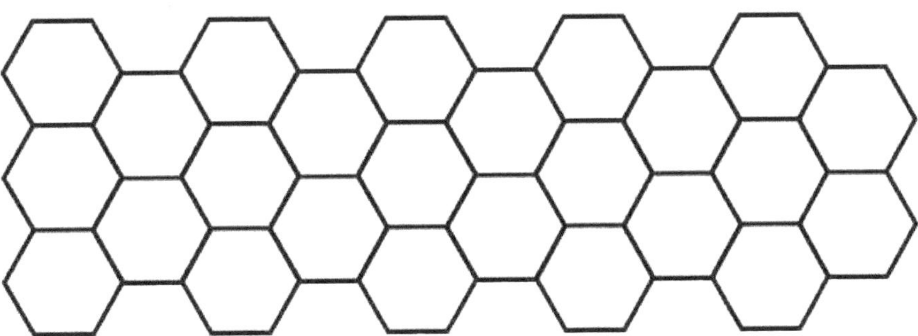

12: Find out area of each of the following.

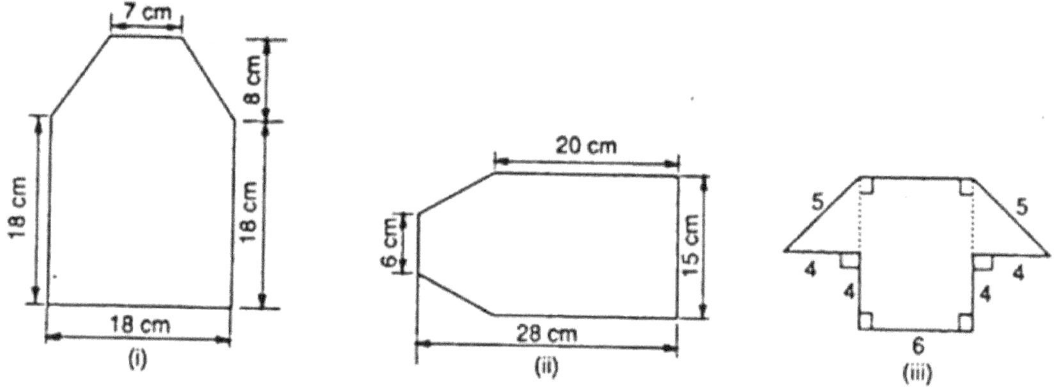

13: Calculate area of the shaded portions.

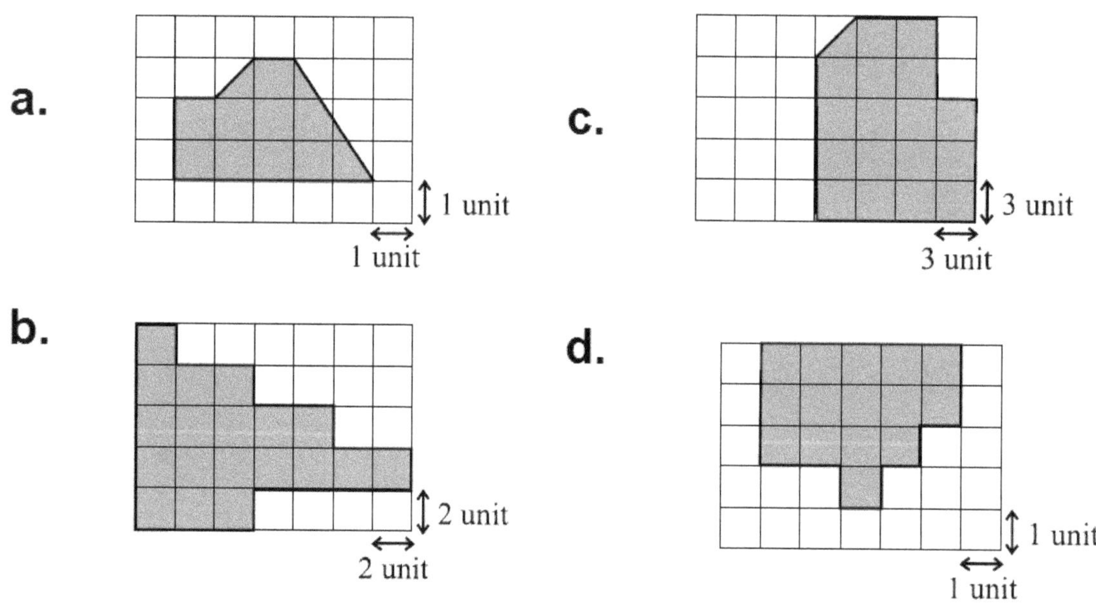

***

2. Property of Triangles

A closed figure bounded by three sides having three angles is called a triangle..

The smallest polygon in terms of number of sides is a triangle. It has three sides, three vertices and three angles.

Sum of all the interior angles of a triangle is equal to a straight angle. It is not possible to draw a triangle by using two or more right angles. An obtuse angled triangle can have only one obtuse angle.

By using angle sum property of a triangle we can find out magnitude of any of the unknown interior angles.

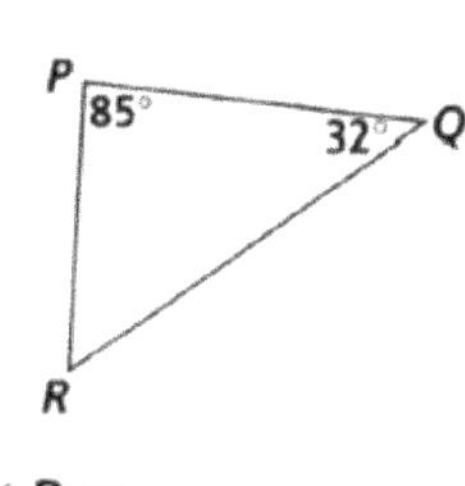

$\angle R =$ ______

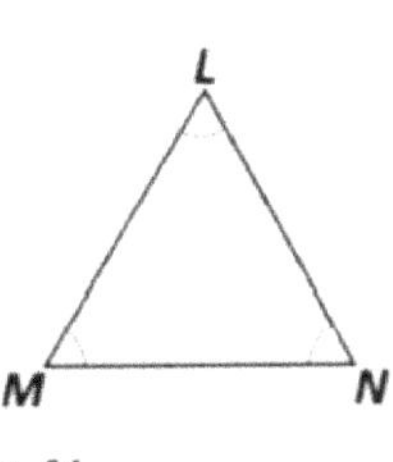

$\angle N =$ ______

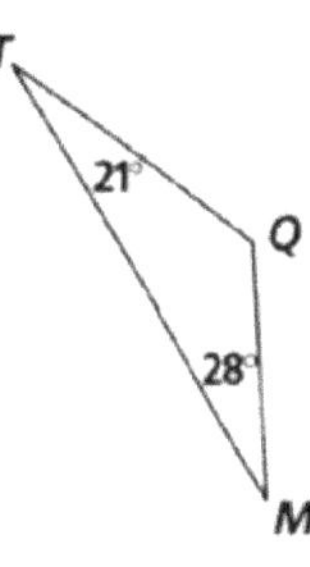

$\angle Q =$ ______

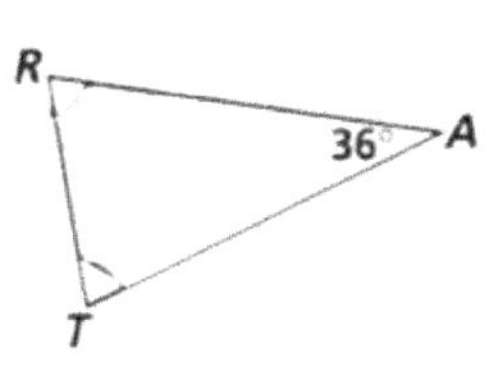

$\angle R =$ ______

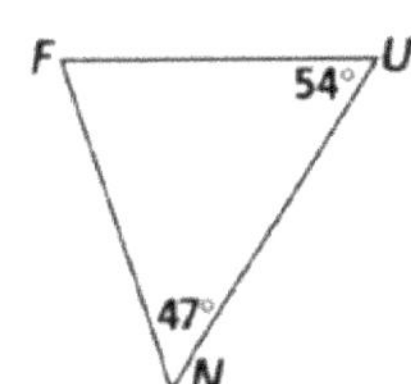

$\angle F =$ ______

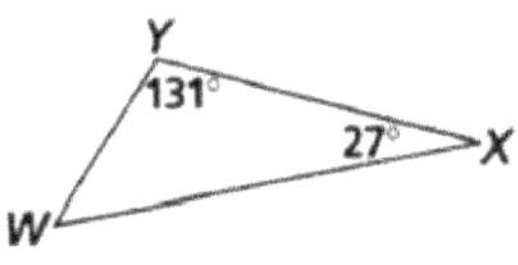

$\angle W =$ ______

Naming a Triangle

Acute angled	All the interior angles are acute angles.
Right angled	Any one interior angle is a right angle.
Obtuse angled	Any one interior angle is an obtuse angle.
Equilateral	All the three sides are equal in length.
Isosceles	Any two sides are equal in length.
Scalene	None of the sides are equal in length.
Equal angled	All the interior angles are equal to each other.

Condition required for constructing a triangle:

Condition 1: Difference of two sides will be greater than the smallest side. Sum of two sides should be greater than the greatest side.

Condition 2: Sum of all the three interior angles of the triangle should be equal to a straight angle.

Condition 3: All the three angles and all the three sides should lie on same plane.

Condition 4: Greatest side of a right triangle lies opposite to the right angle.

Condition 5: Obtuse angled triangle can have only one obtuse angle.

It is not possible to draw any diagonal in a triangle. We can use three non-collinear points and join any two of such points by using a line to construct a triangle.

Let us Work: Find out values of x in the following and verify the angle sum property.

(i)

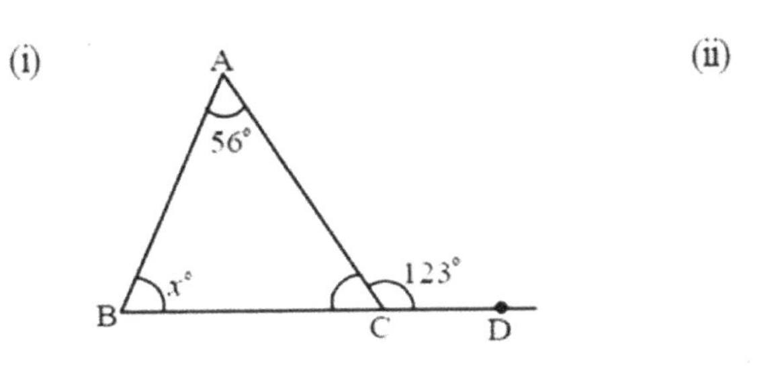

(ii)

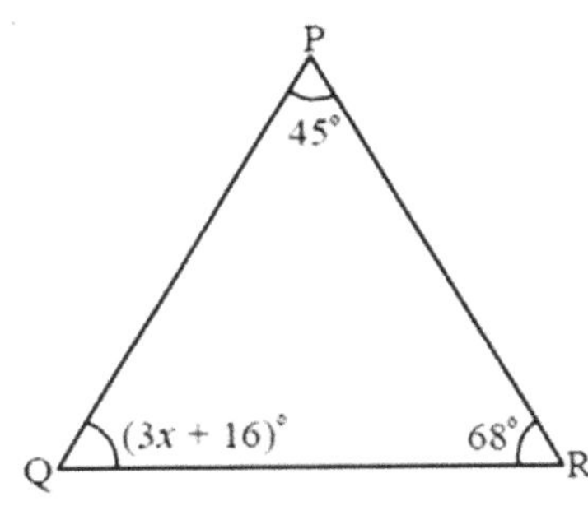

(iii)

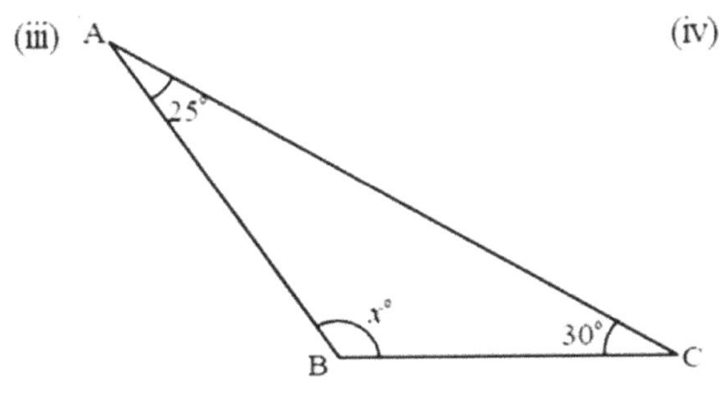

(iv)

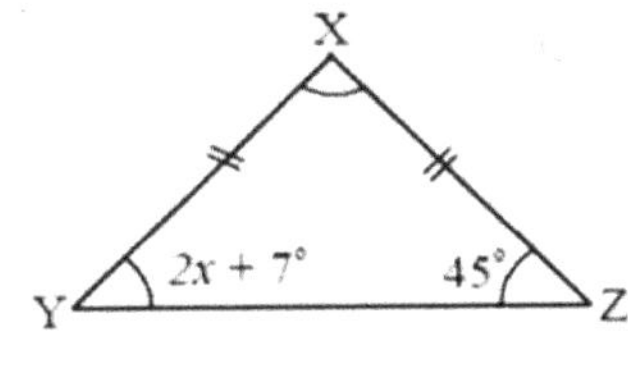

(v) Three given angles are 121^0 , 21^0 and m. What will the value of m so that we can use these three angles to construct a triangle?

(vi) Two angle bisectors of base angles of an isosceles triangle intersect each other at point O and make an angle of 120^0. Find out magnitude of each of the base angles of the given triangle.

(vii) Three interior angles of a triangle are in the ratio of 1: 2: 3. Find out magnitude of the smallest angle.

(viii) Sonalika observed that all the interior angles of a triangle are multiples of 30. Help her to work out magnitude of all the interior angles of that triangle. Also try to coin suitable names for that triangle.

(ix) Triangles in the following figures are trapped in between parallel lines. Find out values of x.

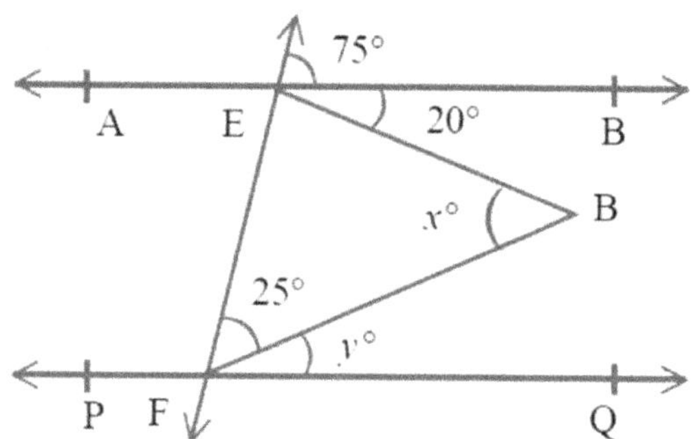

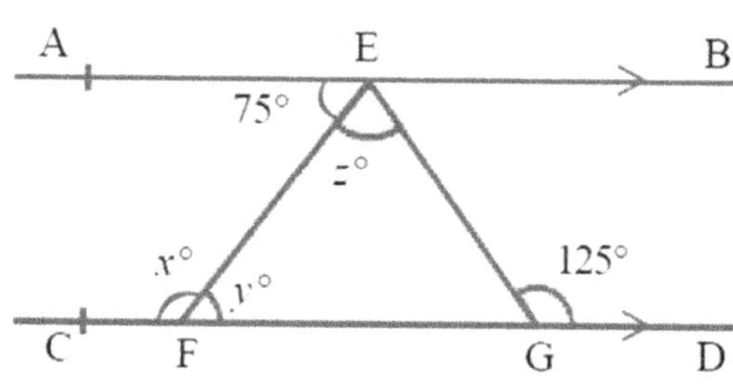

(x) Find out unknown angles in the given figures.

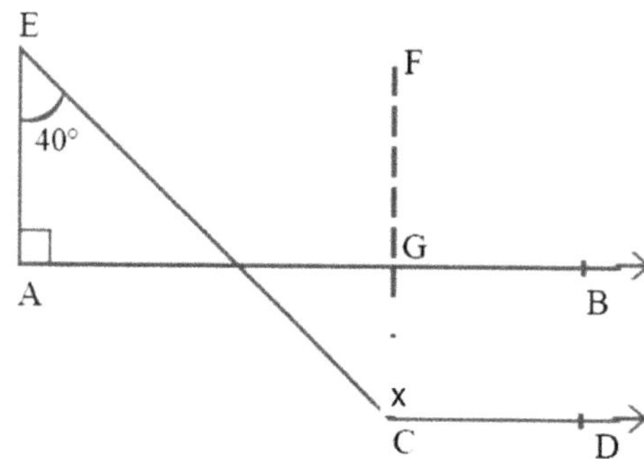

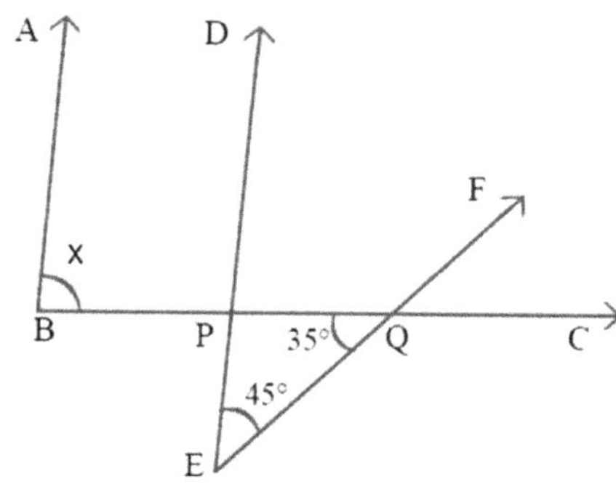

***.

3. Temperature Scales

We use different temperature scales for measuring hotness of a given substance. Two of such scales are Celsius and Fahrenheit scales.

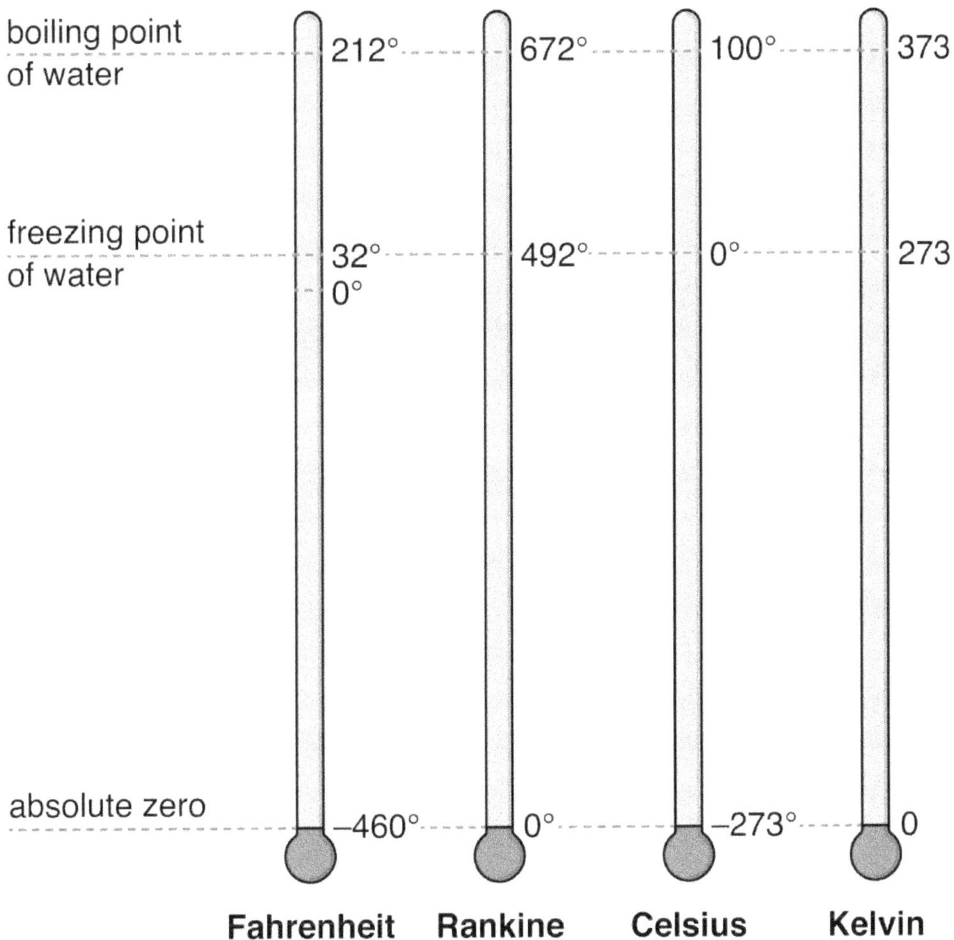

Boiling point of water is considered as upper fixed point and freezing point f water is considered as lower fixed pint for designing thermometers. The gap in between these fixed points are divided equally as per scales to designate equal intervals. All such intervals are called fundamental interval. We can use these figures to compare two scales.

	Celsius	Fahrenheit
Upper Fixed Point	$100\ ^0$C	$212\ ^0$F
Lower Fixed Point	$0\ ^0$C	$32\ ^0$F
Fundamental interval	100	180

As per the comparison if there is an increase of $1\ ^0$C then the corresponding increase in Fahrenheit scale will be $1.8\ ^0$F. Temperature scales are thus related to each other as follows :

C = (F – 32) / 1.8 and F = 1. 8 X C + 32;

Example 1: Convert 98.6° Fahrenheit (normal body temperature) to Celsius

First: 98.6° – 32 = 66.6 Then: 66.6 × 5 = 333 Then: 333 / 9 = 37° C

Example 2: Convert 20° Celsius (A nice day) to Fahrenheit

$1\ ^0$C increase = $1.8\ ^0$F increase. (20 X 1.8 = 36) ; Now 36+32 = 68° F

***.

4. Date and Time

We use date and time format throughout the world as per a standardised globally recognised system of calculations; which also follows relationship of the Earth and the Sun; dates, in the Gregorian calendar (including the proleptic Gregorian calendar); times, based on the 24-hour timekeeping system, with optional UTC offset; time intervals; and combinations thereof.

While writing each date and time value has a fixed number of digits that must be padded with leading zeros. We have 60 seconds a minute; 60 minutes an hour; 24 hours a day; seven days a week; 2 weeks a fortnight; 30 days a month and 365 days a year; 10 years a decade; 10 decades a century. Smallest unit of time is second. Vertical sun rays take 4 minutes to cross 1 meridian (projected on surface of the earth). Gap of 15 such meriidians experience a gap on 1 hour; in that way all the meridians jointly experience a gap of 24 hours or 1 day.

According to such relations of time and meridians we have different time zones. Time zone specified for India is called Indian Standard Time (ISD). Time Zone linked to Prime Meridian is called International Standard Time. Time zones are spaced at an interval of half of an hour.

We use 12 hour notation in our daily life; another notation (24 hour format) is used by institutions like Indian Railways. 13 HRS in 24 hour notation is similar to 1 p.m. in 12 hour notation. 00 Hrs in 24 hour clock denotes 12 midnight.

We can use some prominent steps while adjusting our time; adjustment is generally made on the basis of local time, Standard Time and International Standard Time. Such adjustments (if we do in any digital instrument) may involve some steps to be followed: select your date and time zone; see live date, time, day at the top instantly; enter any desired date and click "Get Day & Formats"; view day of week plus all main formal date formats; digital instruments provide some standard date and time formats; even some instrument have preloaded formats of analog clocks; use any of such formats to obtain a desired one; it can be any of the suitable type.

Light Year is not a unit of time. It indicates distance travelled by light in space in one year. This unit is used to measure distance of stars from our planet.

AM stands for "ante meridian" (before mid day) and PM stands for "post meridian" or after midday. 7 hours before 5 PM denotes 10 AM.

Self Study

1: Tim ran the marathon in 4 h 13 min. Neil ran the marathon in 310 min. Who ran the marathon in less time?

2: Marina Petro worked from 8:15 A.M. to 5:30 P.M. on Monday. She spent 45 min for lunch. She was told she had worked only 7 hours. Marina disagreed and asked her employer to check her time card. Who was correct?

Find the elapsed time.

3. from 2:15 P.M. to 5:30 P.M. 4. from 6:55 A.M. to 8:30 A.M.

5. from 9:30 A.M. to 4:15 P.M. 6. from 8:20 A.M. to 5:30 P.M.

7. from 10:25 P.M. to 6:38 A.M. 8. from 3:10 P.M. to 7:23 A.M.

.

***.

5. Measurement

We use definite units to measure objects of unknown quantities.

We use different measurement instruments for measuring quantities. Some of such quantities are called Standard measurement quantities.

Three popular measurement quantities (CGS, FPS and MKS) are used to denote three scales of fundamental quantities.

We use measurement scales, measurement tapes for measuring lengths, beam balance for measuring mass and clock for measuring seconds.

Self Study

A: Pinto wanted to buy 300 g of honey. The beekeeper had 1 kg of honey on hand. Was Pinto able to purchase the amount of honey he wanted? Why or why not?

B: A leaky faucet drips 2 ml of water each minute. About how many litres of water are lost from the faucet in a week? in a month? in a year?

C: A sign on a cross bridge lists a load limit of 14 tons. Can a truck with a loaded weight of 12,000 kg safely cross the bridge? Give reasons. [1 ton = 1000 kg]

D: A barrel holds 140 L 18 ml of liquid. After removing 121021 ml qt, how much liquid is in the barrel?

E: It is 10:45 A.M. in Savannah, Georgia. Sharon wants to phone her friend when it is 10:00 A.M. in Denver, Colorado. How much longer must she wait before phoning her friend?

F: There are 4 carts at the mall. Each cart is 4 in. taller than the previous one. The tallest cart is 6 ft 2 in. What are the heights of the two shortest carts?

G: Select best estimation.

1. length of a bed a. 6 in. b. 6 yd c. 6 ft
2. weight of a bag of flour a. 6 lb b. 6 oz c. 6 T
3. capacity of a large bowl a. 4 gal b. 4 pt c. 4 qt
4. temperature on a cold, snowy day a. 0°C b. 10°C c. 10°C
5. temperature on a good day to swim a. 5°F b. 45°F c. 90°F

G: Lisa works at the library 3 h 15 min each morning and 2 h 45 min each afternoon, 5 days a week. How many hours does she work in 2 weeks?

H: Every morning Alan jogs once around his property, which is a rectangular block 230 m long and 160 m wide. How far does Alan jog in five mornings?

a. 390 m b. 780 m c. 3900 m d. not given

I: Which is the smaller unit of measure in each pairs? Write the letter of the correct answer.

1. a. milliter	2. a. meter	3. a. gram	4. a. centimeter
b. liter	b. decimeter	b. kilogram	b. millimeter

***.

Combination Worksheets

Model Paper I

1: How many seven digit numbers are there in all?

2: Is there any pair of number having HCF 121 and LCM 1690?

3. How many diagonals can be drawn in a pentagon?

4. Total 3 and half cakes are there to be divided equally amongst 14 fellow friends. Calculate share of each of the fellow friends.

5. $1/11^{th}$ of 121,242,055 = …………

6. Three angles of a triangle are in the ratio of 1: 2: 3. Find out each of the angles.

7. Complementary angle of a given angle is equal to one ninth of a straight angle. Find out the angle.

8. Half of a quarter of a given number is equal to 10,20,300. Find out the angle.

9: How many square centimeters of cardboard were used to make a cubical carton that is 3.5 cm on each edge?

10. 20% of tank A, 30% of tank B and 50% of tank C are equal to each other in terms of volume. Total capacity of all the three tanks is 4,000 m^3. Find out individual volume of the tanks.

11. Volume of a cubical tank is 1331 m^2. Find out edge of this water tank. Also find out area of the bottom.

Work out best estimation

12. crayon box a. 500 m^3 b. 500 dm^3 c. 500 cm^3

13. tissue box a. 90 in.^{3} b. 90 ft^3 c. 90 yd^3

14. CD a. 140 mm^3 b. 140 cm^3 c. 140 m^3

15. Tina made a design by pasting an isosceles right triangle in the center of a square of side 10 cm. If the length of each perpendicular side of the triangle is 5.2 cm, what is the area of the square that is still visible?

16. A special pop-up birthday card has a mass of 12.5 g. The card store sells these cards in a pack that weighs about 2.5 kg. About how many pop-up cards are in each pack?

17. A birdfeeder is 36 cm by 30 cm by 12 cm. A sack of birdseed has a volume of 14 dm3. Is this enough birdseed to fill the feeder? If there exists any difference then calculate such difference.

18. Nikita took a test paper having 45 questions. She had 21 answers correct. What is the ratio of the number of correct answers to the number of incorrect answers?

19. What percent of greatest five digit number is equal to 1250?

20. A natural number is equal to 1002 greater than third multiple of the greatest three digit number?

21. Is it possible to shade a 10 X 10 grid so that it is 15% blue, 75% red, and 20% green?

22. After selling 11 cards a shopkeeper gained an amount equal to selling price of one card. Find out total gain percentage of the shopkeeper.

23. Half of A, quarter of B, one sixth of C are equal to each other. Find out simplest value of the following:

$$\left(\frac{1}{A}+\frac{1}{B}+\frac{1}{C}\right) X \ (2A+3B+4C)$$

Model Paper II

1. The number system which deals with 10 different digits is called decimal system. 324,432,232 is the number represented by using digits from the collection of 10 different digits, such as 0,1,2,3,4,5,6,7,8 and 9.
2. Expanded form of 213,324,543 can be expressed as follows:

   213,324,543 = ___X 1,00,000,000
   + 1 X 10,000,000
   + 3 X 1,000,000
   + ___X 100,000
   + ___X 10,000
   + ___X 1,000
   + ___X 100
   + ___X 10
   + ___X 1
3. We can construct 6 different three digit numbers by using digits 2, 4 and 8 only once.

   Six such numbers constructed by using digits 3, 6 and 9 are:

   369, 396, 639, 693, 963 and 936
4. There are two different types of numeration, one is Indo-Arabic system of numeration and the another one is International system of numeration. All numbers can be expressed in any of the given system of numeration.

   The given number : 125894534

   Indo- Arabic Numeration : 12,58,94,534

   Twelve crore, fifty-eight lakh ninety four thousand five hundred and thirty four

   The given number : 125,894,534

One hundred twenty five million, eight hundred ninety –four thousand five hundred and thirty four.

5. Sum total of all the interior angles of a triangle is 180^0 .
6. Hour hand, minute hand and second hand of a clock completes one rotation by forming a complete angle at the center (360^0).
7. The greatest five digit number without repeating any digit twice is 98,765.
8. The smallest five digit number without repeating any digit twice is 10,234.
9. 3 must be subtracted from the greatest five digit number to make the value divisible by 4.

   [99,999 – 3 = 99,996 ; $\frac{99,996}{4}$ = 24,999 ;]
10. Numbers having only 2 factors, 1 and the number itself, are called prime numbers. 1 is not a prime number. 2 is the smallest and only even prime number.
11. Any natural number and whole number can be represented in a number line.
12. All basic shapes having length and breadth are called 2 dimensional shapes.
13. All basic shapes having length breadth and height are called 3 dimensional shapes.
14. All basic shapes occupy a definite space.
15. All 2 dimensional shapes lie on a definite plane.
16. Two planes meet through a straight line.
17. Decimals are special types of fractions having denominators in the form of a multiple of 10.
18. Percentage is a special type of fraction having denominator 100.
19. What fraction all the numbers starting from 1 to 1,050 are multiples of 105?
20. Find out a smallest possible number which can be subtracted from the greatest six digit number to make the number divisible by 8.
21. One sixth of one eleventh of 66,066 = ...
22. [1 + 2 + 3 + … + 10] = ...

Model Paper III

1: A got Rs. MCLXXXV while B got Rs. MLXXXVII By how much amount A is greater than B?

a) Rs 108 b) Rs 98 c) Rs 88 d) Rs 94

2: A ship was moving at a distance of 52 km from a light house. It takes 1 hr. 30 min for the ship to travel 1 km. How many hours will it take to reach the light house?

a) 4 days and 2 hrs. b) 4 days and 4 hrs.
c) 3 days and 6 hrs d) 2 days and 6 hrs

3: The exam lasted for 3 hrs and 40 min. If it started at 2 hrs and 11 min, What time did it end?

a) 4 hrs and 32 min b) 4 hrs and 52 min
c) 5 hrs and 52 min d) 5 hrs and 51 min

4: What is the value of CLVII plus CLVII tens plus CLVII hundreds?

a) 17727 b) 17427 c) 17327 d) 17527

5: The temperature in the morning was 15˚C less than that at night and in the evening it was 4˚C less than that it was in the morning. In the afternoon the temperature was the summation of fall of the temperatures in the morning and that in the evening. If the temperature at night was 25˚C , what was the temperature in the afternoon?

a) 32˚C b) 34˚C c) 33˚C d) 37˚C

6: Out of the certain number of pens in the box, 1/5th were used in stationeries and 1/6th were used in offices. If there are 240 pens in the box, how many are used?

a) 152 pens b) 120 pens c) 201 pens d) 210 pens

7: Out of 150 students 87 are girls. What fraction of the students are boys?

a) 21/50 b) 11/25 c) 23/50 d) 13/25

9: In a convocation ceremony, there were 366 students and the number of cap and gown is equal to 28 more than 1/3rd of the number of students. How many more gowns are needed if each student gets 2 pair of cap and gown?

a) 516

b) 375

c) 400

d) 432

10: On a rainy day, Keerti's reporting time at the office was at 9.00 am sharp. She was 25 min late with respect to her reporting time. Anushka reached 18 min late after Keerti and Rakesh reached 55 min after Anushka. At what time did Rakesh reach?

a) 10:10 am

b) 10:05 am

c) 10:20 am

d) 10:00 AM

11. What least number should be subtracted from four digit greatest number to obtain a common multiple of 2 and 4?

12. How many five digit numbers are there in all?

13. Richardson jogs 50 m in 12 seconds and Smita jogs at an average speed of 18 km/h. Who jogs faster?

14: 20% of 30% of 60% of 209,000 = ...

Model Paper IV

1: Amit has worked on a project for 336 hours. In his project report, he needs to mention the number of working days so that he can get his salary as per the number of days. If he gets Rs. 100 per day, then how much money will he earn in total?

a) Rs. 1400
b) Rs. 2400
c) Rs. 3300
d) Rs. 3500

2: Ankita had a bar of chocolate which has 12 pieces. She gave one-fourth of it to Snehal, one-third of it to Menaka and one-sixth of it to Gracy. After distribution, how many pieces of chocolate is left with her?

3: Your friend walks 1.749 metres in 3.3 hours. You start walking along with him but your speed is slower than his speed. You both have a common destination. It took you 5 hours to reach the destination then what will be the distance that your friend will cover in 10 hours?

4: In an orchard, 70.3 kg of guavas is picked by the evening. Over the next hour, 5 workers add 3 kg 300 g of guavas each and 6 workers remove 8.1 kg of bad fruits each. What is the total weight of the remaining guavas?

a) 32.8 kg
b) 32 kg
c) 38.2 kg
d) 35 kg

5: Polad wanted to give some vegetables to his friends. He had 20 tomatoes and 18 potatoes. He gave his friend 1/5th of the tomatoes and 1/3rd of the potatoes. How many tomatoes and potatoes did his friend get respectively?

6: Your relatives gave you Rs. 5605. You went to your nearby bank and open a fixed deposit with that amount. You filled up the form but there was a field which asked for the amount of fixed deposit in Roman Numerals. What will you enter in that field if you remove Rs. 705 out of the existing money?

7: Sakira has a farm in which she grows only apples. In this year she has grown 392,600 apples. She needs to pack them to send it to the city. It took 1208 boxes to pack them all. How many apples were packed in 1 box?

8: What number do you get by adding 59 hundred to 31 thousandths?

a) 590.0031 b) 5900.031

c) 0.629 d) 5896.031

9: Mishutka drove 63.9823 km to visit his grandmother. When he reached his grandmother's house he noticed that the car had used up 3.31 litre of petrol. How many km can the car go in 1 litre?

a) 19.65 km/l

b) 19.33 km/l

c) 19.5 km/l

d) 20.33 km/l

10: A person sold 148.19 litres of apple juice on Monday and 17.12 litres more than this quantity on Tuesday. In total, how many litres of apple juice did he sell?

a) 313.5 litres

b) 323.5 litres

c) 330 litres

d) 350 litres

Model Paper V

1. Add : 32 tens + 32 hundreds + 32 thousandths = _________
2. What least number must be added to 19.016 to make it a multiple of 19?
3. Find a smallest value having ratio of all the three digits as 1:2:3.
4. Find the ratio of the greatest and the smallest three digit numbers formed by using digits 3, 4 and 0 only once.
5. Half of dozen banana costs Rs 32. Find the cost of 200 such bananas.
6. Mohan, Ravi, Kanika and Maneka are standing at four vertices of a rectangle having length 200 m and breadth 80 m. distance between Mohan and Ravi is greater than that of Kanika, but greatest distant from him is Maneka. Identify the types of intermediate distances in between these friends in terms of length, breadth and diagonals. Which of distances indicate diagonals of the rectangular shape?

7. What least number must be subtracted from 121.212 to make it divisible by 121?

8. Ravi purchased five dozens of banana at the rate of Rs 50 per dozen and sold them all at the rate of Rs 10 per pair. Calculate his gain or loss.

9. A wall mount clock strikes 2 bells in 2 seconds. This clock will take ______ seconds in striking 10 bells at 10 O'Clock.

10. Write the number in expanded form:
    32 hundreds 21 tenths and 39 thousandths =
11. Write the number in word form: 109.908

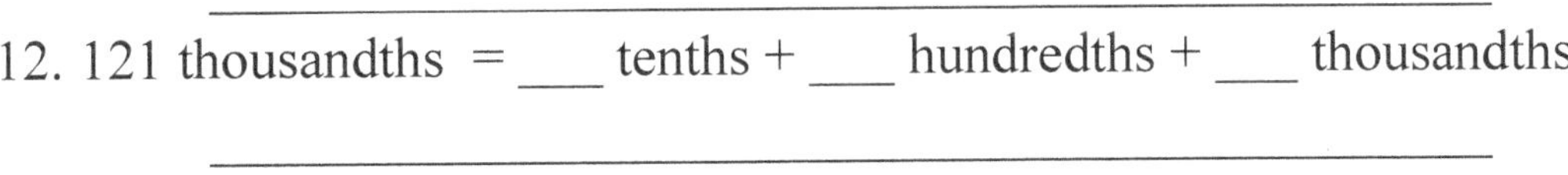

12. 121 thousandths = ___ tenths + ___ hundredths + ___ thousandths

13. A straight angle is ____ times bigger than a right angle and ____ times smaller than the complete angle.

14. Certain number becomes a three digit greatest even number after subtracting _______ from the smallest four digit number.

15. A segment that connects any two nonconsecutive vertices is a _______________.

16. A ___________ polygon can have all the sides equal to each other.
17. A polygon is ___________ if any part of a diagonal contains points in the exterior of the polygon. If no diagonal contains points in the exterior, then the polygon is _____.
18. Write the given decimal in expanded form.

$$182.536 = 1 \text{ X } 100 + \text{X}10 + \quad + \frac{}{10} + \frac{3}{100} + \frac{}{1000}$$

19. Express the following decimal in mixed number:
   a. 800.03 = ______ $\frac{3}{100}$;
   b. 29.029 = ______

   c. 8.019 + 2.881 + 3.008 = __________.

20. A wall mount clock takes 2 seconds to ring two bells at 2 O Clock. Calculate the time taken by the same clock to ring seven bells at 7 O Clock.

A: 14 seconds　　B: 7 seconds
C: 12 seconds　　D: 10 seconds

21. There are two combinations of packs containing pens and pencils. Packet one containing 6 pens and 5 pencils costs Rs 128. Packet B containing 5 pens and 6 pencils

costs Rs 103. Calculate the cost of a new pack containing 10 pens and 10 pencils of such type?

A: Rs. 250 B: Rs. 120 C: Rs. 135 D: Rs. 210

22. Complete the expansion in Indo-Arabic Numeration

a. 98,76,54,321 = 90,00,00,000 + 8,00,00,000 + _______ + 6,00,000 + 50,000 + _______ + 300 + 20 + 1

b. 32,54,03,320 =

23. Multiples of 16 are also multiples of 4 and 8, but all multiples of _____ and ________ are not multiples of 16.

24. A football is 27 times heavier than a tennis ball. A tennis ball is 9 times lighter than a rubber ball. _____ rubber balls will be equal of three footballs.

Model Paper VI

1. How many six digit numbers are there in all?
2. 1080 more than __________ is 30080.
3. Last two digit of the greatest seven digit even multiple of 3 is ____.
4. ______ must be subtracted from six digit greatest even number to make it a multiple of 4.
5. The greatest seven digit number which is not a multiple of 9, but a multiple of 3 is ___________.
6. Which digit should come at the blank space to make the statement true?
7. Digit 7 used _________ times while writing all the numbers starting from 1 to 100.

8. The speed of a car is increased from 60 km/h to 70 km/h. calculate the time saved by the rider while driving through a distance of 420 km.
9. The sum total of 4 consecutive two digit even numbers is 12 more than eight times ten. Find the numbers.
10. Five years ago Nikita reached at her teenage. Five years hence she will be at her ___________ years of age.
11. Rishabh paints a wall in 12 days and his counterpart Chelladurai paints it in 16 days. They jointly started working to finish the wall painting in _____days.
12. Anamika measured a length of 1.2 m, 1.6 m and 2.8 m ribbons by using her greatest possible measuring scale. Find the length of her scale.
13. Three bells toll at in intervals of 12 seconds, 16 seconds and 18 seconds respectively. After what interval of time do they toll together?
14. Complete the following:

$$\frac{121}{144} X \frac{12}{169} X \frac{26}{225} X \frac{15}{242} X \frac{15}{77} X \frac{91}{100} X \frac{11}{100} X \ \_\_\_ = 0.0001$$

15. Sixteen square shaped uniform tiles of side 4 cm each are arranged in two different patterns. In the first pattern tiles are joined to form a largest possible square. In the second pattern tiles are joined side by side to form a longest possible rectangle. Find out the difference in their outer boundaries.

16. Mr Ravikumar observed that the hour hand and minute hand of a wall mount clock makes _________ and ___________ complete turns on the dial throughout a day.

17. Vijayan installed two cisterns for filling up the water tank . First cistern alone can fill it in 1 hour 40 minutes and second cistern can fill it in 2 hours 30 minutes. Both the cisterns can fill the water tank in _____hours ___ minutes.

18. Three interior angles of a triangle are in such a way that sum total of first two angle is equal to the third angle, and first angle is twice the second. Find out all the interior angles.

19. ________ is the greatest possible six digit number divisible by 2, 4 and 8 without leaving remainders.

20. Half of a quarter of six tenths of a number is 120. Find the number.

21. Nikitha travels 360 km on three fifths of the petrol tank of her car. How far would she travel at the same rate with a full tank of petrol of her car?

22. A six digit number is exactly divisible by 101. Find the greatest number of this type.

23. Which greatest number of six digits is divisible exactly by 8?

24. 20% 0f 10% of a number is 80. Find the number.

25. _____ is the greatest prime number of two digits.

26. There are …… vertices and ……. Sides in a pentagon.

27. ……... lines can be drawn by using any two out of three non-collinear points lying on a plane.

Worksheet 1

1. How many vertices does a pentagonal prism have?
2. There are _____ tens in 45,6065.
3. Observe the figure and find out the number which is common to all the three shapes.

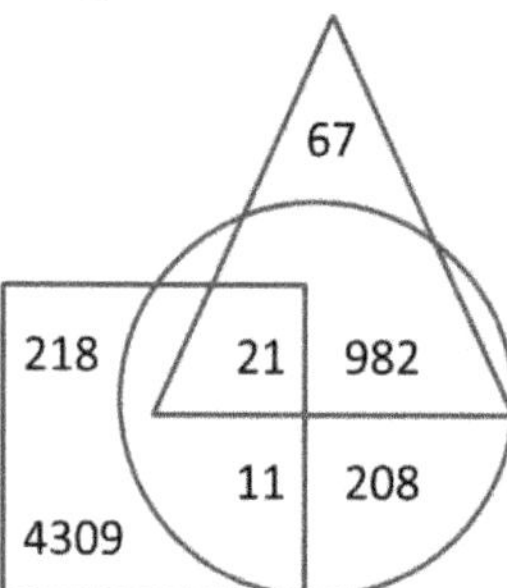

4. _________ is the greatest possible five digit even number divisible by 3.
5. All multiples of 9 are divisible by ____ and ____, but all multiples of ____ and 6 are not divisible by 9.
6. ______ can be added to or _____ can be subtracted from the four digit greatest number to make the number an odd multiple of 5.
7. Observe the following statements. It describes the population of cats, dogs and rabbits in a city duly recorded last year.
   Number of Cats < Number of Dogs
   Number of Dogs > Number of Rabbits

Which could be the number of cats and dogs?

	Cats	Dogs	Rabbits
A	192	232	176
B	306	127	176
C	432	542	675
D	541	329	767

8. Complete the following:

   1, 4, 9, __a___, __b___, ___c___;

Options	**a**	**b**	**c**
A:	16	25	36
B:	21	27	29
C:	12	15	19

11. The digit at one's place of a number which is 3 less than the third multiple of 1427.

A: 6 B:7 C: 8 D: 9

9. There are two combinations of packs containing pens and pencils. Packet one containing 6 pens and 5 pencils costs Rs 128. Packet B containing 5 pens and 6 pencils costs Rs 103. Calculate the cost of a new pack containing 10 pens and 10 pencils of such type?

   A: Rs. 250 B: Rs. 120

   C: Rs. 135 D: Rs. 210

10. Last Thursday in the calendar it was 27th February 2020. The forthcoming Thursday will be _________March 2020.

A: 4 B: 5 C: 6 D: 7

11. The product of 10th multiple of 11 and the 7th multiple of 109 has ________ at its one's place.

A: 0 B: 1 C: 2 D: 3

12. Find <A in the following figure.

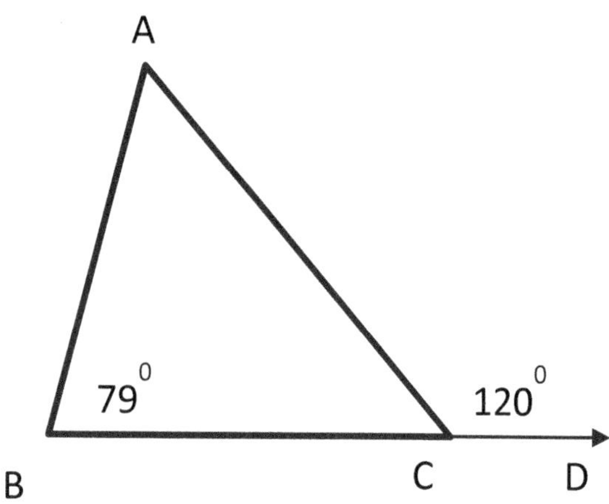

13. Ravikumar completes a work in 12 hours and Donald can complete the same work in 18 hours. Both of them started working together to finish the work earlier for saving their respective times.

Time saved by Ravikumar = ____________.

Time saved by Donald = ________________.

Who saved more time and by how much?

13. What least number can be added to the five digit smallest odd number to make it a multiple of 11?

14. what should be subtracted from the greatest even number of five digit to make it a multiple of 8?

Worksheet 2

1. 36 has _______ factors:

   Statement : 36 is a composite numbers.

   Reason : 36 has more than two factors.

   A: The given reason is appropriate.

   B: The given reason is not correct.

   C: The given reason requires more explanation.

   D: Both the statement and reason are wrong.

2. Observe following statements:

   I: 2 is an even prime number.

   II: 2 has no factors other than 1 and the number itself.

   III: 2 has another factor which is also a factor of all the other natural numbers.

   IV: All the other even numbers are multiples of 2.

   Select which of the statements mentioned above are true.

   A: Only I B: Only II C: Only I and III D: All

3. All multiples of 99 are divisible by ___, ____ and ____, but all multiples of ____, _____ and ___ are not divisible by 9.

4. _____ is the factor of all natural numbers and all the natural numbers are multiples of ____.

5. Shantakumar joined two different linear scales of the ratio of length 4:3 and managed to measure a length of 4 m 90 cm long steel rod by using the scale for an

exact number of times. Find the greatest possible measure of both the scales which Shantakumar used to make his scale.

6. Some of the statements regarding prime and composite numbers are given below.

I : 1 is not a prime ***or*** composite number.
II : Two is the only even prime number.
III: All odd numbers are not prime.
IV: All composite numbers can be written as product of prime numbers.
V: 101 has only two factors 1 and the number itself. That is why it is a prime number
Which of the above statements are true?
A: Only I   B: All
C: I, II and III   D: Only II, III and IV

7. Observe the following numbers represented in expanded form.
30,550 = 50 + ____a____ + 500
809,100 = 800,000 + 100 + ____b__
c. 725,608 = 20,000 + 700,000 + 8 + _c__+ 5,000
I: Numbers are represented in the International System.
II: All a, b and c are in thousands.
III: Sum total of a, b and c exceeds 60,000.
IV: In ascending order c > b > a.
Which of the statements are true?

A: I, II and IV   B: Only IV   C: None

8. Observe factors of 12 and 36 ….

Factors of 36 are 1,36,2,18,3,**12**,**6**,9,4

Factors of 12 are 1,**12**, 2, **6** , 3, **4**,

If common factors of 12 and 36 arranged from least to greatest are a, b, c, and if a x b + c = d, then d = ____

A: 24 B: 36 C: 72 D: 48

9. Observe the figure and answer the question as follows:

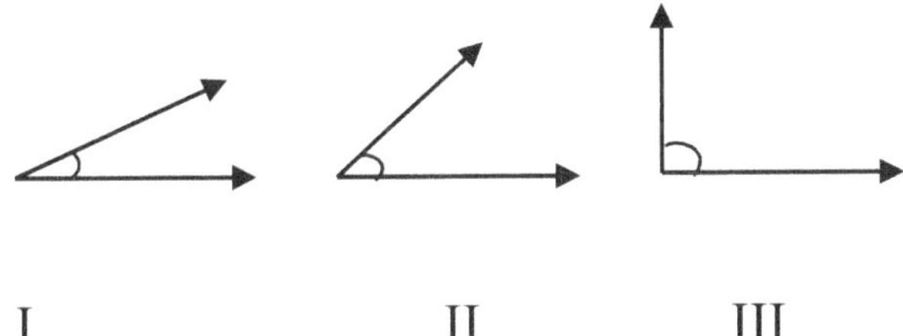

I II III

P : Angle I and II are acute angles.

Q: Angle II is not an acute angle.

R: Angle III is an obtuse angle.

S: Sum total of angle I and II exceeds a right angle.

T: Sum total of all the three angles is more than a straight angle.

Which of the above statements is/are not true?

A: Only P B: Only Q

C: Only P, Q and R D: All

10. ______ is the smallest number which can be added to 1321 to make the value divisible by 11.

11. Rohit planted a sapling which grows at the rate of 8 cm per week. After a gap of 10 fortnight he has observed that the plant is about to reach the height of _____ .

I: Less than 2 m but more than 1 m.

II: More than 1.5 m but less than 9th multiple of 20 cm.

III: We can measure it exactly by using a 40 cm scale.

IV: The height is two times shorter than another tree of 3.2 m height.

Which of the statements mentioned here are true?

A: Only I B: Only I, II and IV C: Only II, III and IV D: All

12. Observe the following:

13. Observe the information related to a pair of solid figures carefully and answer the question as follows:

Fig 1 is a cube and Fig 2 is a cylinder.

I: Fig 2 has a curved face. II: Fig 1 has six flat faces in all.

III: Fig 2 has 4 flat faces less than that of flat faces.

IV: Fig 2 resembles a cylinder.

V: Fig 1 has 8 corners. VI: Top view of Fig 1 is a square.

Which of the above statements regarding solid shapes are true?

A: Only I and II B: Only III C: All D: None

14. Observe the expanded form of two numbers:

12,345 = I + 2,000 + 300 + 40 + 5;

29,658 = 20,000 + II + III + 50 + 8;

I is ____________ more than II + III;

A: 4 B: 40 C: 400 D: 4000

15. There are some similarities between a parallelogram and a rhombus.
I: None of the interior angles are right angles.
II: Opposite sided are parallel to each other.
III: Opposite sides are equal to each other.
IV: Sum total of interior angles of each polygon is 3600

Which of the statements are not true?

A: Only I, II and III B: Only I C: All D: None

16. Observe the figure.

a. It is a polygon.
b. It has 4 sides.
c. Opposite sides are parallel to each other.
d. None of the interior angles are 90^0.
e. Opposite sides are equal in length.

Which of the above statements are not true?

A: a and b B: Only b C: none D: all

17. There are some similarities between a regular pentagon, regular hexagon and a square.

I: They have lines of symmetry equal to number of sides .
II: They can be divided into two equal halves. .
III: Number of Vertices = Number of Sides.
IV: Their opposite sided are parallel to each other.

Which of the statements are not true?

A: Only I, II and III | B: Only IV
C: All | D: None

18. A train covers 200 km in 2 hours and another 400 km 8 hours. The speed of the train during second time is ____ times less than that of the first time.

19. The product of the place values of 6 in the following number is ______________

36,436

20. Sanya is taller than Mira, but shorter than Jena. Jena attained 119 cm of height this year. Gap of their heights is uniform. It is 4.5 cm. Mira among them is the tallest. Who is shortest? What is the height of Sanya?

21. Sergey Bubka's Olympic gold-medalwinning pole vault in 1988 was 5.90 m. Would a vault of 595 cm be higher or lower than Bubka's jump?

22. Isabel needs 350 mL of milk to make a loaf of bread. How many liters of milk does she need to make 8 loaves of bread?

23. Marco was running in the 600-m race. He had run 45 000 cm. How many meters farther did he have to run to complete the race?

24: Which metric unit would best measure the capacity of each?

Write mL, L, or kL.

A. a fish tank
B. an oil tanker
C. an ice tray
D. a milk truck
E. a baby bottle
F. a washing machine

Worksheet 3

1. The greatest possible six digit even number has digit ___ at the unit place.
2. _____ should be subtracted from the digit of hundreds place of the given number to make it exactly divisible by both 3 and 6.

4,325,876

3. How many diagonals can be drawn inside a regular pentagon?
4. Is it possible to draw a triangle by using sides 3 cm, 5.6 cm and 9.02 cm?
5. Sixteen rows of plants in a crop field contain 160 plants in each row. How many plants are there in that garden?
6. 147 ÷ 49 = ___ ÷ _____. [Write values in simplest form.]
7. Arrange in ascending order.
   29%, 2.9 hundredths, 290 tenth, .029 hundreds.
8. Half a dozen banana costs Rs 24. Cost of 39 bananas = ______.

9. In a queue A is eighteenth from the front and B is 16th from the back. C is standing in the middle of A and B. C is 25th from the front. How many persons are there standing in the queue?

Options: A: 45 B: 46 C: 47 D: 48

10. In the given pattern letters are changing by following certain rules. Observe the rule and complete the series.

ACFH, BDGI, EGJL, ______, _______

11. Observe the figure and complete the statements as follows:

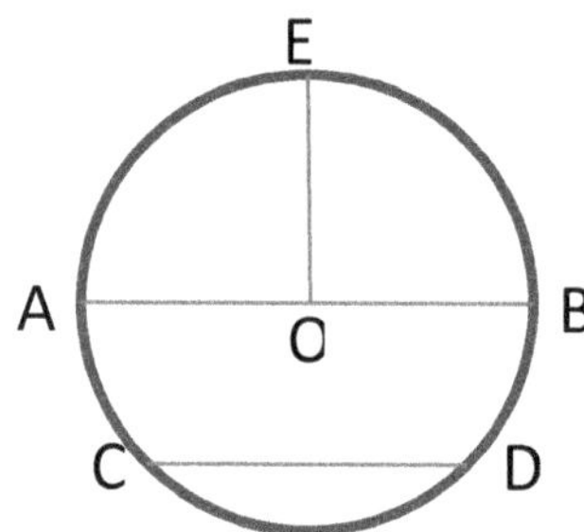

a) ____The distance from the center of a circle to its edge.
b) ____ - The distance across a circle through its center point.
c) _____ - The distance around the edge of a circle, better known as the circles rim.
d) _____ - Two or more circles of different radii that share the same center.
e) _____ - Line across a circle that does not pass through its center.
f) _____ - one fourth (quarter) of a circle.
g) ______ half of a circle.
h) ________ is the greatest chord of a circle.
i) ________ X 2 = Diameter.

12: 19th multiple of 20 is _____ more than 5th multiple of 60.

13: 2,008 g = ______ kg _________ g.

14: 19,019 m = ______ km _______m.

Worksheet 4

1. 144 students were standing in the assembly in such a way that number of rows and number of students in each row is equal. How many students are there in each row?
2. 293 marbles are there. Six friends wanted to share these marbles equally. How many marbles each of them will get? How many marbles remain undivided?
   [share of each friend = 48; marbles left = 5]
3. In certain office one third all workers are women. 16/17th of all the working women are married. If number of unmarried women in the office is 10 then find the total number of men working in that office.
   [$\frac{1}{3}$ of $\frac{1}{17}$ = 10; therefore $\frac{2}{3}$ of all workers (men) = $\frac{510X2}{3}$ = 340;]
4. Complete the number series by providing two consecutive values.

   385, 365, 340, ____, ____, 235, 190…..

   [the numbers decreases at the rate of 20,25, … respectively]
5. (1/5th of 105 + 1/6th of 606 = P; P has _____ at its ten's place and ____ at its one's place.
6. 6. Sum total of place values of 4 in the following numbers = _____
7. 14,647; 51,480; 14,505
8. 7. Day before yesterday was Friday. Day after tomorrow will be __
9. 8. The greatest possible 6 digit number divisible by 8 is ______ less than the smallest 7 digit number.
10. 9. Fraction of "C" in the word "SCIENCE" = ______________.
11. 10. _____ must be subtracted from 121,124 to make it divisible by 11.

Worksheet 5

1. If 3 is added to a number it becomes a 6th multiple of 120,100. Find the number.
2. Find the sum total greatest and smallest 3 digit number without repeating any digits.
3. Find the perimeter of a semicircular crop field of diameter 56 m = ________________.
4. What must be added to 10109 to make it a multiple of 5?
5. ______ is the 100th multiple of the smallest odd composite number of 3 digits.
6. 1/3rd of 4/5th of 15,015 = _________.
7. 11th multiple of 11 is _____ more than 10th multiple of 12.
8. _______ numbers have only two factors, _____ and the number itself.
9. Minerva Multiplex can accommodate 1,500 viewers at a time. Last Sunday 11/15th of it was full. Find the number of seats remained vacant last Sunday.
10. $\frac{121}{139} X \frac{139}{100} =$ ________.[Find the value in decimal]
11. If 1 is subtracted from a number it becomes a 4th multiple of 101122. Find the number.
12. Find the greatest and smallest 6 digit numbers without repeating any digits. Also find their difference.
13. A square of side 20 cm is exactly fitted uniformly inside another square of side 30 cm for obtaining a design. Find the area enclosed by linings of both the squares.
14. What least number must be added to 3,989 to make it a complete square number?
15. ____________ is the 90th multiple of the smallest composite number of 3 digits.
16. $\frac{4}{19}$ $of \frac{19}{20}$ of 505,000 = _________
17. 100th multiple of 19 is _____ less than 20th multiple of 100.

18. $\frac{7}{19} X \frac{19}{39} X \frac{39}{100} =$ _______ [in decimal]

19. $\frac{1}{10} X \frac{1}{100} X \frac{1}{1000} = \frac{1}{\ldots\ldots\ldots\ldots}$

20. __________ is the three digit greatest number divisible by 4.

21. If 9 is added to a number it becomes a 6th multiple of 100100. Find the number.

22. Find the greatest and smallest 3 digit number without repeating any digits. Also find their sum total.

23. A circle of diameter 280 cm is exactly fitted concentrically inside another circle of diameter 2.8 m for obtaining a design find the area enclosed by linings of both the circle.

24. What must be added to 8,885 to make it a complete square number?

25. _____ is the 12th multiple of the smallest composite number of 4 digit.

26. $\frac{13}{190}$ *of* $\frac{190}{2003}$ *of* $8{,}012 =$ ________

27. 100th multiple of 1001 is _____ more than the greatest four digit number.

28. 2.0121 X 125 X 8 = …………

Worksheet 6

1. Show different ways to form 25,704.

   i) ______thousands + _____ hundreds + ____ ones
   ii) _________ hundreds + ____ ones
   iii) __________ ones.

1. There are two different types of arrangements:
   a. P = 29,000 + 400 + 20 + 8
   b. Q= 20,000 + 9400 + 28

   Establish the relationship in between P and Q: P _____ Q.
2. Circle the numbers divisible by 4:

   12,984, 214316, 3204348, 43054082

3. There are five apples in a shelf. There are 109 other fruits on the other shelf. How many fruits are there in all in the kitchen shelf?

   [add both the value.]
4. Suneeta draws 12 comics books from the library on Monday. She draws 15 more books on Thursday than compare to books drawn on Monday. How many books were drawn in all does Suneeta draw in Monday and Thursday?

5. During the basketball game, Pinaki makes 5 baskets worth 2 points each, 3 baskets worth 3 points each, and 5 free throws worth 1 point each. Calculate the total point earned by Pinaki.

6. Roger's classroom bench can seat 4 students each. Find the number of benches required for accommodating 21 boys and 24 girls in the classroom.

7. Complete the following:

2065 X 25 = _______ X 25 + ____ X 25 + 5 X 25;

8. Complete the fractional relations: $\frac{12}{19} = \frac{24}{38} = \frac{48}{76} = \frac{\_\_\_}{}\ X\ \frac{\_\_\_}{152}$.

10. Find the rule:

30, 27, ______, 21, _______, ________, __________

11. Compare: 305 hundreds _______ 30 thousand and 50 tens.

12. Mark rounded a number to the nearest hundred and got 6000. Which number could be Sally's original number?

a. 6403 b. 4000 c. 5220 d. 7001 e. 5620

13. Round 734,678…

To the nearest ten: _______________

To the nearest hundred: _______________

To the nearest thousand: _______________

To the nearest ten thousand: _______________

To the nearest hundred thousand: ____________

14. Which two numbers round to 300,000 when rounded to the nearest hundred thousand?

a. 306,999 b. 352,384 c. 399,999
d. 245,678 e. 289,653

15. Find the product:

a. 6.09 X 1000 =__________.

16. A number multiplied by itself is called a ________ number.

17. Observe the number pattern and complete the series:

11X 11 = 121
111X 111 = 12321
1111X 1111 = ____________.
11111X11111 =________________.

18. Complete the following:

1.1X 0.1X 0.01 X 0.001 = ____________.

19. Half a dozen banana costs Rs 20. Cost of 30 dozen banana is Rs ______.

20. Write a number sentence that matches the following pattern:

	5000	400	70	5
9	45000	3600	630	45

Worksheet 7

1. A rectangular flowerbed in the Regent Park has an area of 120 meter square. The breadth of the bed is 5.5 m. Find it length.
2. Fractions represented in the following tape diagram are _________ fractions having values: ____, ______ and ______.

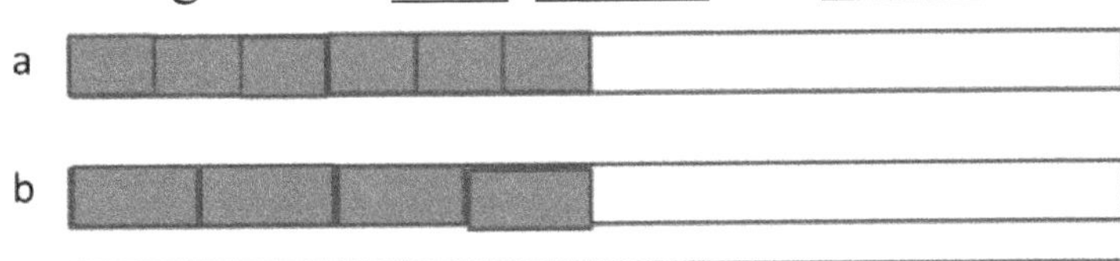

3. Half of the first bucket, quarter of the second, one fifth of the 3rd and 1/8th of the 4th are filled with slaked lime. All the buckets are of same capacity. What fraction of all the buckets are filled with slaked lime?

4. What solid figures can be made by folding the following patterns?

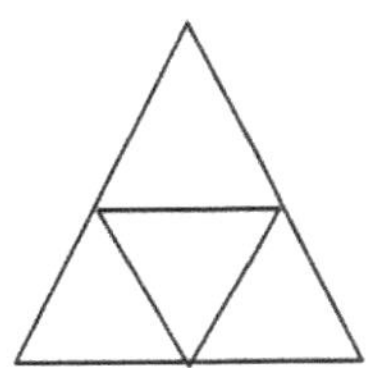

5. ________ must be added to 998.089 to make the value equal to the greatest three digit multiple of 3.

6. What fraction of the big square box is yet to be filled by small square boxes of identical types?

Hints : [(No,of boxes present in it)/(Maximum number of box is it can hold as per its capacity)]

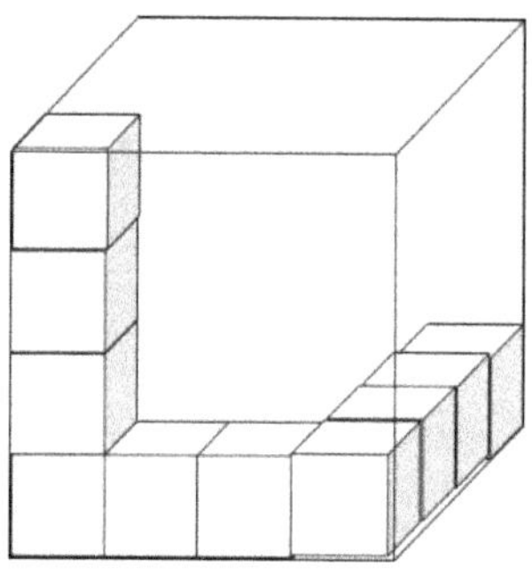

7. What fraction of the following figure is shaded?

8. Which of the following value is the greatest?
   a. 29% b. 29 tenths c. 29 thousandths d. 29 tens
9. Nikita can do her project works by herself in 12 hours. Along with Ruchira she can finish it in 4 days. Ruchira alone can finish the same project work in ______ days.
10. What fraction of all the numbers starting from 1 to 1,000 are multiples of 200?
11. Simplify: $\frac{13}{100} + \frac{303}{100} + \frac{1201}{1000} + \frac{16}{25} =$ ....

Worksheet 8

1. If $\frac{2}{5}$ of 40 $= \frac{2}{5}$ X 40 $= \frac{2X40}{5} = 2X8 = 16$
   a. What is $\frac{3}{5}$ of 60 ?
2. Add : $\frac{2}{10} + \frac{33}{100} + \frac{121}{1000} + \frac{6}{5}$
3. 19 + 19 tenths + 19 thousandths = __________.
4. $3\frac{1}{2} + 11\frac{7}{8} =$
5. Half of a quarter of 64 = ________________.
6. Multiply : $\frac{10}{121}$ X $\frac{11}{100}$ X $\frac{13}{24}$ X $\frac{11}{26}$ X $\frac{4}{5}$ =
7. Tap A can fill up a water tank in 30 minutes and tap B can empty the same water tank in 45 minutes. Tap A will take ____ minutes to fill the tank when both the taps remain open.
8. A cistern can fill a water tank in 45 minutes and a tap can empty the same water tank in 1 hour 30 minutes. Find the time taken up by the cistern to fill the tank when the tap kept open.
9. Three triangles joined side by side to form a polygon having ___ sides. Sum total of all the interior angles of this polygon is ____^{0}.
   [Angle Sum Property of a Triangle: Sum total of all the interior angles of a triangle is 180^0.]

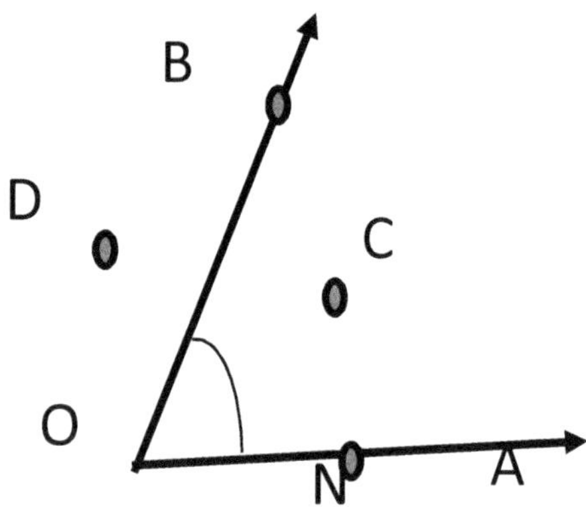

:

10.Observe the figure and complete the following:

a) Write names of different rays present in the given figure. Example: **OB**
b) There are ____________ arms and ______ vertex.
c) _____ and ________ are two arms of this angle.
d) Point ____ is lying inside the angle.
e) Name of this angle is __________.
f) Two rays meeting at a point. This point is called __________________ of the angle.
g) Point _____ and _____ are lying on the angle.
h) Point ______ is lying at the exterior of the angle.
i) Point ______ is lying in the interior of the angle.
j) < AOB is an angle because:

I. It has two ____________;
II. It has a ______ ;
III. It has a definite___________ .

11. Fill in the blanks:

a. Exterior angles of a polygon are 1st , 2nd 3rd and 4th multiple of 36^0. Find all the interior angles of this polygon.
[Exterior angle along with corresponding interior angle of any polygon are supplementary to each other.]
b. Interior angles of a triangle are first second and third multiples of 30^0. Find the angles. What is the special name of that triangle?
c. A triangle having _______ right angles is not possible.
d. A triangle having ______ obtuse angles is not possible.
e. Sum total of all the interior angles of a polygon is 540^0. Find the number of sides it has. There are _____ diagonals in this polygon.
f. Sum total of all the interior angles of a polygon is equal to four right angles. It must have at least one _____ angle or at least ______ right angles. They cannot have less than _____ obtuse angles.
g. Identify following triangles:
h. Supplementary angle of complementary angle of 56^0 is equal to ___________________.
i. A quadrilateral having maximum number of _____ right angles is possible.
j. What fraction of right angle is 30^0?
k. A quadrilateral having maximum number of ____ acute angles is possible.
l. A triangle having two ______ angles or two ______ angles is not possible.

12. How many vertices are there in a pentagon?
13. What least number should be added to 11,011,064 to make the number a common multiple of 3 and 9?

Worksheet 9

1. Complete the following number pattern:

a) 88,______, __________, __________, 33, __________. _________.

b) 121, ________, __________, ________, _____, 55, ____, ________, 22, 11

c) 12, ___, ______, 12,345, ______________.

d) 10204, _____, __________, ______________, ___________, 12,204, 12,404.

e) 144, _____, __________, ______________, 96, 84 , ________, ______.

2. Add : MMDCXX + MCDXCLVI

3. Subtract: MMMCLX – MCMLXXXV

4. Arrange the following in ascending and descending order:

a) MDC, MCMLXV, MCDXCLV, MDLXVIII

b) XXII, XXXVIII, XCLXXVI, XVI

c) MMMCMXCIX, MMMXII, MMMCMXXII,

5. Compare:

a) MMMCMXCIX _____ MMMDCXCIX;

b) CMCCX ________ MCCX

c) XXIV ______XXXIII

6. Complete the following:

36,653 = _____ + ___ + ____ + ___ + ______.

7. 2,892 = X 1000 + ... X 100 + ... X 10 + ...X 1

8. Complete the following:

a) ____________ are what we can multiply to get numbers.

b) ____________ are what we get after multiplying the number by any other number.

c) ____________ is a factor of all the numbers.

d) All the numbers are one of the multiple of ____________.

e) All ____________ numbers have only two factors, 1 and the number itself.
f) 36 has ____________ factors in all.
g) 36 has ____________ prime factors in all.
h) All the factors of 18 are also ____________ of 36, but all the ____________ of 36 are not the factors of 18.
i) ____________ are always greater than or equal to the number.

9. Multiples of 4 are also multiples of 2, but all multiples of 2 are not necessarily multiples of ____________.
10. ____________ is the smallest three digit number divisible by 8.
11. ____ must be added to the three digit smallest number to make it exactly divisible by 9 .
12. The greatest possible five digit number formed by different digits without repeating any of the digit twice.

13. Find the number of triangles in each figure.

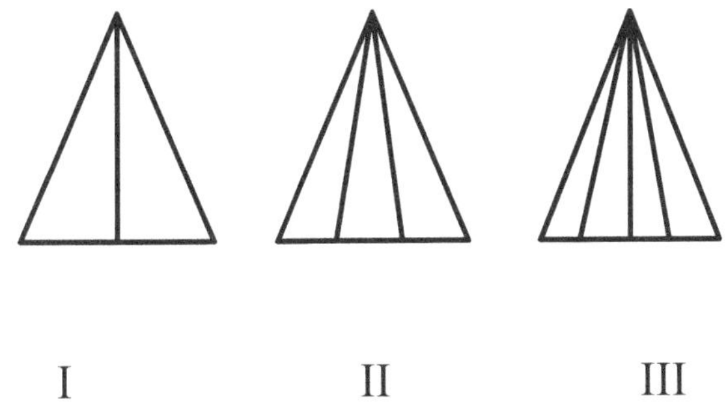

I II III

Worksheet 10

1. Dana has only 2 rupees coins in her hand, and Ajah has exactly the same number of 5 rupees coins and no other coins. Together they have a total of Rs. 210. How many coins is each person holding? Find their individual shares in the collection.
2. When 2 pieces of rope are placed end-to-end, they measure 40 meters in length. When the 2 pieces are laid side-by-side, one is 10 meters longer than the other. How long is each piece of rope? Show your work.

3. If 1 is added to a number it becomes a third multiple of 900900. Find the number.
4. Find the greatest and smallest 4 digit number without repeating any digits. Also find their difference.
5. A circle of diameter 14 cm is exactly fitted concentrically inside another circle of diameter 28 cm for obtaining a design find the area enclosed by linings of both the circle.
6. What must be added to 12109 to make it a complete square number?
7. _____ is the sixteenth multiple of the smallest composite number of a digit.
8. Half of 20% of 1600 = ________
9. 9th multiple of 9 is _____ more than 7th multiple of 7.

10.5. Calculate the fraction of "M" present in the word "Mathematics."

11.6. Mandela wanted to find out a number which is a sum of square values of three consecutive even numbers. The sum total was 308. Find all the three numbers.

12. What least number must be subtracted from 1332 to make it a multiple of 11?
13. Half of 4/9th of 810 = ___________
14. Mohan scored full marks in Mathematics. Dinesh got 6 less than Mohan in Mathematics. His score was 12 more than Latika. Full Marks in Mathematics was 100. Find the score of Latika.
15. _____ Dozens is just half of a gross.

16. Average age of 12 students was 12.8 years. After a new admission in their group the average age of the group became 13 years. Find the age of newly admitted fellow.

17. Sum total of place values of 5 in the following numbers = _____ 15,647; 51,780; 12,505

18. Day before yesterday was Sunday. Day after tomorrow will be __

19. The greatest possible 5 digit number divisible by 4 is ______ less than the smallest 6 digit number.

20. Monika added 3210 to number for obtaining the greatest even number of four digits. Find the number.

21. What least number must be subtracted from a five digit smallest odd number to make it a multiple of 11?

22. How many three digit numbers can be formed by using digits 3,5 and 0? Arrange these numbers in ascending order.

23. What least number should be subtracte4d from five digit greatest number to obtain a common multiple of 2, 4 and 8?

24. 125 X 8 X 40 X 25 X 1.009 = ……….

Worksheet 11

1. Find value of the given expression:

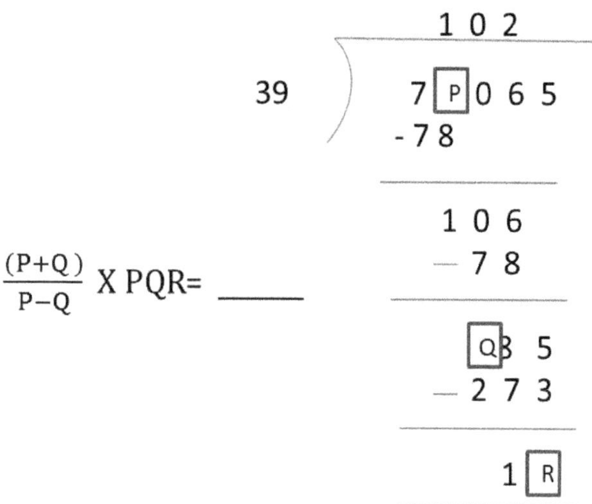

$\frac{(P+Q)}{P-Q}$ X PQR= _____

2. There are _____ triangles more in Fig 1 than in Fig 2.

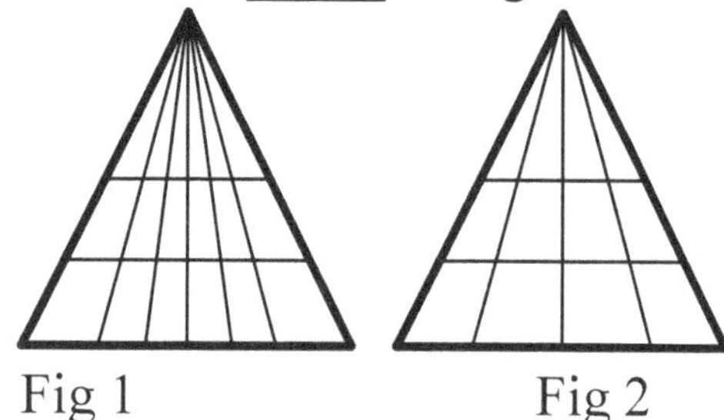

Fig 1 Fig 2

3. Observe the sequence of the arrangement of polygons.

If above mentioned sequence continues, then number of sides present in the seventh figure will be _____ more than that of the number of sides present in the 1st figure.

4. If 10 is added to a number it becomes the 10th multiple of 10100. Find the number.

5. Find the greatest and smallest number of four digits having different digits at their respective places.

6. Form the greatest and smallest 4 digit number by using digits 8,4,0 and 3. Also find their difference.

7: Find the perimeter of a rectangle having length 32 cm and breadth 20 cm.

8: Total cost of 3 pens and 2 pencils is Rs 25. In another combination total cost of 2 pens and 3 pencils is Rs 20.

a. Find the total cost of 2 pens and 2 pencils.
b. Also find the total cost of 5 pens and 4 pencils.
c. Find the cost of 1 pen.
d. Find the cost of 1 pencil.

9: _____ million is the 1000th multiple of the greatest even number of 5 digit.

10: $\frac{11}{29}$ of $\frac{29}{709}$ of $\frac{1418}{1,001}$ of $\frac{7,007}{12100}$ $=$ ________

11: 30th multiple of 11 is _____ more than 6th multiple of 50.

12: ____ is the smallest number to be subtracted from 1009 to make it a multiple of 6.

13: Rina used different digits to form six digit numbers. Find out sum total of greatest and smallest such numbers formed by her.

14: Four interior angles of a pentagon are first four multiples of 45^0. Find out magnitude of fifth interior angle of that pentagon.

Worksheet 12

1. Difference of digits of a two digit number is 7. If digits are reversed then sum total of both the number becomes the predecessor of the three digit smallest number. Find the second multiple of this number.

2. 121, 169 and 225 have following things in common:
   I. All these numbers are square numbers.
   II. These are square numbers of odd primes.
   III. These numbers have equal numbers of prime factors.

   Select which of the statements mentioned above are true.

   A: Only I B: Only II

   C: Both I and III D: All I, II and III

b) Complete the following to obtain values in the form of product of prime factors:

I. 1410 = _____ X___;

II. 1331 = ____________________.

III. 169 = __________________.

IV. $1/10^{th}$ of $9/17^{th}$ of 5100 = _______________.

V. 21 hundredths added to 11 tenths = _____________.

VI. $\left(\frac{84}{0.004}\right)$ = ____________________;

VII. 363 = __________ X __________;

VIII. 3,000 = 2 X 2 X 2 X _____________

IX. 729 = __ X __X___ X ___X___;

X. __________ = 89 X 11

XI. 9th multiple of 11 is _______ multiple of 9.

XII. After subtracting ___________ we can obtain 3rd multiple of 13 from the 4th multiple of 10.

c) Complete the following:

I. 1, 4, 9, __i___, __ii___, ___iii___;

II. (i + xxxiv) +(cii – viii) = _______________

III. 1, 8, 27, ________, ___________, _____________ .

IV. 121, ________, ___________, ___________ 161.

V. 64, ________, ______, ________, 16, 9.

d) Some of the statements regarding prime and composite numbers are given below.

I : 1 is not a prime ***or*** composite number.

II : Two is the only even prime number.

III: All odd numbers are not prime.

IV: All composite numbers can be written as product of prime numbers.

V: 101 has only two factors 1 and the number itself. That is why it is a prime number

Which of the above statements are true?

A: Only I B: All

C: I, II and III D: Only II, III and IV

e) A racing car covers 100 km in 2 hours and another 400 km 4 hours. The speed of the car during second time is ____ times more than that of the first time.

A: 1 B: 2 C: 3 D: 4

f) A wire of a square sized shape of side 32 cm is reshaped to form a circle. Find the circumference of that circle. [Circumference of a circle is the outer boundary of a circle].

g) There are 35,278 students in Class III, 32,184 students in Class IV and 25,375 students in Class V in the schools of a city. Find the total number of students reading in Classes III, IV and V. Among these students 60,324 are girls. Find the number of students who are boys.

h) There are 4021 students in a school. Each section can accommodate a maximum number of 25 students. There are equal number of students in each section, find their number in each section. Is there any section having less than 25 students? How many such sections are there?

i) Sum total of place values of 6 in the following set of numbers = __ .

26,754,   64,543   23,362

A: 66,600   B: 66,060

C: 60,606   D: 16,000

j) There are 2,983 boys and 2,175 girls in a school. Find the total enrolment of the school. Find also the number of more boys than girls on the rolls of the school.

k) What should be added to 79,415 to make it the greatest five-digit number?

l) By how much is 89283 is greater than 79382?

m) What should be subtracted from 98989 to get 88888?

n) There are ____ vertices, ____ faces and _____ edges in a cuboid.

o) Two cubical block of edge 30 cm each joined side by side to form a cuboidal block. Find the surface area of the top and bottom part of that cuboid.

p) Two sets of pillars counted by a visitor from standing in the middle. He has counted number of pillars from right hand side along with the pillar that he was holding as 10. From left hand side his counting in the same way was 9. How many pillars were there? Consider the fact that none of the pillars were identical.

q) Monika calculated 15th multiple of 5 added to 5th multiple of 15. Find the digit that she might have in the one's place of the product.

r) There are ______ flat faces and ___ curved faces in a cuboid.

s) Find the difference of place values of 5 in 22,543 and 54,432.

t) Renuka prepared a bar graph that shows the number of kg of food eaten each day by each animal. What information goes on the horizontal axis? What information can be placed on the vertical axis?

u) Tim lives in New Delhi. He prepares a line graph that shows the amount of LPG used in his home kitchen for a year. Will the line graph show any change throughout the year?

29. A regular pentagon has ______ lines of symmetry less than that of a regular hexagon.

Worksheet 13

1. What least number of six digits can have 2, 3, 4 and 6 as common multiples?
2. Kim gathered information about the population of individual states of her country. If she prepares a bar graph of this data, what information will be displayed on the vertical axis? What information will be displayed on the horizontal axis?

3. Total cost of 3 snacks and two breads is Rs. 11. In other combination total cost of 2 snacks and 3 breads is Rs. 9. What will be the total cost of a snacks and bread?

4. What least number must be multiplied to 72 to make the value a perfect square?

5. There are some similarities between a parallelogram and a rhombus.
I: None of the interior angles are right angles.
II: Opposite sided are parallel to each other.
III: Opposite sides are equal to each other.
IV: Sum total of interior angles of each polygon is 360^0
Which of the statements are true?

A: Only I, II and III B: Only I
C: All D: None

6: What digit will be there at unit place of the product of 108, 101, 2008 and 4001?

7: How many digits will be there in the product of 10, 200, 3000 and 40000?

Worksheet 14

1. A segment that connects any two nonconsecutive vertices is a ______________.

2. A ___________ polygon can have all the sides equal to each other.

3. A polygon is __________ if any part of a diagonal contains points in the exterior of the polygon. If no diagonal contains points in the exterior, then the polygon is _____.

4. A _____________ polygon is always convex.

5. How many diagonals can be drawn in a hexagon?

6. ________ non overlapping triangles can be fitted inside a hexagon.

7. How is 106.076 written in word form?

____

8. Write 16 tenths and 16 thousandths in standard form?

____

9. Write a decimal with 7 in the ones place, 4 in the tenths place, and 5 in the hundredths place. _________

10. Find the difference of place values of 4 and 3 in 107.423 ?

____

11. Write the given decimal in expanded form.

$$182.536 = 1 \text{ X } 100 + \text{X}10 + \quad + \frac{}{10} + \frac{3}{100} + \frac{}{1000}$$

12. Express the following decimal in mixed number:

a. 800.03 = ______ $\frac{3}{100}$;

b. 29.029 = ______

c. 8.019 + 2.881 + 3.008 = __________.

Worksheet 16

1. Find the value of $20 \div 5 + 10 \times (8 - 4)$.

2. Find the value of $10 - 5 + 3$.

3. Find the value of $25 \div 5 + 20 \times (10 - 5)$.
4. Tell whether the number 3 is prime, composite, or neither.
5. Write the prime factorization of 49 using exponents.

6. Your local bakery has 3 3 + 4 flavors of bagels. How many bagels does the shop have?
7. How do you know that a number is prime?
8. Every composite number can be expressed as a product of ……

9. When you find the value of an algebraic expression by replacing variables with numbers, you ____________________ the expression.
10. A is a relationship that assigns exactly one __________ value to one input value.

11. A __________ or symbol used to represent an unknown quantity is a language of symbols we use for representing variables.
12. ____________ is the number of square units needed to cover the inside of a region or plane figure.

13. _________________ are combinations of variables, numbers, and at least one operation.

14. 21 tens + 21 tenths = ______________ .

15. 15th multiple of 20 is equal to 20th multiple of ________.

16. 121 tens + 121 tenths + 21 hundredths = ___________.

17. There are ______________ more flat surfaces in a cube than compared to a rectangular pyramid.

18. We must add __________ to 1243 to make it exactly divisible by 4.

19. At least _____________ lines can be drawn by using any two of three non collinear points located on a plane.

20. 3089 mm = _______ m _____ cm _____ mm.

21. Complete the following:

$$\left(10+\frac{1}{2}\right)\left(10+\frac{1}{3}\right)X\frac{16}{93}\ X\left(1-\frac{19}{42}\right)X\frac{36}{61}\ X\left(1-\frac{17}{200}\right)=\_\_\_\_\_\_\_\ X\ 0.005$$

22. Base angle of an isosceles triangle is twice that of the vertex angle. Find measures of all the angles of the triangle.

23. All the ________________ are special types of parallelogram, but all the parallelograms are not __________________.

24. What least number must be added to 131.102 to make the value divisible by 131?

25. Sum total of all the numbers starting from 1 to 1000 = ______________.

26. What must be added to make 19832 a multiple of 11?

27. Find a common factor of 121,1331 and 13431. Is this factor a greatest one? Is there any other common factor?

28. Mohan is twice as old as Mohini. Three years ago, he was three times as old as Mohini. How old is Mohan now?

29. Nitin added 3 to obtain a four digit smallest number divisible by 5. What least number must be added to this number to make it a multiple of 8?

30. After attempting all the 80 questions a candidate secured 140 marks. As per rule there were 5 marks for each correct answer and 1 marks for every incorrect answer. What is the number of questions he attempted wrongly?

31. What least number should be subtracted from 32,098 to get a multiple of 3?

32. Two angles of a triangle are 110^0 and 39^0 43'. Find out the third angle.

33. 30% of 20% of 1,00,300 = ...

Worksheet 17

1. The table below shows the water used by a family having 5 members.

Activity	Water in Litres(l)
a. Cooking and drinking	30 l
b. Washing	105 l
c. Cleaning pots, pans	40 l
d. Bathing	120 l
e. Gardening	85
Total water used by them ______	

   i. Find the average per head consumption of water.
   ii. Which activity requires least amount of water?

2. A wall mount clock strikes three bells in three seconds at 3 O' Clock. Find the time taken by that clock to strike 10 bells at 10 P.M.

3. Mr Ravikumar checked his mobile at 9 a.m. and found that it is showing a time which is ________ hours more than the GMT. The place where Mr Ravikumar residing is at 90^0 East to the GMT time zone. Time increases at the rate of 4 minutes per one degree change in the meridian towards eastern direction. What was the GMT ?

4. Pressure of a gas increases when volume is decreased. The product of pressure and volume of certain mass of gas always remains constant. The volume will be decreased by ________ fraction when pressure of the gas is doubled.

5. Which number is equal to the difference of fifth multiple of 20 and fifteenth multiple of 3?

6. Complete the following expansion:

$$102.2032 = 100 + \quad + \frac{2}{10} + \frac{}{100} + \frac{}{1,000} + \frac{2}{10,000}$$

7. Find the value :

$$\left(\frac{1}{2} X \frac{2}{3} X \frac{3}{4}\ X \ldots \ldots . X \frac{999999}{1,000,000}\right) X\ 11,00011\ =$$

8. Which number comes at the fifth step if we continue multiplying 1.10011 repeatedly by 10?

9. Rajan completes his assignment in 12 days and Nikitha completes the same assignment alone in 16 days. If they work jointly upon the same assignment, then in how many days do they complete the same assignment?

10. The minute hand of a clock makes 360^0 at the dial during a complete rotation. Find the angle made by the minute hand at the dial during a day.

11. Rishabh observed that if we multiply 15 to a number then it becomes 60 times greater than 4. Find the original number.

12. Namitha made a decimal representation in such a way that the number was a least value of 5 digits without repeating any digit twice. Also the number had five places of decimals. Find the product of digits at thousandths and ten thousandths place.

13. By heating 100 kg sandstone 44 kg carbon dioxide is obtained. Calculate the mass of sandstone required for obtaining 8.8 kg carbon dioxide.

14. Arrange the following in ascending order:

    12%, 1.2, 12 tenths, 12 thousandths, 12 tens, 12 hundredths, (12 X 0.101)

15. Is there any prime number located in between 80 and 90? If yes, then find their sum total.

16. Cost of 3 pencils and 4 pens is ₹ 77. Total cost of 4 pencils and 3 pens is ₹ 63. Find the total cost of 10 pens and 11 pencils.
17. Monika prepared a chart to show two different closed figures each of which are made of 81 identical square sized silver papers in such a way that one of the shapes has maximum possible outer boundary and the other shape has least outer boundary. If the area of each silver paper is 1 sq. inch, then find the dimensions of both the shapes made by Monika.
18. What least number must be added to the smallest six digit number to make it a multiple of 9?
19. Find the values of the following:
    a) 11 tens + 11 tenths + 11 hundredths + 11 thousandths
    b) $\frac{11}{100} + \frac{101}{1000} + \frac{1001}{1000} + \frac{10001}{10000} + 101$

c) $\left(1+\frac{1}{10}\right) X \left(1+\frac{1}{11}\right) X \ldots \ldots . \left(1+\frac{1}{999}\right) =$

d) $5-5+5-5+5-5+\cdots$ 170 times =

e) $\left(1+\frac{1}{1-\frac{1}{1+\frac{1}{10}}}\right) =$

20. 20% of 100,100 = ……………

21: Rikin covers 20 m in 4 seconds. Calculate his speed in km/h.

22. 7th multiple of 7,000 is added to the successor of the 7 digit greatest number. The sum total will be . ____________ more than 10 million.

23. 7th multiple of 9,000 and 9th multiple of 7,000 added to obtain a value which is __________ more than the smallest 6 digit number.

24. 1,000th multiple of the product of all the factors of 101 is ______ more than the 5th multiple of 20,000.

25. $\frac{11}{23}$ of $\frac{23}{48}$ of $\frac{48}{97}$ of 194 = ____ .

26. How many seven digit numbers are there in all?

Worksheet 18

1. Roderick took a car for reaching his office in time. The car was moving with an average speed. It took 4 hours to reach his office which is 240 km away from his house. The car was moving through the second lane of express way having a speed limit of 60 km/h. The speed limit of first lane of that express way is 80 km/h. find the total time which could be saved by Roderick if he prefers moving through the first lane instead of the second.

2. 20 % of a number is 8 more than the 8th multiple of 100. Find the original number.

3. Find the value:

$$\frac{11}{100}+\frac{11}{1000}+\frac{11}{10000}+0.101+1.01=$$

4. What least number must be subtracted from 121019.049 to make this value exactly divisible by 8 without extending the place of decimals beyond hundredths?

5. The average of six person's age is 12 years. After joining a senior person the average is increased by 3 years 2 months. Find age of the senior.

6. A number is increased by 6.6 to make it a five digit smallest natural number exactly divisible by 11. Find the original number.
7. Donadoni is 4 years older than Mike, who is again 3.5 years younger than Rick. Rick will enter his teenage after 3 years. Find the age of all the fellows.
8. Add the following:
   40% of 64 + 25% of 81 + 50% of 125

9. Subtract 14 thousandths from 14 tenths and multiply the result by 5 hundredths.
10. Richardson throws a baseball at a speed of 72 km/h and his counterpart Ambarish throws it at an average speed of 20 m/s. who throws the ball at a greater speed?

11. Add the following fractions:

$$6\frac{2}{11} + 5\frac{3}{33} + 4\frac{5}{55} + 3\frac{1}{22}$$

12. First angle of a scalene triangle is two times of the second angle and half of the third angle. Find all the three angles.

13. Simplify the following:

8 + {22 X [15 + (14 X 2)]}

14. Which decimal is equivalent to the following expression?

$$\frac{101}{1000} \text{ X } \frac{11}{100} \text{ X } \frac{1}{10}$$

15. A cistern can fill up an empty tank of water in 45 minutes, while another cistern will take 1 hour 30 minutes to fill up the same tank. Find the time taken by both the tank to fill up the same empty water tank.
16. Pamela calculated the sum total of all the prime number located in between 1 and 22 and found that her result was 21 less than the original result. Which of the two prime numbers were missing in her sum total chart?

Worksheet 19

1. A wall mount clock strikes 4 bells at 4 p.m. in 4 seconds. Find the time taken by that clock to strike 11 bells at 11 p.m.
2. Nithin got Rs. 124 as an interest form a bank for his deposit of certain amount for the period of 2 years. Find the principal amount.
3. Mohan is 4 times older than his sister Mohini. Before a couple of years he was five times older than Mohini. Find their ages after ten years.

4. $\frac{5}{6}, \frac{5}{8}, \frac{5}{11}, \frac{5}{13}$ are examples of ________ fractions having identical numerators.

5. 12% of 29 = 14% 0f _____.

6. Mohini deposited a sum of money in a bank and received a simple interest of Rs 1250 after five years of time period at a rate of 6.5% per annum. Find the amount that she can receive on the same principal after 10 years.

7. A number having only two factors is a ________.

8. All ______________ numbers have more than ___ factors. All such factors are ______________ than or equal to the number.
9. John makes and sells juice drinks. The juice drinks are sold in six-packs and boxes. A six-pack has 6 juice drinks and costs $2.
10. 4, 14, 10, 28 These are all multiples of: _
11. There are _____ prime factors in 507.

12. The grocer at a shop arranged 10 rows of cans. There were 2 cans in the first row, 4 cans in the second row, and 6 cans in the third row. The grocer continued to add 2 cans to each new row.
    a. How many cans did the grocer put in the fifth row? Show or explain how you got your answer.
    b. What is the total number of cans the grocer arranged in all 10 of the rows? Show or explain how you got your answer.
    c. Describe the relationship between the row number and the number of cans in each row.
13. Determine the sum of the measures of the exterior angles of following regular polygons.
    a. Hexagon
    b. Octagon
    c. 23-sided polygon
    d. 100-sided polygon

14. Nine times of a number added to ten thousand is 10,999. Find the number.
15. Fraction of "M" in the word "MATHEMATICS" = __
16. One fifth of 3 score is ______% of 500.

17. Rosi is walking around the outside of a building that is in the shape of a regular polygon. She determines that the measure of one exterior angle of the building is 30°. Find the number of sides that the outer lining of the building have.

18. Complete the following table to display the relationship of number of sides of a regular polygon with its measure of interior angles.

a. **an Interior angle**	**No. of sides**
b. 120°	______
c. 72°	______
d. 135°	______
e. 90°	4
f. 60°	______

19: A wall mount clock takes 8 seconds for striking 3 bells. Calculate the time taken by the same clock for striking …

g. 6 bells b. 8 bells c. 10 bells

20: Half of a water container is filled up by a cistern in 20 minutes. Quarter of another cistern is filled up by the same cistern in 10 minutes. The cistern will fill up both the water tanks completely in …. h and …….. minutes.

21: What fraction of all the numbers starting from 1 to 100 are multiples of 4?

22: What fraction of 121,121,121 is equal to 10,01,001?

23: Four non - overlapping triangles are accommodated inside a polygon. How many sides are there in that polygon?

Worksheet 20

1. Complete the following:
    a. The reciprocal of a _______ fraction is an improper fraction.
    b. The reciprocal of an improper fraction is a _______ fraction.
    c. Product of two fractions =
       Product of their ___________/ Product of their _________
    d. The product of two __________ fractions is less than both the fractions.
    e. A ____________ of a fraction is obtained by inverting it upside down.
    f. To multiply a decimal number by _______, we move the decimal point in the number to the right by three places.
    g. To divide a decimal number by _______, we move the decimal point in the number to the left by two places.
    h. _____ is the only number which is its own reciprocal.
    i.

.2. Simplify:

$\left(1-\frac{1}{2}\right)X\left(1-\frac{1}{3}\right)X\left(1-\frac{1}{4}\right)X\ldots..\left(1-\frac{1}{100}\right) = 0.$_____

3. A person travelled 2/5th of his journey by train, one third by bus and one fourth by car and remaining 3 km on foot.
    a. What is the length of his journey travelled by bus?
    b. What fraction of the total journey that the person travelled by the car?
    c. Find the ratio of his journey by train, bus and car.

4. If $\frac{1}{891}$ = 0.00112233445566778899........ Then what is the value of $198\frac{198}{891}$?

5. Express 129 as a sum total of two odd primes.

6. A square shaped rod having sides of one tenth of a meter is used for making a circular ring. Find the circumference of the ring. Also find the distance covered by that ring in 360 complete spins.

7. 28, 42, 196, 126 These are all divisors of a greatest 6 digit number ______________.

8. The numbers 3, 5, 7 , 11 , 13, 17, ……., 29 are multiplied together. What is the number of zeros at the right end of the product ?

9. Fill in the blanks …

$$\frac{19}{242} X \frac{11}{144} X \frac{12}{39} X \frac{78}{19} X \frac{12}{37} X \frac{11}{100} = \frac{\quad}{3700}$$

10. 343 tens + 32 hundreds + 12 tenths + 3 thousandths = _________.

11. What is the 25th digit to the right of the decimal point in the decimal of 6/11 ?

12. Fractions obtained on multiplying or dividing both numerator and denominator of a given fraction by the same non-zero number, and the given fraction are called _______________ fractions.

13. A fraction, whose denominator can be expressed as a multiple of 10 , is called a _________________ fraction.

14. For addition or subtraction of like fractions, __________________ are added (or subtracted), _________________ remaining the same.

15. Fill in the blanks .

16. What least number must be added to 1/10th of a six digit smallest number to make it a multiple of 9?

17. The LCM of two numbers is 28 times of their HCF. The sum of their LCM and HCF is 1740. If one of the numbers is 240, find the other number.

18. Four fifth of an angle is equal to quarter of a complete angle. Find the supplementary of that angle.

19. Complete the pattern:

f) 10204, _____, __________, ____________, __________, 12,204, 12,404.

g) 121, 12321, __________, ____________, _______________.

20. A drum contains 20 l of a paint. From this, 2 l of paint is taken out and replaced by 2 l of oil. Again 2 l of this mixture is taken out and replaced by 2 l of oil. If this operation is performed once again, then what would be the final ratio of paint and oil in the drum ?

21. Two persons A and B walk round a circle whose diameter is 1.4 km. A walks at a speed of 165 m per minute while B walks at a speed of 110 m per minute. If they both start at the same time from the same point and walk in the same direction at what interval of time would they both be at the same starting point again.

22. Three consecutive numbers having sum 300,306. Find out the value of smallest number.

23. How many five digit numbers are there in all?

24: A counter produces a beat after an interval of ten seconds. Another counter produces a beat after 15 seconds. After what time interval both the counters can produce beats jointly?

Worksheet 21

1. Temperature of a city increased by 5 ^{0}C last week. If a corresponding increase of temperature in ^{0}F is 1.8 times more than that of the value in ^{0}C, then find the value of such increase of temperature in ^{0}F

   A: 18^0 F B: 9^0 F C: 8.9^0 F D: 6 ^{0}F

2. A racing car covers 100 km in 2 hours and another 400 km 4 hours. The speed of the car during second time is _____ times more than that of the first time.

   A: 1 B: 2 C: 3 D: 4

3. The product of the place values of 5 in the following number is ________

   32,435

   A: 9,000 B: 90,000 C: 9,00,000 D: 900

4. What must be added to 10932 to make it exactly divisible by 9?
5. $\frac{3}{6}, \frac{7}{6}, \frac{1}{6}, \frac{5}{6}, \frac{11}{6}$

   If we arrange these fractions in ascending order, then denominator of the product of 2nd and 3rd fraction in simplest form will be ___________

   A: 12 B: 24 C: 36 D: 48

6. Half of one sixth of 72 is the ________ multiple of three.
7. A wire of a square sized shape of side 32 cm is reshaped to form a circle. Find the circumference of that circle. [Circumference of a circle is the outer boundary of a circle].

8. A solid cylinder has _____ flat faces and _____ curved faces.

9. The product of all the factors of 121 is _______ less than its greatest factor.
   A: 1 B: 11 C: 1,452 D: 1331

10. Two bells toll at an interval of 6 seconds and 8 seconds respectively. They toll together at 11:55 a.m. When do they toll together again for the second time?
    A: 12:19 pm B: 12:19 am C: 12: 24 pm

11. Ruchika observed that a 300 m long goods train is taking 45 seconds to cross a light-post. Find the average speed of that train. Also find the time taken by that train to cross a 1500 m long railway platform.
12. Compare the place value of 5 in 235,934 and 54,435. Find difference of both the place values.

13. A milk-dairy produces 25,545 liters of milk every day. It supplies 15,625 liters of milk to a milk-depot and the rest to the market. How much milk is supplied to the market?
14. The sum of two numbers is 94506. One of the numbers is 49605. Find the other number.
15. The sum of two numbers is 45650. One of the numbers is 22587. Find the other number. Which part of the sum is the given number?
16. There are 35,278 students in Class III, 32,184 students in Class IV and 25,375 students in Class V in the schools of a city. Find the total number of students

reading in Classes III, IV and V. Among these students 60,324 are girls. Find the number of students who are boys.

17. A person had $ 197,865. He gave $ 50,753 to his wife and $ 75,928 to his son. The rest of the money he gave to his daughter. How much did the daughter get?
18. What should be added to the sum of 3,46,068 and 3,24,263 to get the sum of 8,05,400?
19. Sum total of a number and its reciprocal is 8.125. Find the product of that number and the respective reciprocal.

20. There are 4021 students in a school. Each section can accommodate a maximum number of 25 students. There are equal number of students in each section, find their number in each section. Is there any section having less than 25 students? How many such sections are there?
21. Write in standard form:
    32 tens + 54 hundreds + 121 = __________.

22. Sum total of digits of a two digit number is 9. If 27 added to it its digits are reversed. Find the number.
23. $2[\left(1-\frac{1}{10}\right)\left(1-\frac{1}{11}\right)\ldots.\left(1-\frac{1}{1000}\right)] = ?$

24. A plant grows at a rate of certain fixed rate per week and attained a height of 208 cm in a year. Finds its regular rate of growth.
25. A shopkeeper increased the price for certain item by 20% and issued a discount of 20%. Find the total profit or loss percentage on his overall transactions.
26. Half of a number exceeds quarter of 800,800 by 1,004. Find out the number.

Worksheet 22

I: Compare

01 3 L 390 cL 02 21 L 9 ml 03 21 L 2009 ml

04 21098 ml 05 210980 cL 06 12 L 98 cL

07. 2 L 250 cL 08. 13 L 130 mL 09. 36 kL 36 000 L

10. 52 L 515 dL 11. 2600 L 26 kL 12. 35 dL 4 L

13. 760 cL 75 L 14. 12 L 12 000 mL 15. 173 L 1730 cL

16. 860 mL 8.6 L 17. 17.3 kL 1730 L 18. 2.5 L 25 dL

Round the following to nearest hundred.

13. 158 14. 426 15. 375 16. 896

17. 719 18. 950 19. 1047 20. 3888

21. 5942 22. 6891 23. 3098 24. 8762

25. 37,405 26. 62,345 27. 88,088 28. 65,097

29. 58,706 30. 66,636

Round the following to nearest thousand

31. 9155 32. 7983 33. 4550 34. 6237

35. 8396 36. 33,888 37. 15,942 38. 93,192

39. 87,983 40. 46,237 41. 326,150 42. 145,706

43. 357,029 44. 563,498 45. 807,476 46. 821,593

47. 450,513 48. 435,127 49. 205,120 50. 761,604

Estimate by rounding then add or subtract.

51. 215 + 687 52. 4306 – 3849 53. 6287 – 318

54. 659 – 286 55. 7583 + 2948 56. 3717 – 839

57. Three hundred seventeen less than thirteen hundred seventy nine.

58. 14th multiple of 1,002 more than 15th multiple of 5,009

59. 11th multiple of 1,002 + 12th multiple of 12,012 + 32,043

60. 309 m long track is attached to 30,0129 m long track. Total length (estimated up to) of the track will be …………………..

II. Fraction and decimal.

Figure	Fraction	Decimal
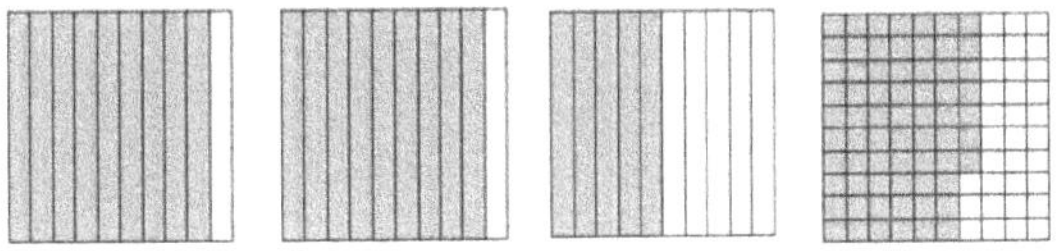		
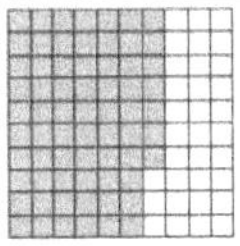	$\frac{67}{100}$	0.67
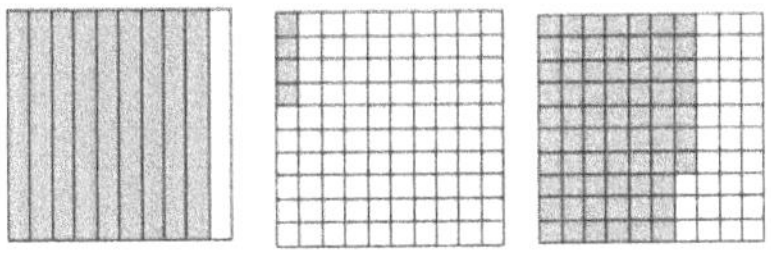		
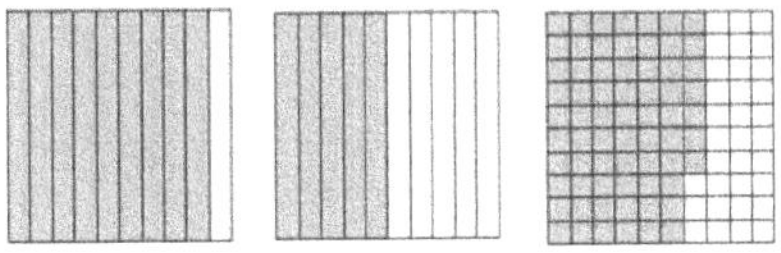		

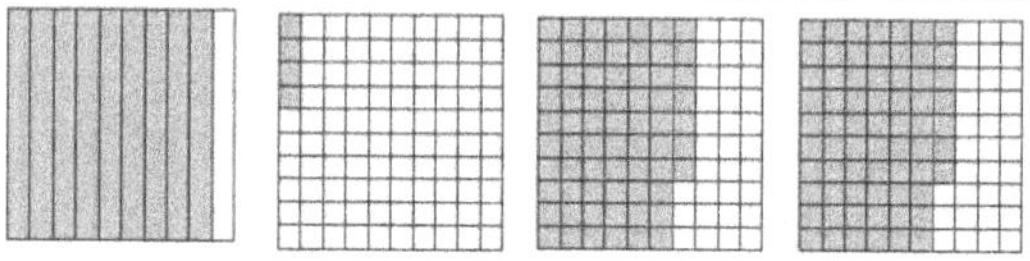		
1/5th of 405 + 1/6th of 618 + 1/7th of 735		
Quarter of 636 + 1/8th of 16,424		
1.1 X 1.01 X 0.001 X 0.01 X 125 X 8		
125 X 40 X 8 X 16 X 0.004 X 0.008		
1/7th of 4,949 + 1/9th 8,181 + 1/11th of 121		
Three thousandths + 103 hundredths + 2.009		

III. Write best units of measurements which can be used for the following.

1. length of an eraser
2. width of a board
3. distance between 2 cities
4. height of a desk
5. length of a soccer field
6. width of a quarter
7. length of a pencil

a. 4 yd b. 4 in. c. 4 ft

8. height of a basketball player

9. Distance of a planet

10. distance of a star from the earth

(a. mile b. light year)

11. Distance of the Sun from the Earth

(a. mile b. light minute

c. light year)

12. juice in a pitcher

13. ice cream in a carton

14. paint in a can

15. water in a swimming pool

16. milk in a recipe

17. water in a bucket

18. length of a car

19. depth of the ocean

20. height of a person

21. width of a tape

22. thickness of a sandwich 24. Half of the capacity of water tank.

Answer the following.

25. A goods train spends 45 seconds to cross a light post. Speed of that train is 36 km/h. calculate length of that train.

26. Somnath jogs 1.2 m in a second while Nikita jogs at an average speed of 3.6 km/h. Who is jogging faster?

27. Namrata observed that her school bus reaches school in 38 minutes. It has five stoppages of duration 3 minutes each. Average speed of the bus is 36 km/h. What is the distance of her school ?

28. 1.9 km + 2 km 89 m + 21 km 121 m = ………………..

IV. Round each to the nearest whole number, tenth, and hundredth.

1. 1.001 X 0.11 X 0.001 X 125 X 8 X 0.0001

2. (1 + 2 + 3 + …….. 1,000) X 1001 X $\left(\left(\frac{125\ X\ 8}{1001\ X\ 1001}\right)X\ 10232\right)$

3. 1/4th of 16,0128 + 1/5th to 55,0525 + 1/6th of 1,21,212

4. Seventh multiple of 17,019 X 0.001 X 0.01

5. Half of a quarter of 2,009 + half of one fifth of 1,008

6. 11 tenths + 11 hundredths + 11 thousandths

7. 101 tenths + 1001 hundredths + 11.011 + 101.101

8. 12.012 9.121,032

10. 324.980 11.205.509

12. 21.12 13. 21 X 0.901

14. 134.980 15. 43.980

16. 2.1 X 2.001 17. (2.01 X 0.002 X 0.04)

18. 43 X 4.04

19. (Quarter of 104 + One seventh of 4,949 + 1.001) X 0.3

20. $\left(\frac{11}{19} + \frac{33}{38} + \frac{109}{190}\right) X\ 0.003\ X\ 0.09$

21. 6.148 22. 1.792

23. 3.732 24. 24.873

25. 39.925 26. 73.159

27. 29.866 28. 548.501

29. 112.549 30. 332.532

33. 121.098 34. 32.098

Round each to the nearest dollar, ten dollars, and hundred dollars.

35. $427.89 36. $642.87

37. $792.46 38. $225.98

39. $146.72 40. $119.28

41. $542.76 42. $125.58

39. $918.92 40. $699.45

41. $15042.706

V. Solve the following:

1. There are 106 books on a shelf A, 121 books on shelf B, 98 books on shelf C and 721 books on shelf D. Nikita takes 17 books from each of the shelves. How many books are left on the shelves in all?

2. There are 11 more girls in class III and 9 more girls in class IV than the number of girls in class II, which is 17 less than the number of girls in class I, which is again 19 less

than the number of girls in class V. Number of girls in class II is equal to second multiple of 11. Strength of the school is 250. How many boys are there in the school?

3. Record of rainfall of a state is displayed in the following chart. Each unit of icon is equal to 10 mm.

April	∇∇
May	∇
June	∇∇∇
July	∇∇∇∇∇∇∇∇∇
August	∇∇∇∇∇∇∇∇∇∇∇∇∇∇∇∇∇
September	∇∇∇∇∇∇∇∇∇
October	∇∇∇∇∇∇∇
November	∇∇

Calculate average rainfall of the state.

Which pair of months receives maximum rainfall?

4. The day Sonali left home for an outing was Saturday. She came back home after 103 days and resumed her service after 3 days. What was the day when she resumed her service?

5. In a 7-day period, Tina spends 4 h, 3.4 h, 5.02 h, 3 h 12 minutes, and 5 h 32 minutes pruning trees. Her sum exceeded 35 h mark. Duration of remaining two days estimated as a variable H. She then adds to find the total number of hours. What was the value of H? Does the order in which she adds the numbers affect the sum?

6. What least number should be subtracted from six digit greatest number to obtain a common multiple of 4 and 8?

7. Five rivers form a river system and have lengths of 513.11 miles, 247.08 miles, 211 miles, 192.09 miles and 397.03 miles. Altogether, how long are these rivers?

8. Pallavi, Richimon, Nikhil and Snehal planned to use 213, 432, 355 and 431 saplings respectively to cover one side of the roads leading to their crop fields. They kept a uniform gap of 11.5 m in between two saplings. Calculate total length of the roads used by them for the plantation works.

VI. Estimate the following.

1: How many four digit numbers are there in all?

2. what least number should be subtracted from five digit greatest number to obtain a common multiple of 4 and 8/

Find out surface area and volume of the following.

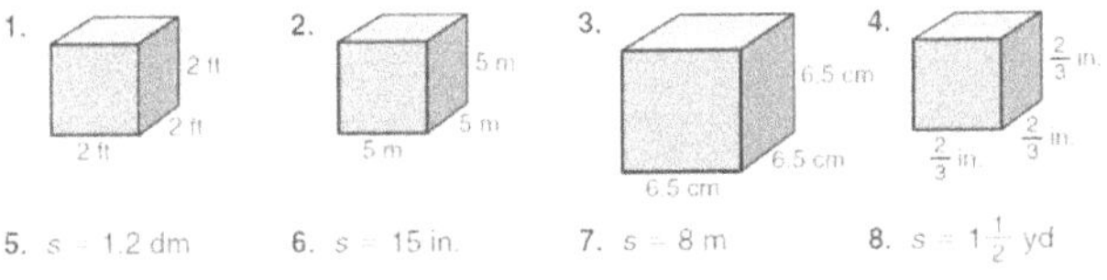

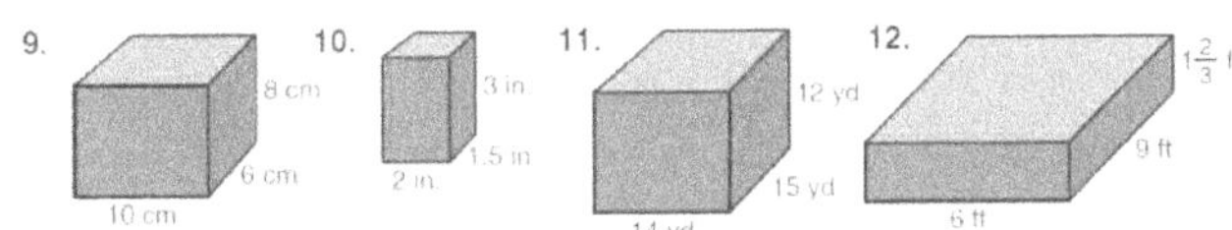

13: l = 12 cm, b = 8 cm, h = 6 cm   14: a cube of edge 12 cm

15: l = 20 cm; b = 18 cm; h = 10 cm;   16: a cube of edge 12.5 cm;

17: Three angles of a triangle are in the ratio of 2: 4: 7. Find out the angles.

18. Half of an angle is equal to quarter of its supplementary angle. Find out the angle.

19. Quarter of angle A, 3/5th of angle B and 6/19th of angle C jointly form a straight angle. Find out the angles.

20. Complementary of an angle is 39^0 32'. Find out the angle.

21. Angle A and B of a triangle jointly forms a right angle. Find out the third angle.

22. What fraction of all the natural numbers from 1 to 600 are common multiples of 30, 15 and 60?

23: What is the surface area of a utility cabinet that is 60 cm long, 46 cm wide, and 32 cm high?

24. Half of a cubical water tank of edge 1.5 m is filled with water. calculate total volume of water present in the tank. A cistern throws 200 cm^3 water in a second. Calculate total time to be taken by that cistern to fill up remaining parts of the tank.

25. What is the difference between the surface area of a cube that is 30 cm on an edge and a rectangular prism that is 40 cm long, 20 cm wide, and 10 cm high?

26. Quarter of a water tank is filled up by a cistern in 20 minutes. One fifth of another water tank is filled up by that cistern in 15 minutes. Calculate total time to be taken by that cistern to fill up both the water tanks completely.

27. Sonali and Monali jointly works to finish an assignment in 12 days. Monali alone can finish it in 18 days. Sonali alone can finish it in …. days.

Worksheet 23

I: Estimate the following.

1. 36,587 + 87,943 + 13,156

2. 28,764 + 64,537 + 35,936

3. 65,446 + 1,915 + 47,291

4. 49,765 + 18,976 + 7,359

5. 26,542 − 17,986

6. 34,896 − 15,984

7. 41,132 − 17,545

8. 62,764 − 58,685

9. 115,609 + 205,399 + 411,111

10. 356,789 + 141,217 + 222,888

11. 471,009 + 180,007 + 277,777

12. 365,786 + 274,982 + 186,214

13. 672,244 − 456,688

14. 681,337 − 278,456

15. 524,700 − 316,672

16. 938,400 − 619,711

II. Observe the following

Arena	Seating Capacity
Yankee Stadium, NY	57,545
Cleveland Browns Stadium, OH	73,200
Wrigley Field, IL	36,765
Angel Stadium, CA	45,050

A: Which arena could be preferred for accommodating near about seventy thousand viewers?

B: Arrange the given places as per their increasing seating capacity.

C: Which stadium holds minimum seating capacity?

D. Which stadium could be preferred for a mass of 35,000?

E. Average seating capacity of all the four stadium is equal to ....

III. Earth's total surface area is about 199,560,000 square miles. Approximately 139,692,000 square miles are covered with water. About how much of Earth's surface is covered by land?

IV. Write the following in standard form.

1. CCLXIII = 100 + ___ + 50 + ___ + ___ + ___ + ___ = ___
2. CMXCIV = (1000 − ___) + (___ − 10) + (___ − ___) = ___

3. XXXIV	4. MVII	5. LV	6. DXXI
7. CCLXX	8. DCCXC	9. XCIX	10. MDIII
11. XLVII	12. MCCLVI	13. CXLV	14. MDCCXCI
15. MMCLI	16. MMDCCCIII	17. MDCCLXXXV	18. MDCCCXLV

V. In the number 308,610,547,823, write the digit in the ten billions place, millions place and ten thousands place.

VI. While writing the following expanded form in standard numeration Nikhil placed digit 7 at ten thousands place. Find out difference of the actual result and result obtained by Nikhil.

1,000,000,000 + 13,000 + 1,300 + 32,098 + 28,202 + 40,000 + 80 + 3

VII. Car A travels 30 m in 4 seconds, Car B covers 76 km in 1 hour, Car C covers 600 m in a minute and Car D covers 39 m in 5 seconds. Which car is moving with fastest speed?

VIII. Arrange following numbers from least to greatest:

6,135,936; 6,315,396; 6,531,639; 6,153,693

Worksheet 24

I: Find product in each of the following:

a. 10 X 20 X 30 b. 80 X 10 X 700 c. 40 X 50 X 8000

d. 20 X 40 X 50 e. 60 X 50 X 200 f. 20 X 30 X 6000

g. 20X X 30 X 40h. 30 X 50 X 100 i. 20 X 40 X 9000

II. Solve the following.

1. Smith made three stops during his 150-mile bike trip. He first stopped after 20 miles. His second stop was 54 miles away from the starting point, his third stop was 18 miles before the end of the trip. How many miles did he travel between his first and third stops?

2. A multiple theater complex in a shopping center has 40 rows of seats with 9 seats in each row, 50 rows having 11 seats in each row and 60 rows of seats having 12 seats in each row. Total 200 seats are reserved for VIPs. How many seats are available for non-VIP visitors?

3. How many bricks each of 16 sq. inches can be used to construct a wall of length 12 m, breadth 10 inches and height 2 m?

6. Complete the following numeration chart.

The Numbers	Places			
	Th	H	T	O
2432				
3009				
4098				

7. What fraction of all the numbers starting from 1 to 200 are multiples of 25?

8. P = 2143 + 7856; Q = 21098 – 21000 + 992 ; R = 3209 + 6790;

Calculate the value of $Q + P - R + \frac{R}{P} + 109{,}802\ X\ (R - P)$

9. What fraction of all the numbers starting from 1 to 100 can be divided exactly by 5?

10. Two interior angles of a triangle are 20^0 and 40^0 respectively. Find out magnitude of the third interior angle of this triangle.

11. Simplify:

$$\left(\frac{121}{999} + \frac{1021}{9999} + 12.098 + 0.0909\right) X \left[\left(1 + \frac{1}{100}\right) \div \left(1 - \frac{1}{101}\right) - (1.01^2)\right]$$

12. Interior angles of a given quadrilateral are p, 2p, 3p and 4p. Sum of all the interior angles is equal to 360^0. What is the value of p?

13. Find out variables in each of the following:

(i) $\frac{n}{5} - \frac{5}{7} = \frac{2}{3}$ (ii) $\frac{x}{3} - \frac{x}{4} = 14$

(ii) $\frac{z}{2} + \frac{z}{3} - \frac{z}{6} = 8$ (iv) $\frac{2p}{3} - \frac{p}{5} = 11\frac{2}{3}$

(v) $9\frac{1}{4} = y - 1\frac{1}{3}$ (vi) $\frac{x}{2} - \frac{4}{5} + \frac{x}{5} + \frac{3x}{10} = \frac{1}{5}$

(vii) $\frac{x}{2} - \frac{1}{4} = \frac{x}{3} + \frac{1}{2}$ (viii) $\frac{2x - 3}{3x + 2} = \frac{-2}{3}$

(ix) $\frac{8p - 5}{7p + 1} = \frac{-2}{4}$ (x) $\frac{7y + 2}{5} = \frac{6y - 5}{11}$

(xi) $\frac{x + 5}{6} - \frac{x + 1}{9} = \frac{x + 3}{4}$ (xii) $\frac{3t + 1}{16} - \frac{2t - 3}{7} = \frac{t + 3}{8} + \frac{3t - 1}{14}$

14. A cistern takes 2 minutes to fill up quarter of a water tank and one fifth of another water tank. Calculate total time to be taken by that cistern to fill up both the water tanks completely.

Worksheet 25

1: Find out value of variables in each of the following.

(i)

A, 56°, B, x°, C, 123°, D

(ii)

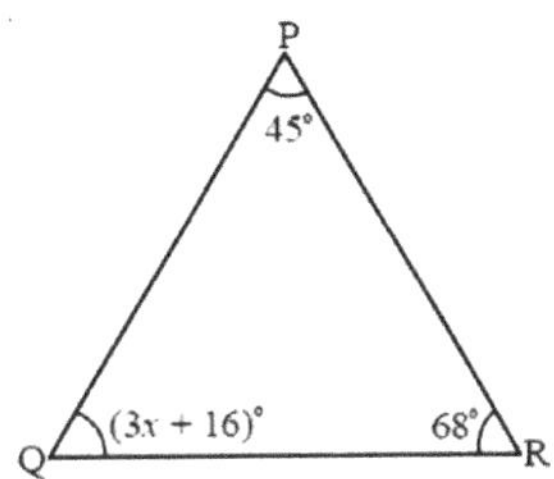

(iii)

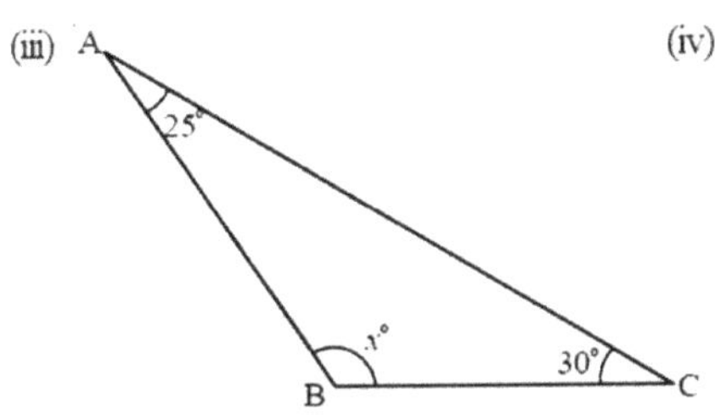

(iv)

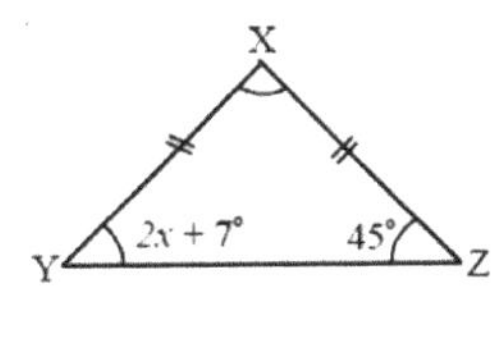

2. Complete the following:

$\frac{2}{3}, \frac{7}{8}$

Then $\frac{2}{3} \div \frac{7}{8} = \frac{2}{3} \times \frac{8}{7} = \frac{16}{21}$ which is a rational number

Check this for two more example.

$\frac{5}{7} \div 2 = \frac{5}{7} \div \frac{2}{1} = \frac{5}{7} \times \frac{1}{2} = \frac{5}{14}$

$-\frac{2}{3} \div \frac{6}{11} =$ ________ = ________ = ________

$3 \div \frac{17}{13} = \frac{3}{1} \div \frac{17}{13} =$ ________ = ________ = ________

3. What fraction of all the numbers starting from 1 to 200 are not divisible by 4?

4. February 4th was Wednesday, what day will be February 27th ?

5. Time taken by minute hand of a clock to complete a spin is ....

6. A passenger train takes 49 seconds to cross a light post. The average speed of that train was 72 km/h. Calculate total length of that train.

7. Find out magnitude of missing angles.

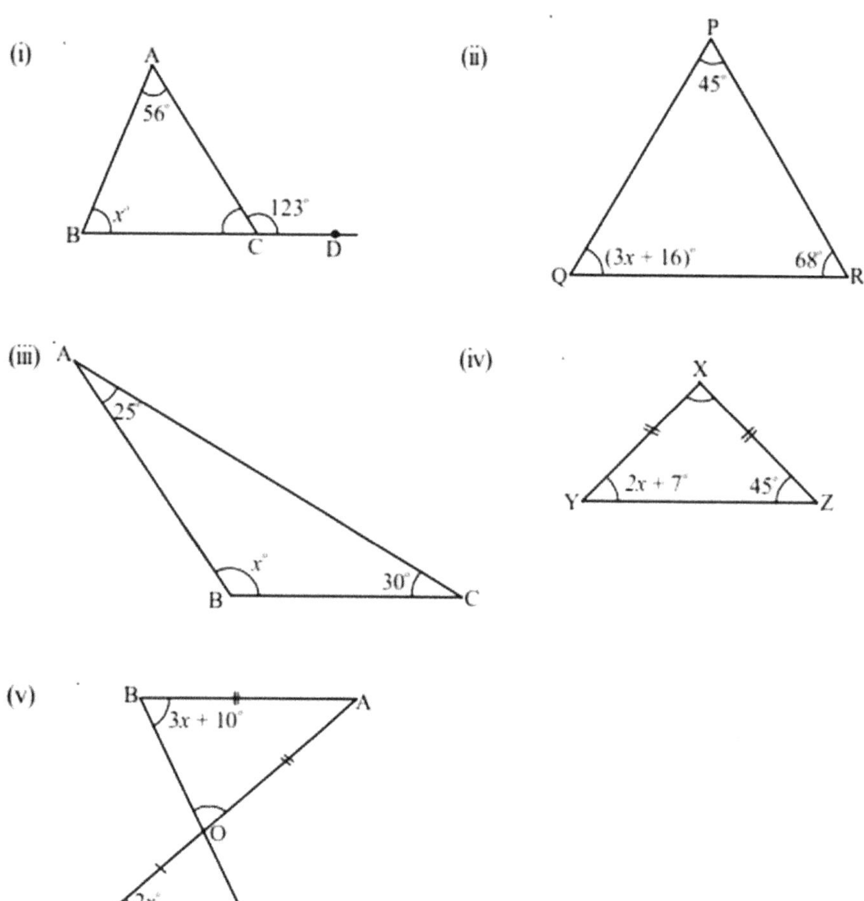

8. Half of a quarter of a natural number is equal to 100,100,101. Find out fifth multiple of that number.

9. Simplify the following:

$$\left(1.001 + \frac{1001}{9999} + \frac{209}{1009} + 2.0909 + 1.90901 + \frac{109}{9001}\right) X \left[1.0001 - \left(1 + \frac{1}{10000}\right)\right]$$

10. (1.01 X 0.01 X 0.001 X 0.0001) 125 X 8 X 40 X 25 = ...

11. Find out the missing angles in the following:

(i)

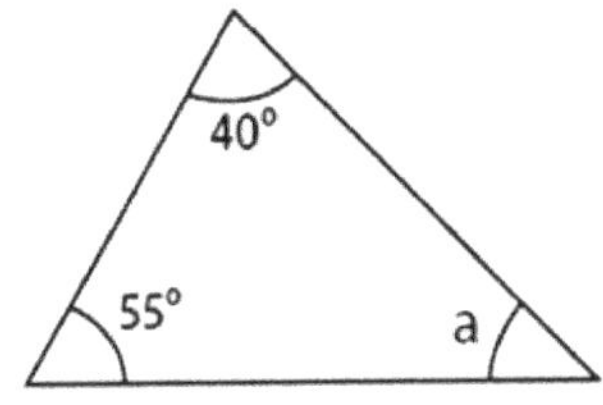

(ii)

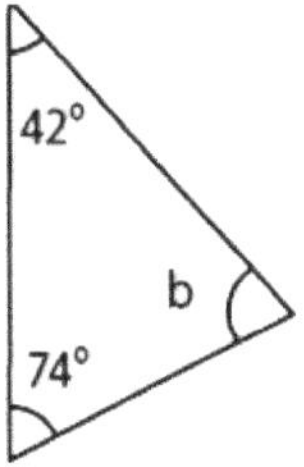

(iii)

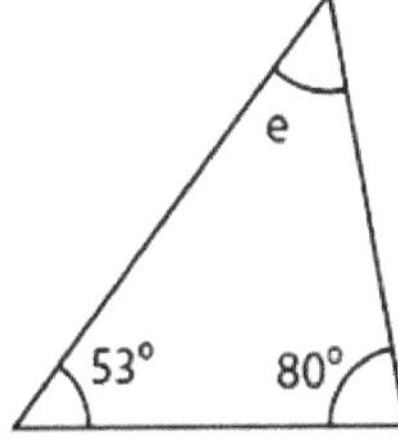

(iv)

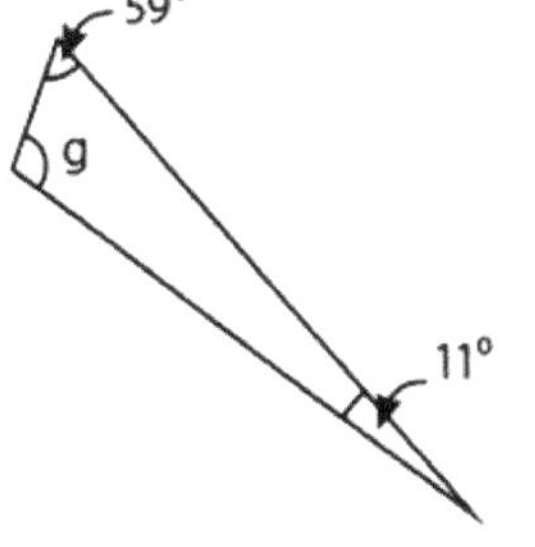

(v)

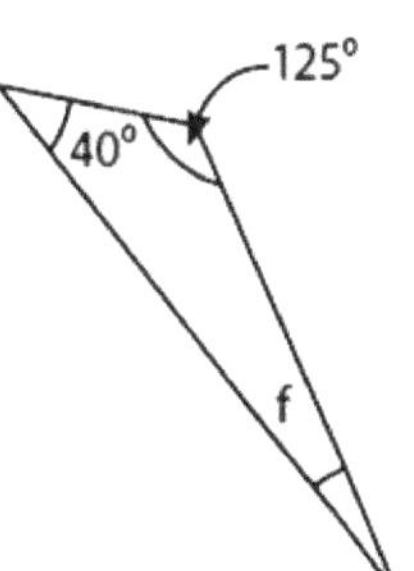

(vi)

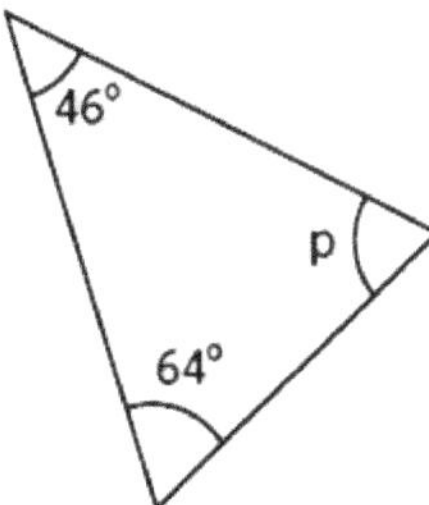

12. Find out area of the following.

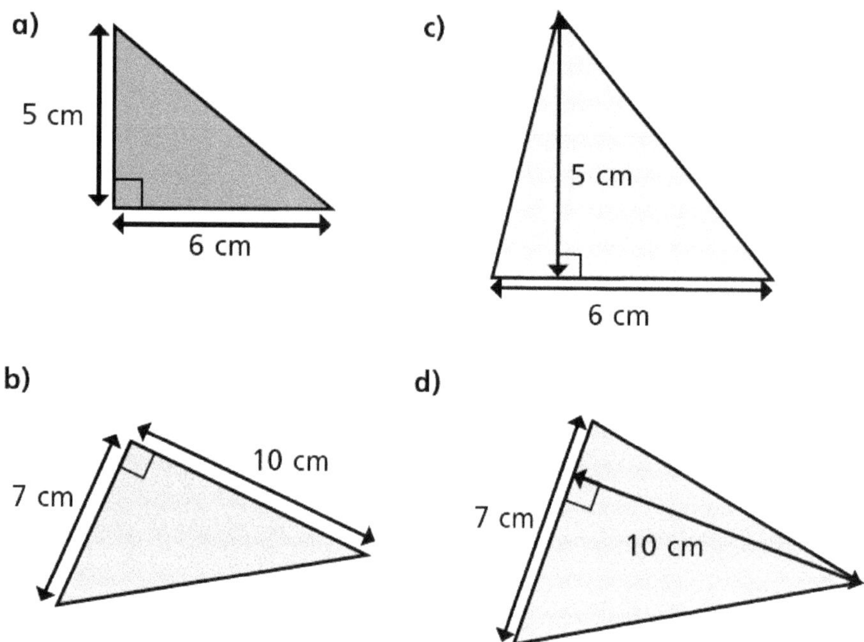

13. What fraction of all the numbers from 1 to 100 are multiples of 5?

14. P = 2.002 X 0.002 X 0.0002 and Q = 125 X 25 X 40 X 8. Find out simplest value of [(PXQ) ÷ 8].

15. Write the following representative fractions.

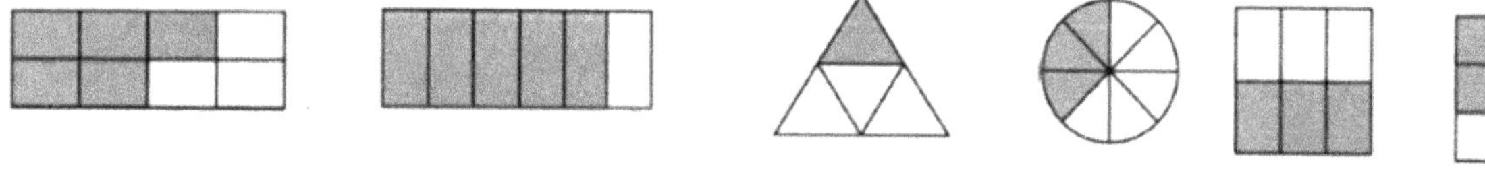

____ ____ ____ ____ ____ ____

16. Find out area of shaded portions.

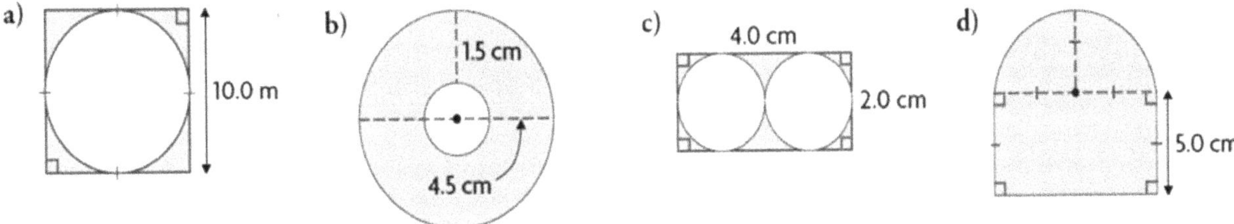

17. Here (P + Q – R) = ……………..

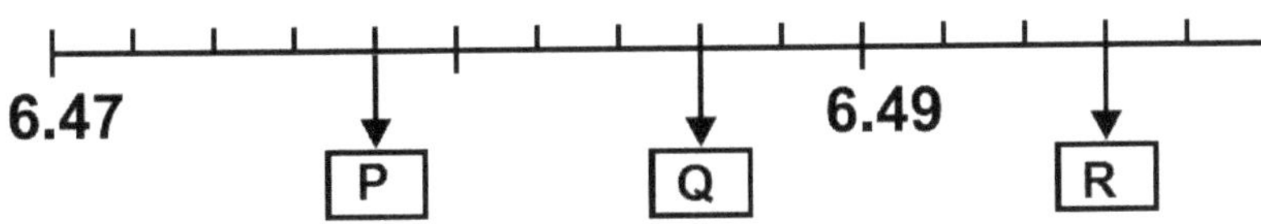

19. Write the following expression in standard form:

Three billion three million three thousand more than three billion two million forty-five thousand and eighty-three.

20. In May, 23,637 people attended the circus, which was 18,478 people less than the attendance in June. In July, the attendance was 5,342 more than June's. How many people attended the circus in July?

21. Find out and compare area of shaded portions.

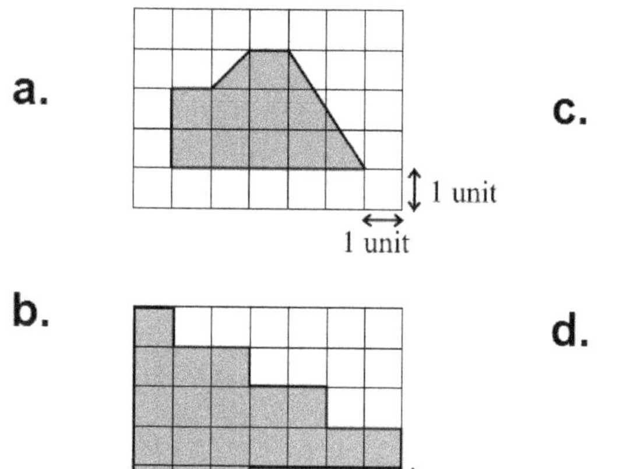

c.

3 unit

3 unit

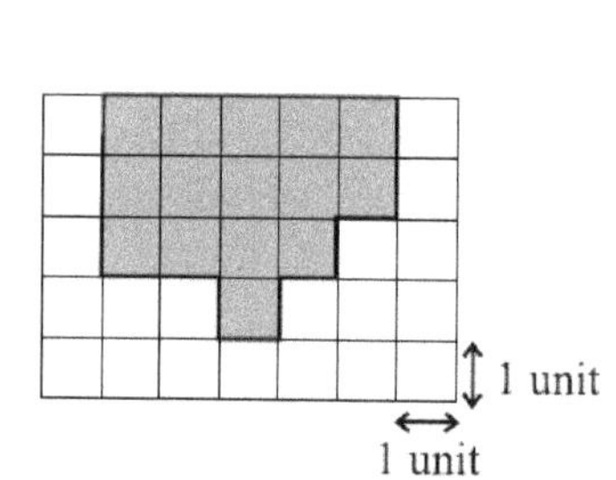

22: .Calculate shaded portions

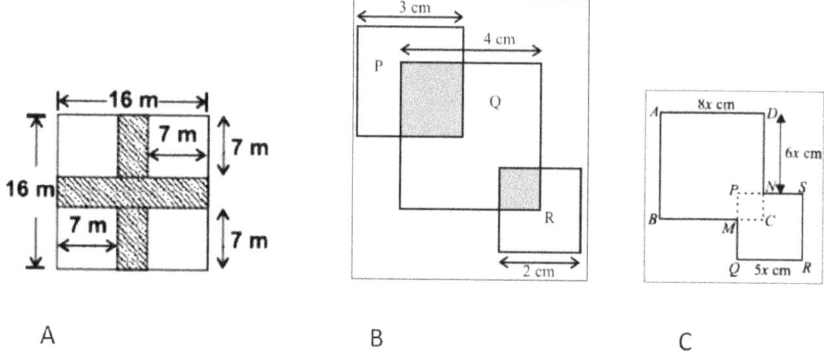

A B C

23. Calculate shaded portions.

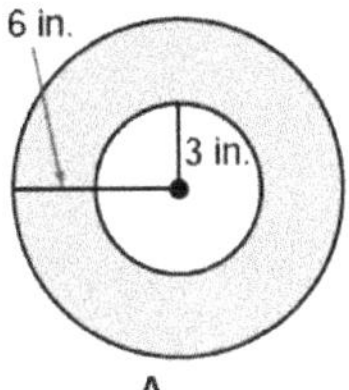

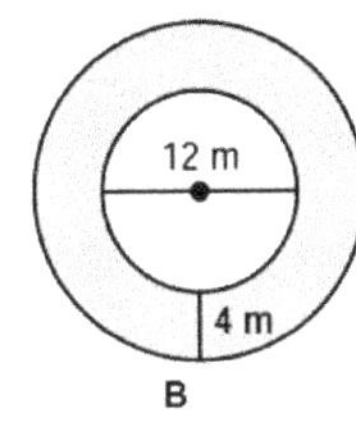

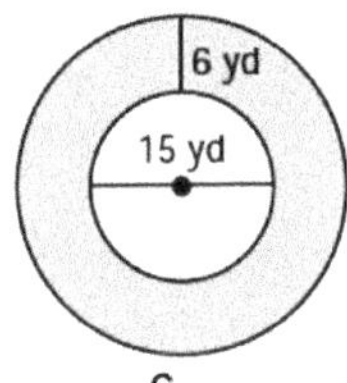

24. How many cubical bricks each of side 16 cm will be used to construct a wall of dimension 6 m 40 cm, 4 m and 32 cm?

25. Increase of 36 ^{0} C is recorded in a city during day time. Calculate corresponding increase in ^{0} F.

26. 20% of a number is 640 more than fourth multiple of six digit smallest number. Find out the number.

27. Write in standard form:

$$125 + \frac{121}{125} + \frac{345}{625} + \frac{39}{40} + \frac{21}{25} + \frac{1001}{1000} + \frac{321}{400} - 121.324$$

28. Neha reached her school 5 minutes earlier than scheduled time. Her wrist watch was displaying 100: 45 a.m. The watch was running late by 9 minutes. Normal schedule of assembly is ....

29: Quarter of a number exceeds 20,20,300 by 10,001. Find out the number.

30: Two line segments to be used for constructing a triangle are 5 cm and 9,8 cm. Find out the greatest possible and smallest possible length of the third side.

Worksheet 26

1: Revision works

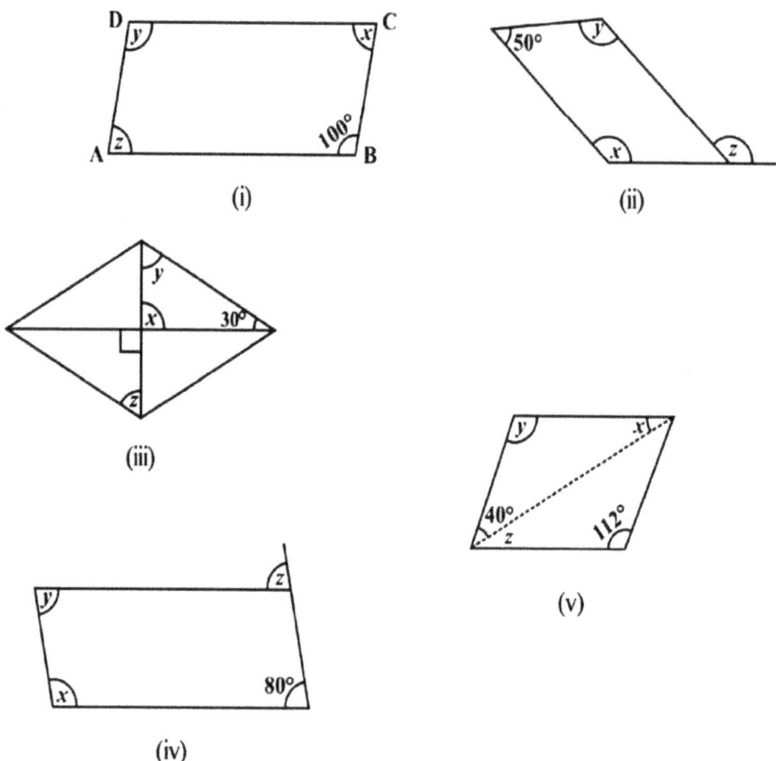

2. Sonali added 1002 to a natural number instead of subtracting it. Her result was equal to sum of five digit greatest and five digit smallest number. Find out the actual result.

3. Find out missing fractions in the following.

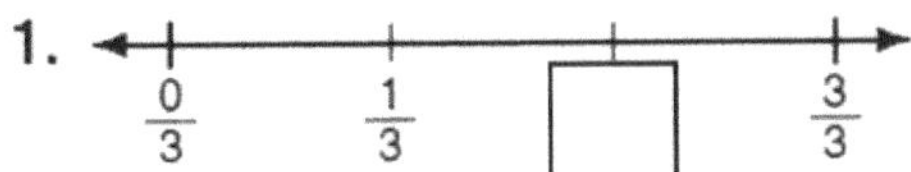

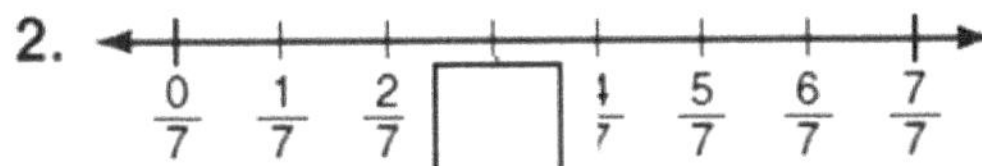

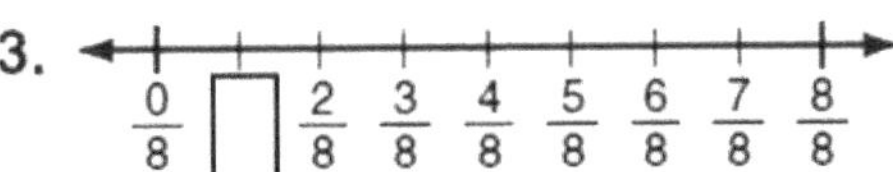

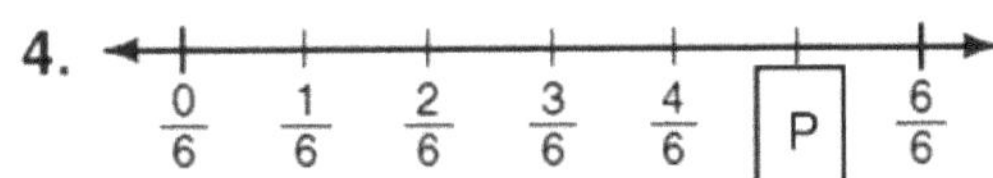

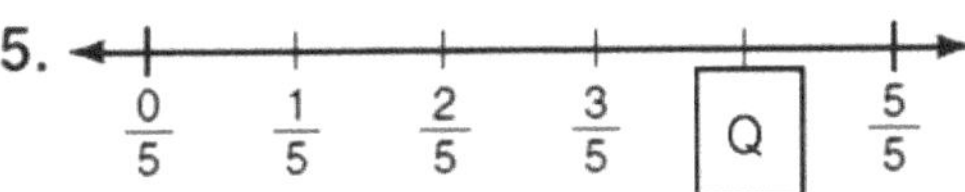

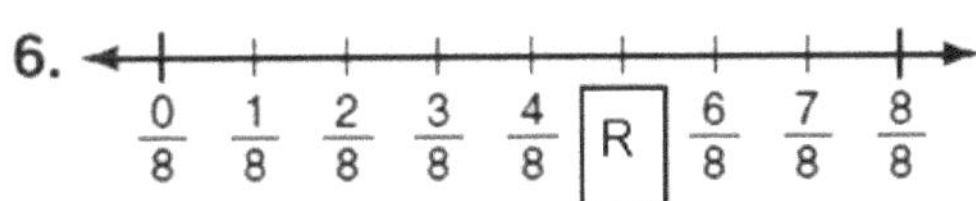

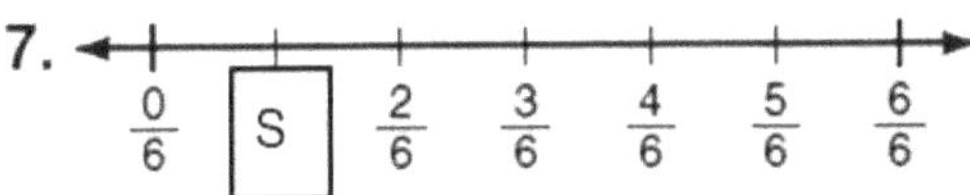

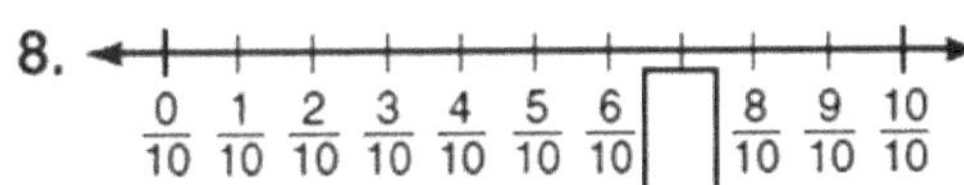

4. Compare the following numerals.

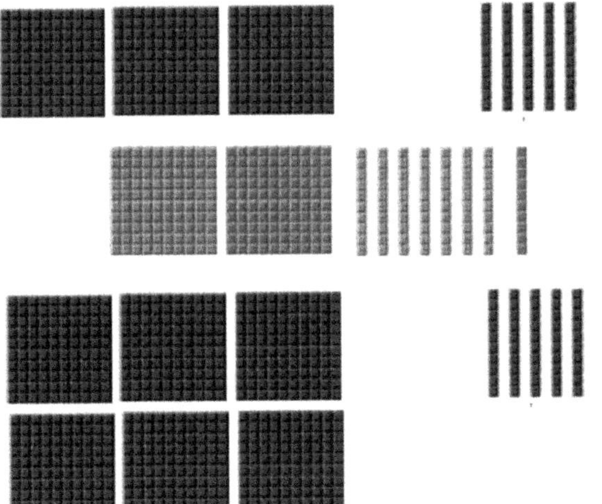

5. What least number should be subtracted from five digit greatest number to obtain a multiple of 8?

6. What digit will be there at ones place if we multiply 99, 999 and 9999?

7. P = 4,000 X 3,000 X 25 and Q = 0.1 X 0.001 X 0.0001; then find out simplest value of (P X Q) $\div \frac{P}{Q} + 29{,}908\, X\, (\, Q - \;10^8$;

8: Average weight of 10 apples estimated as 69 g. Later on it is observed that Weight of each apple is 1.09 g less that the estimated weight. What was the original average weight of apples?

9. P = (1.009 - 1.009 + 1.009 – 1.009 ….. six hundred times);

Q = (4.991 – 4.991 + 4.991 – 4.991 … seven hundred seven times);

P + Q = ……………

10. Represent in decimal form:

$1009 + \frac{109}{125} + \frac{29}{40} + \frac{193}{250} + \frac{19}{25} + 1.009 + 3.991 + 4.891 + 0.109$

11. Rajani has a box with 6 marbles numbered from 1 to 6 on each of them. She picks a marble from it without seeing. What is the probability that the marble picked has the number 3 on it?

12. 20% of 40% of 50% of 100,300 = …………………

Worksheet 27

Q 1. Calculate outer boundary and area of the following.

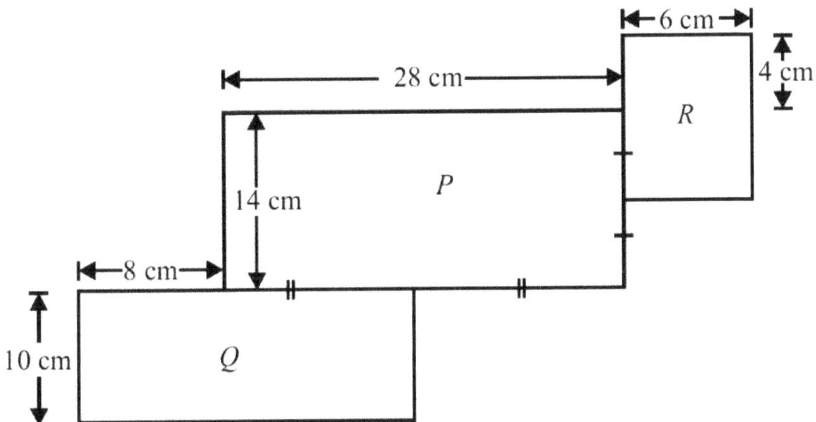

Q 2. How many bricks are there in each of the following?

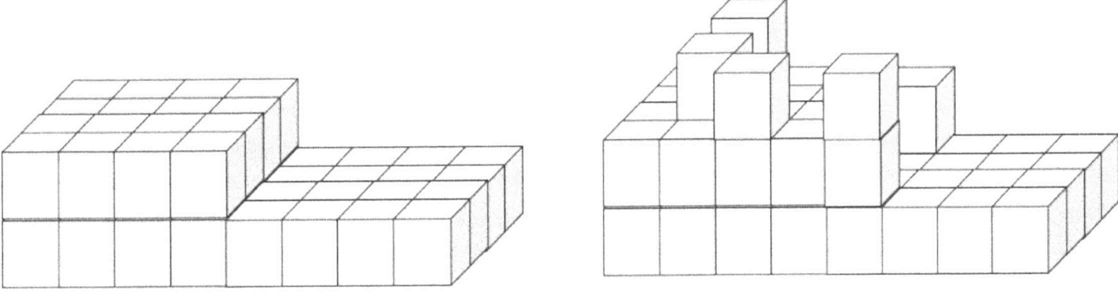

Q 3. What fraction of the following is shaded?

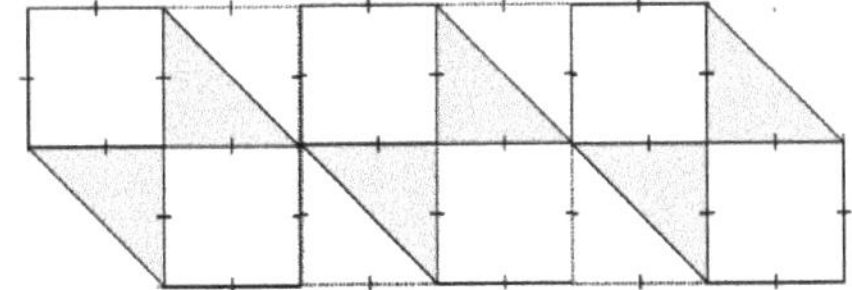

Identify the following angles as acute or obtuse types.

4.

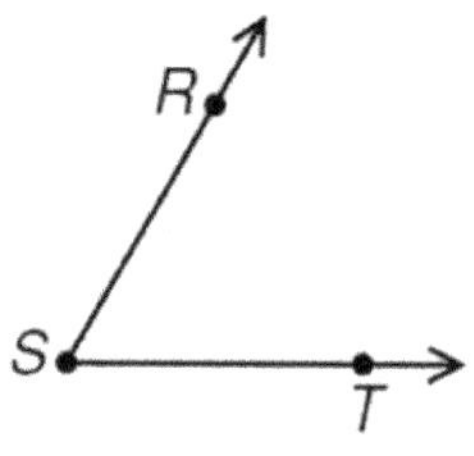

5.

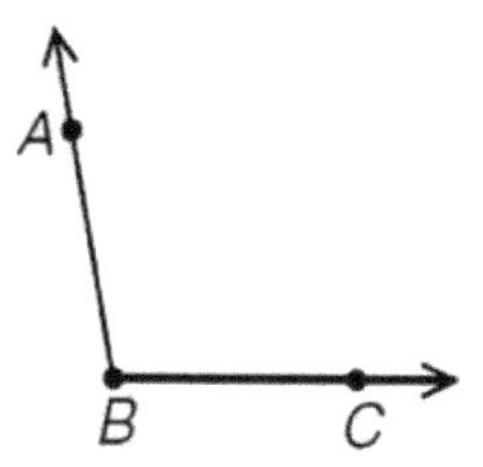

6.

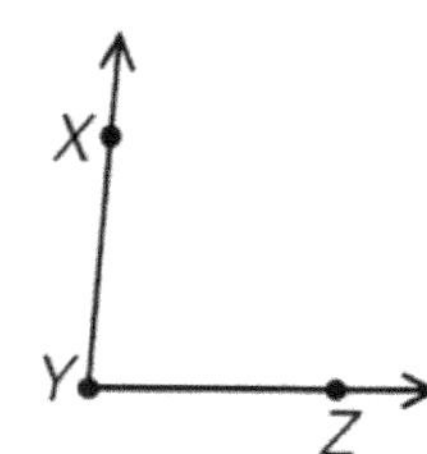

7.

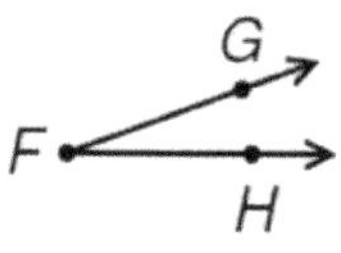

8.

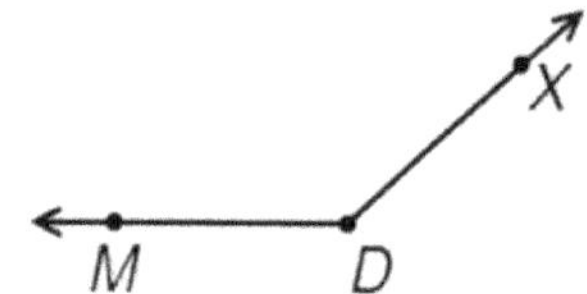

9.

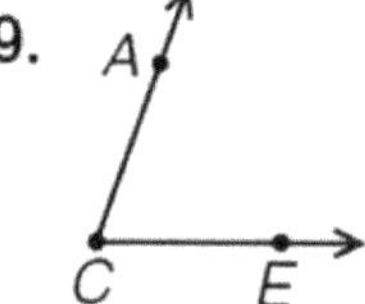

Q 10. Line l and m are parallel to each other and line n is transversal. Find out values of x.

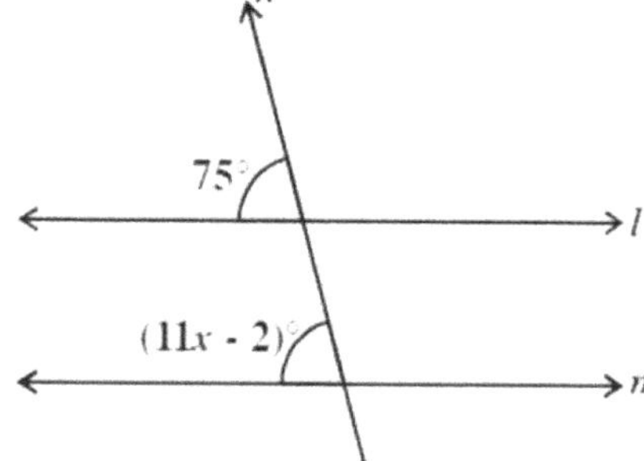

Q 11. What least number should be subtracted from the sum of greatest six digit number and smallest seven digit number to obtain a common multiple of 2, 4 and 8?

Worksheet 28

Q 1. Find out values of the variables in the following.

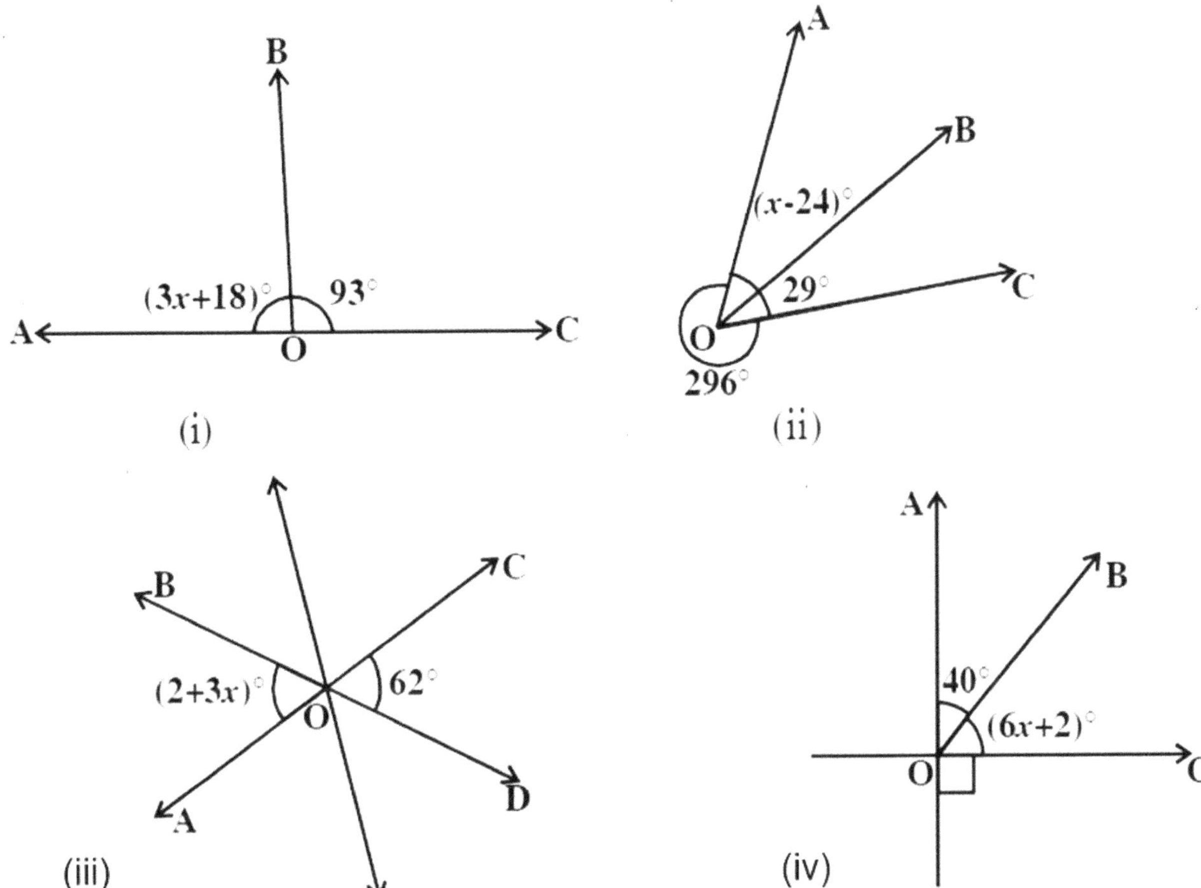

Q 2. Calculate volume.

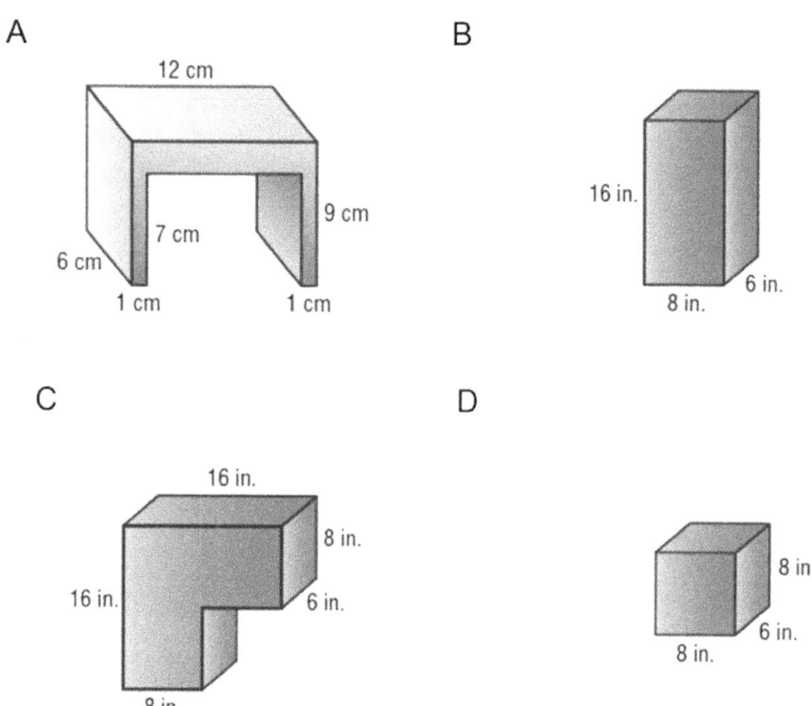

Q 3. Calculate area of shaded portions.

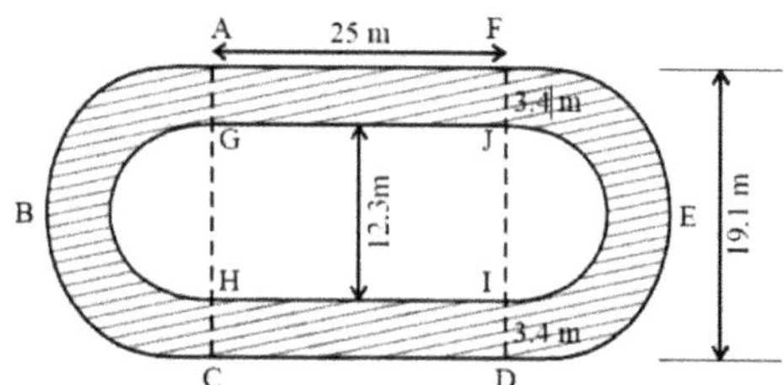

Q 4. Compare area of the following.

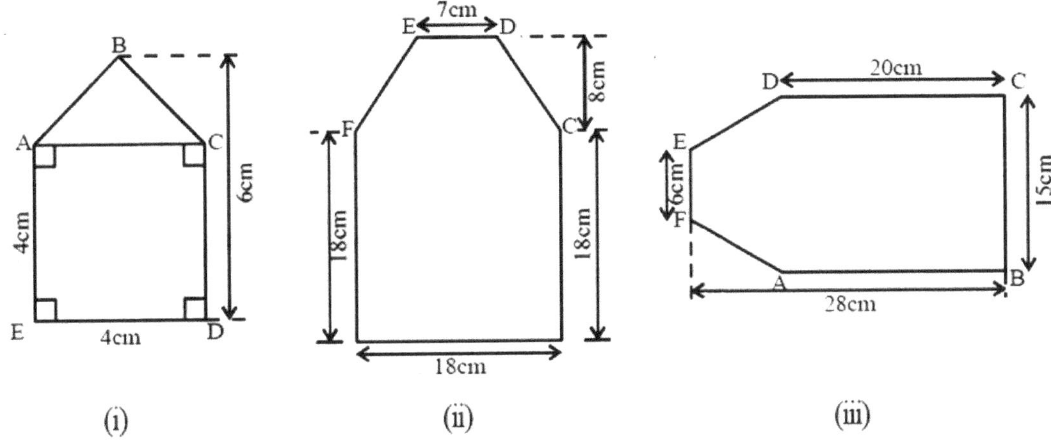

Q 5. Calculate area of the following.

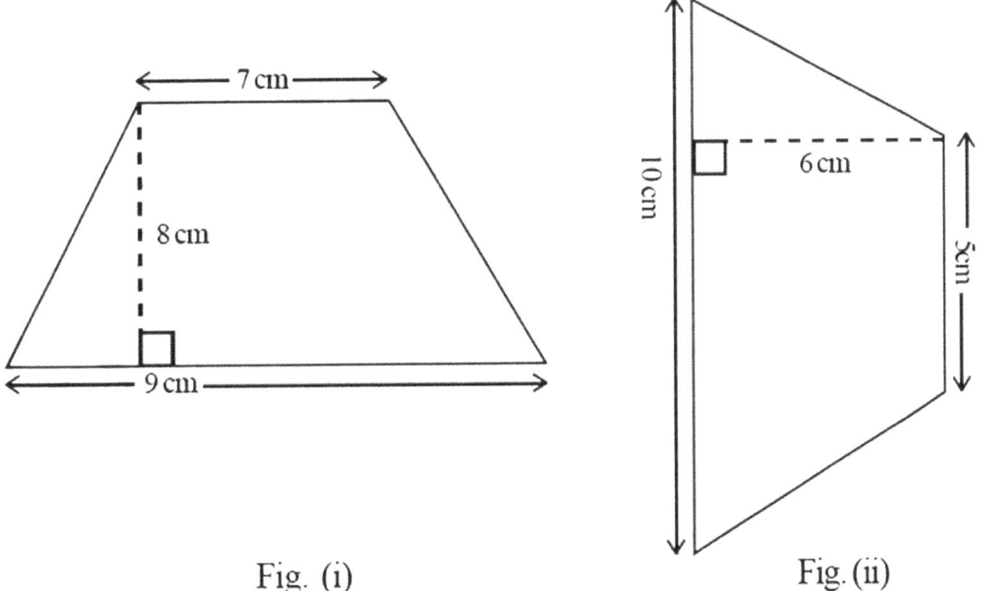

Fig. (i)

Fig. (ii)

Worksheet 29

Q 1. Find out the variables in the following.

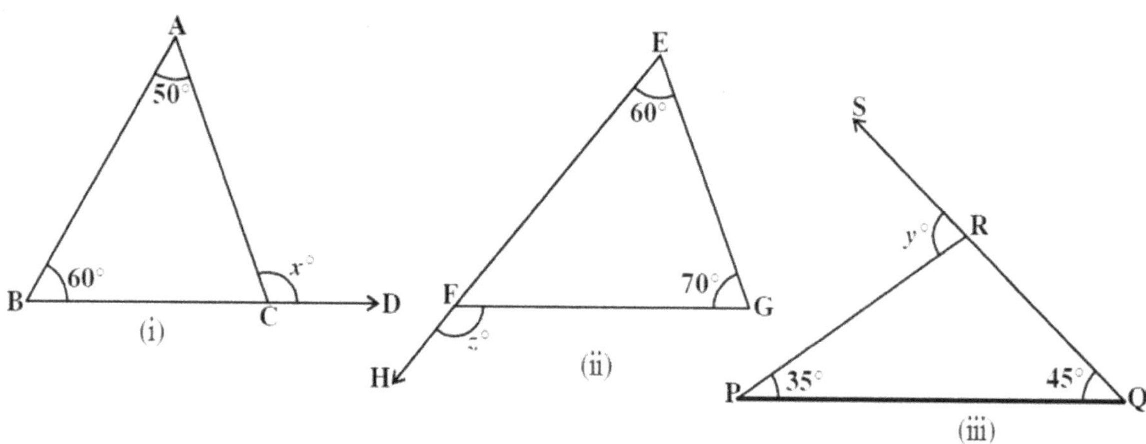

Q 2. Find out x and y in the following.

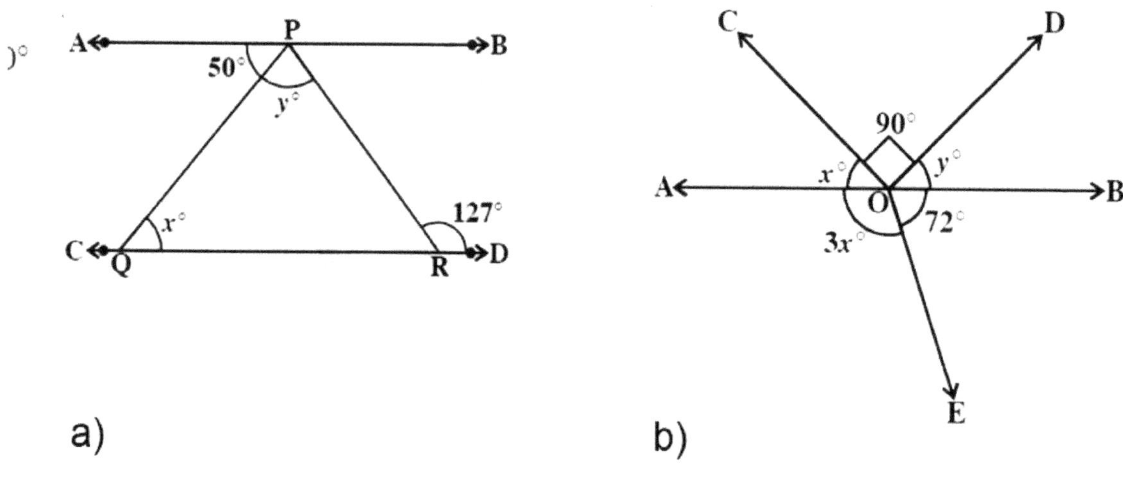

Q 3. Find out missing angles.

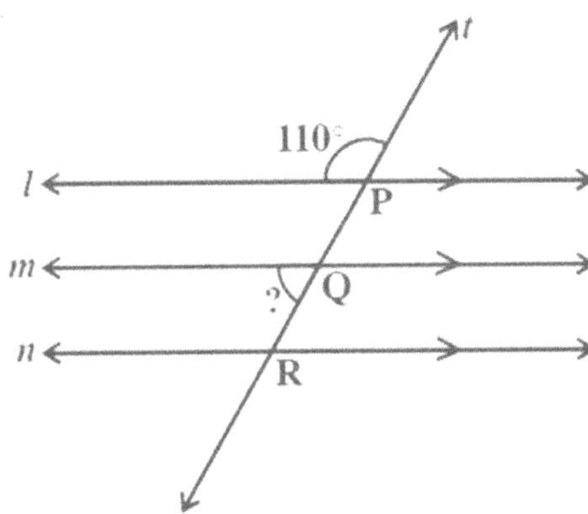

Q 4. Find out magnitude of angles represented by using variables.

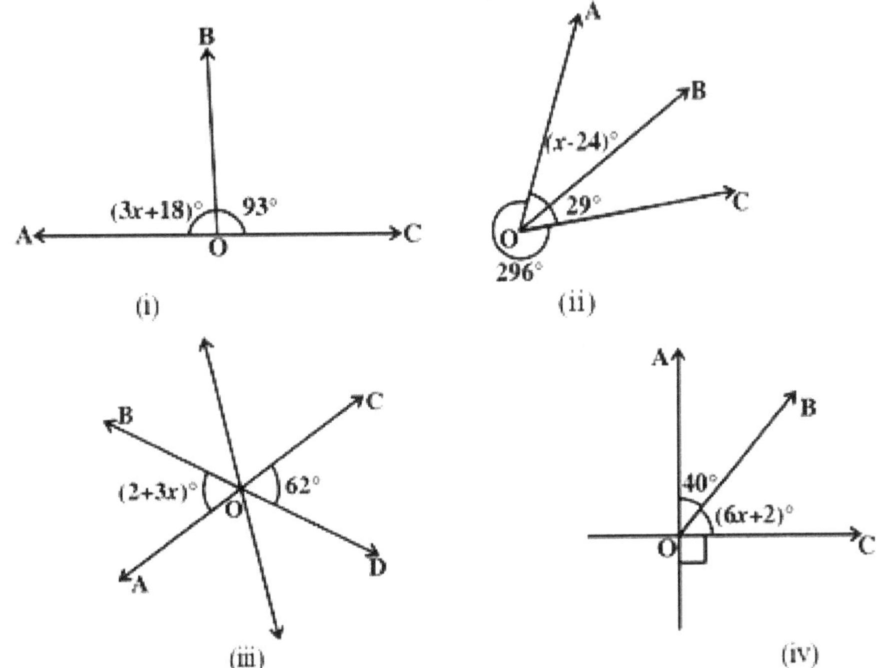

Q 5. Find out missing angles.

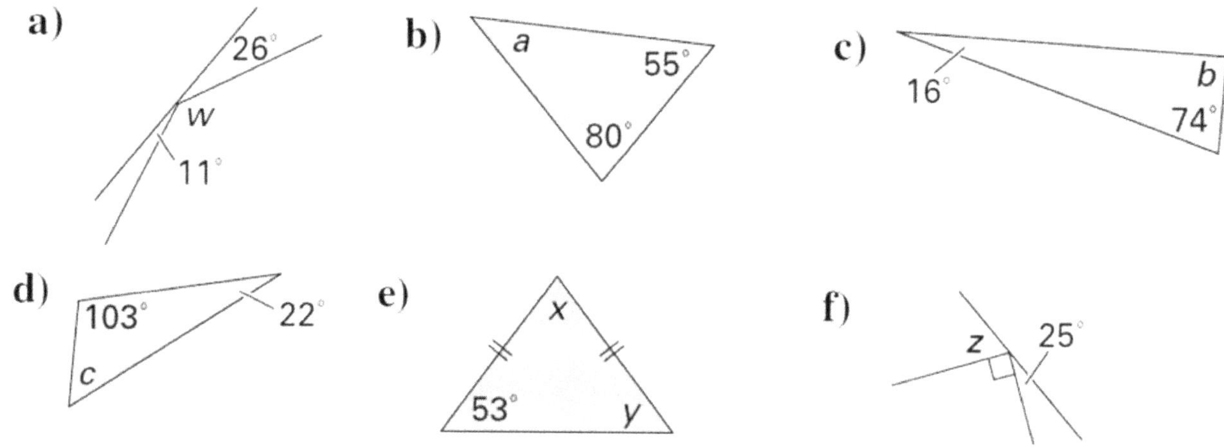

Q 6. What least number should be subtracted from the product of greatest and smallest four digit numbers to obtain a multiple of 9?

Q 7. Half of a quarter of a number is equal to 200,300,101. Find out the number.

Q 8. Seven fifth of a number exceeds seventh multiple of seven digit smallest number by 56. Find out the number.

Q 9. What least number should be subtracted from five digit greatest number to obtain a common multiple of 2, 3, 4, 6 and 12?

Q 10. Nikhil jogs at an average speed of 10 m in a couple of second. Mohini jogs at an average speed of 18 km/h. Who jogs faster and by how much?

Q 11. 19. Which of the following statements is true?

(A) The mean height of the mountains is greater than their median height.
(B) The mean height of the mountains is less than their mode.
(C) The median height of the mountains is less than their mode.
(D) The median height of the mountains is greater than their mean height.

Worksheet 30

Q 1. Calculate area of shaded portions.

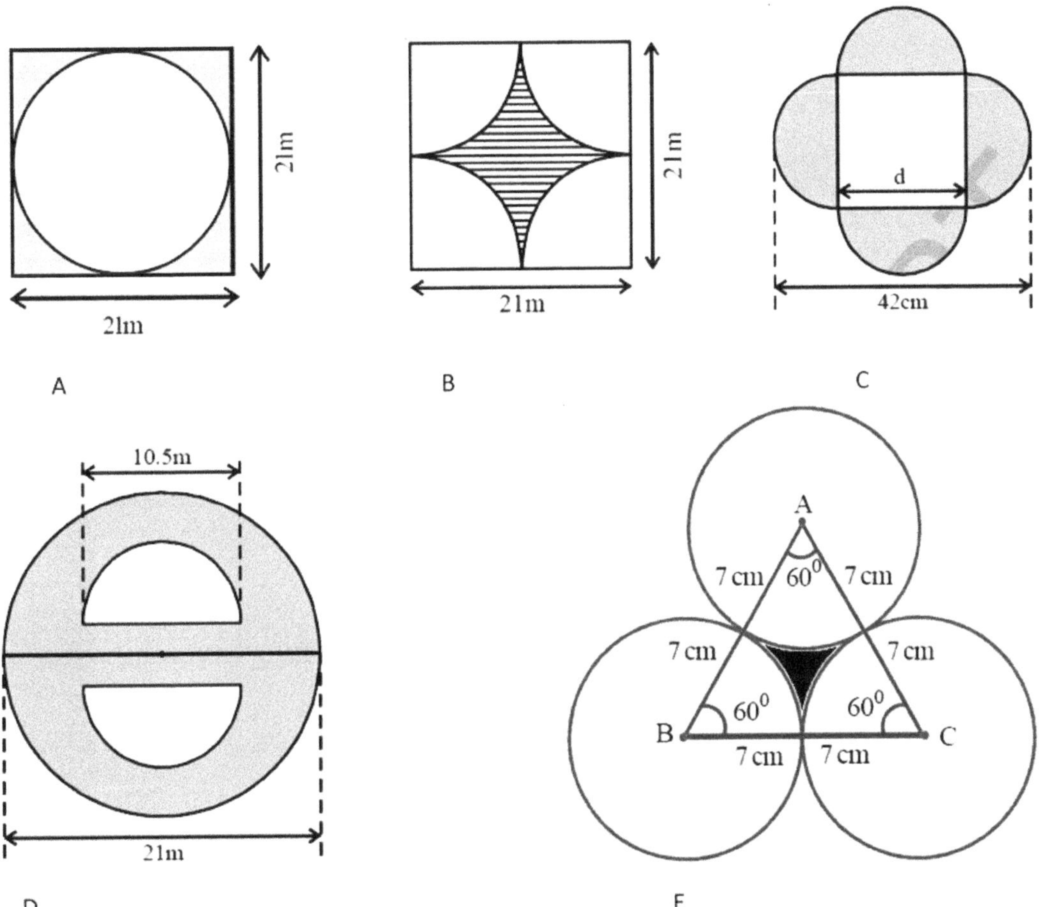

Q 2. Complete the following.

(i) $\left(\frac{-1}{17}\right)+(\_\_\_\_\_)=\left(\frac{-12}{5}\right)+\left(\frac{-1}{17}\right)$

(ii) $\frac{-2}{3}+\_\_\_\_\_=\frac{-2}{3}$

(iii) $1\times\_\_\_\_\_=\frac{9}{11}$

(iv) $-12+\left(\frac{5}{6}+\frac{6}{7}\right)=\left(-12+\frac{5}{6}\right)+(\_\_\_\_\_)$

(v) $(\_\_\_\_\_)\times\left(\frac{1}{2}+\frac{1}{3}\right)=\left(\frac{3}{4}\times\frac{1}{2}\right)+\left(\frac{3}{4}\times\_\_\_\_\_\right)$

(vi) $\frac{-16}{7}+\_\_\_\_\_=\frac{-16}{7}$

Q 3. What least number should be added to the product of smallest and greatest five digit numbers to obtain a common multiple of 3 and 9?

Q 4. Observe the given fractions.

a. 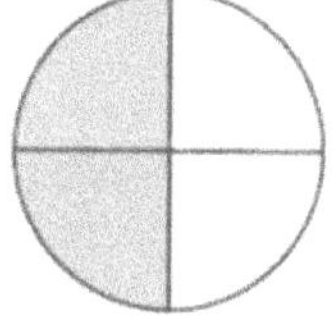

b. 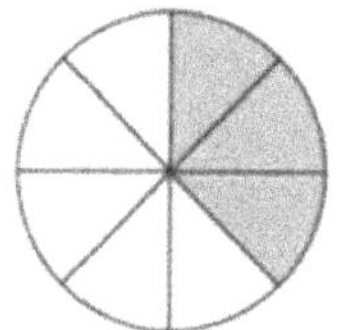

c. 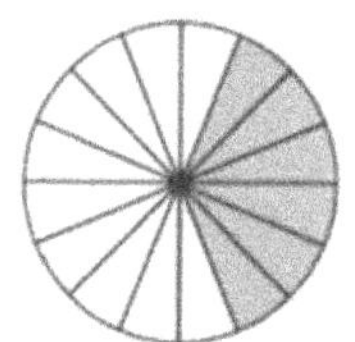

d. 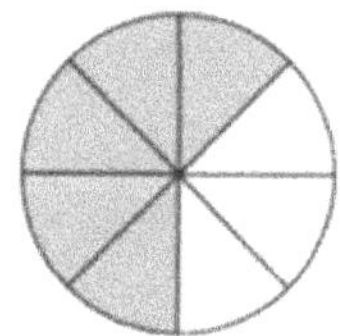

Calculate: (21 a + 12 b + 8 c – 0.02d + 12.009) = ……………

Worksheet 31

Calculate and compare.

1. 36,587 87,943 + 13,156	**2.** 28,764 64,537 + 35,936	**3.** 65,446 1,915 + 47,291	**4.** 49,765 18,976 + 7,359
5. 26,542 − 17,986	**6.** 34,896 − 15,984	**7.** 41,132 − 17,545	**8.** 62,764 − 58,685
9. 115,609 205,399 + 411,111	**10.** 356,789 141,217 + 222,888	**11.** 471,009 180,007 + 277,777	**12.** 365,786 274,982 + 186,214
13. 672,244 − 456,688	**14.** 681,337 − 278,456	**15.** 524,700 − 316,672	**16.** 938,400 − 619,711

Q 17. How many three digit numbers can be prepared by using digits 3, 5 and 8 only once? Find out sum of smallest and greatest number of this series.

Q 18. What least number should be subtracted from 32,43,094 to get a common multiple of 3 and 9?

Q 19. $1/11^{th}$ of $1/10^{th}$ of 220,330,440 = ……………..

Q 20. Half of a quarter of 80,80,072 = ……………………

Q 21. Calculate simplest value.

a. $$\frac{40^{50} - 40^{48}}{2^{96}} \times 10^{-45} =$$

(A) 20

(B) $10^3(1599)$

(C) $10^2(1601)$

(D) 200^6

(E) 200^{53}

b. $$\frac{40^{48}(40^2 - 1)}{2^{96}} \times 10^{-45}$$

c. If $ab \neq 0$, $\frac{a^8 - b^8}{(a^4+b^4)(a^2+b^2)} =$

(A) 1

(B) $a - b$

(C) $(a + b)(a - b)$

(D) $(a^2 + b^2)(a^2 - b^2)$

(E) $(a - b)/(a + b)$

d. $$\frac{2^{16} - 1}{(2^4 + 1)(2^{11} + 2^3)}$$

Q 22. Three numbers are in the ratio of 2: 4: 9. Smallest number is equal to third multiple of 208. Find out sum of all the three numbers.

Q 23. Rita jogs 200 m in a minute, Rina jogs 30 m in 5 seconds and Tina maintains an average speed of 18 km/h. Who jogs faster?

Worksheet 32

Observe the following chart of representation.

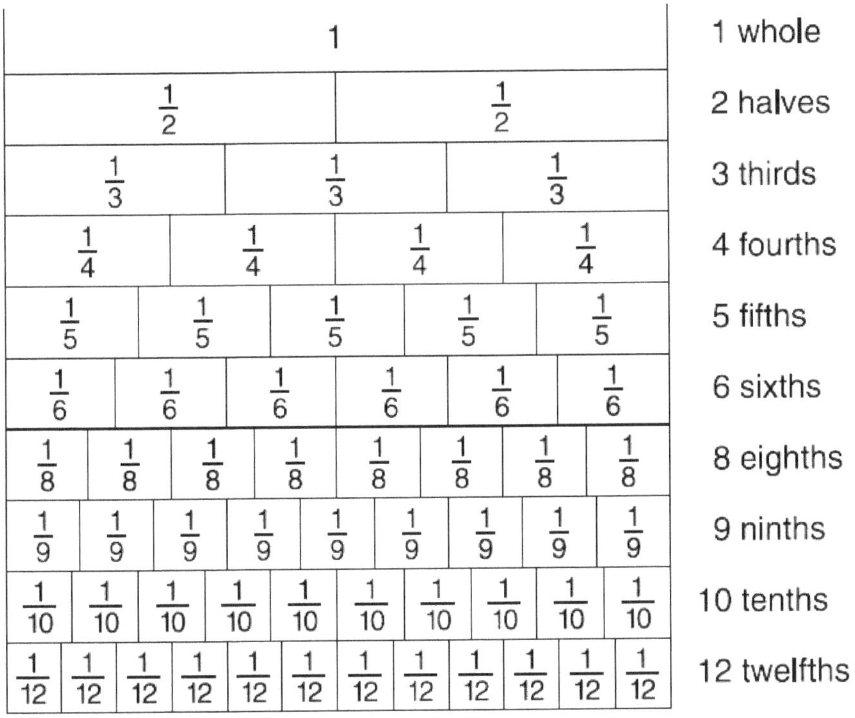

Chart	
1	1 whole
$\frac{1}{2}$ $\frac{1}{2}$	2 halves
$\frac{1}{3}$ $\frac{1}{3}$ $\frac{1}{3}$	3 thirds
$\frac{1}{4}$ $\frac{1}{4}$ $\frac{1}{4}$ $\frac{1}{4}$	4 fourths
$\frac{1}{5}$ $\frac{1}{5}$ $\frac{1}{5}$ $\frac{1}{5}$ $\frac{1}{5}$	5 fifths
$\frac{1}{6}$ $\frac{1}{6}$ $\frac{1}{6}$ $\frac{1}{6}$ $\frac{1}{6}$ $\frac{1}{6}$	6 sixths
$\frac{1}{8}$ $\frac{1}{8}$ $\frac{1}{8}$ $\frac{1}{8}$ $\frac{1}{8}$ $\frac{1}{8}$ $\frac{1}{8}$ $\frac{1}{8}$	8 eighths
$\frac{1}{9}$ $\frac{1}{9}$ $\frac{1}{9}$ $\frac{1}{9}$ $\frac{1}{9}$ $\frac{1}{9}$ $\frac{1}{9}$ $\frac{1}{9}$ $\frac{1}{9}$	9 ninths
$\frac{1}{10}$ $\frac{1}{10}$ $\frac{1}{10}$ $\frac{1}{10}$ $\frac{1}{10}$ $\frac{1}{10}$ $\frac{1}{10}$ $\frac{1}{10}$ $\frac{1}{10}$ $\frac{1}{10}$	10 tenths
$\frac{1}{12}$ $\frac{1}{12}$ $\frac{1}{12}$ $\frac{1}{12}$ $\frac{1}{12}$ $\frac{1}{12}$ $\frac{1}{12}$ $\frac{1}{12}$ $\frac{1}{12}$ $\frac{1}{12}$ $\frac{1}{12}$ $\frac{1}{12}$	12 twelfths

$$1 = \frac{2}{2} = \frac{3}{3} = \frac{4}{4} = \frac{5}{5} = \frac{6}{6} = \frac{8}{8} = \frac{9}{9} = \frac{10}{10} = \frac{12}{12}$$

Complete the following:

Q 1. $\frac{2}{7} = \frac{\_\_}{14} = \frac{\_\_}{21} = \frac{\_\_}{28} = \frac{\_\_}{35} = \frac{\_\_}{56} = \frac{\_\_}{63}$

Q 2. What fraction of 1331 is equal to 121?

Q 3. $1/11^{th}$ of a number is equal to 100,200,311. Find out the number.

Worksheet 33

Q 1. Complete the following.

Standard Form:
2,821,700,000

Billions Period			Millions Period			Thousands Period			Ones Period		
hundreds	tens	ones	hundreds	tens	ones	hundreds	tens	ones	hundreds	tens	ones
		2,	8	2	1,	7	0	0,	0	0	0

Expanded Form:

2,000,000,000 + 800,000,000 + 20,000,000 + 1,000,000 + 700,000

Word Name: ....

Q 2. Find out area of the following in unit square.

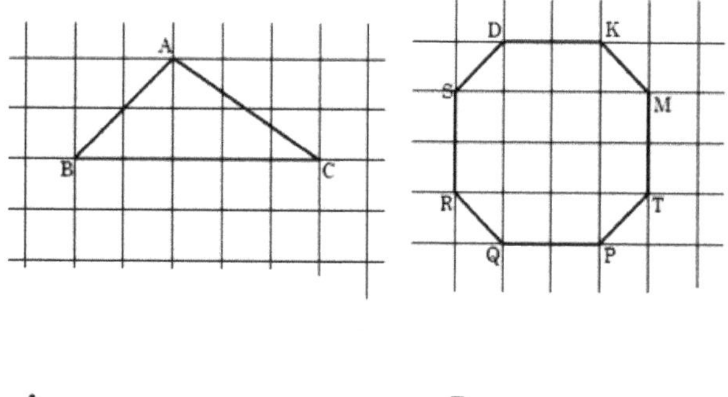

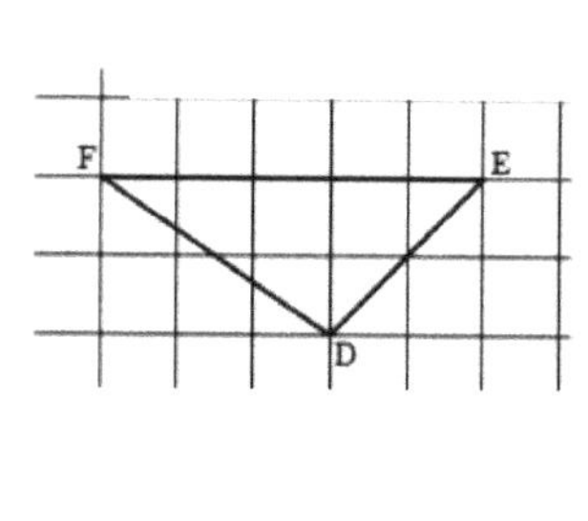

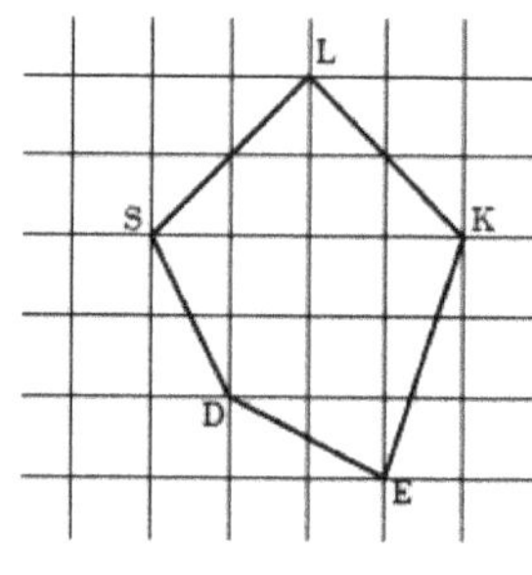

A B C D

Q 3. What least number should be added to greatest six digit number to obtain a multiple of 8?

Q 4. Three bells toll at an interval of 4 seconds, 8 seconds and 12 seconds respectively. After what time interval do they toll together?

Q 5. Find out variables.

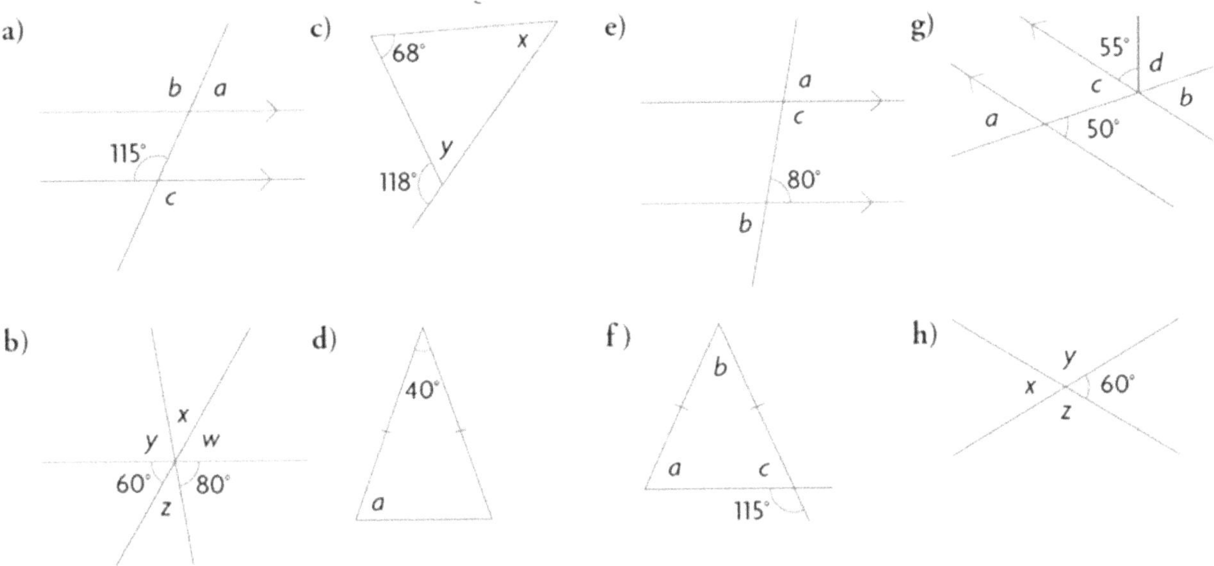

Q 6. Seven seventeenth of a natural number exceeds smallest six digit number by 3. Find out the number.

Q 7. Sum of five consecutive natural numbers is equal to 15 more than 55,000. Find out the smallest number.

Q 8. Find out missing angles.

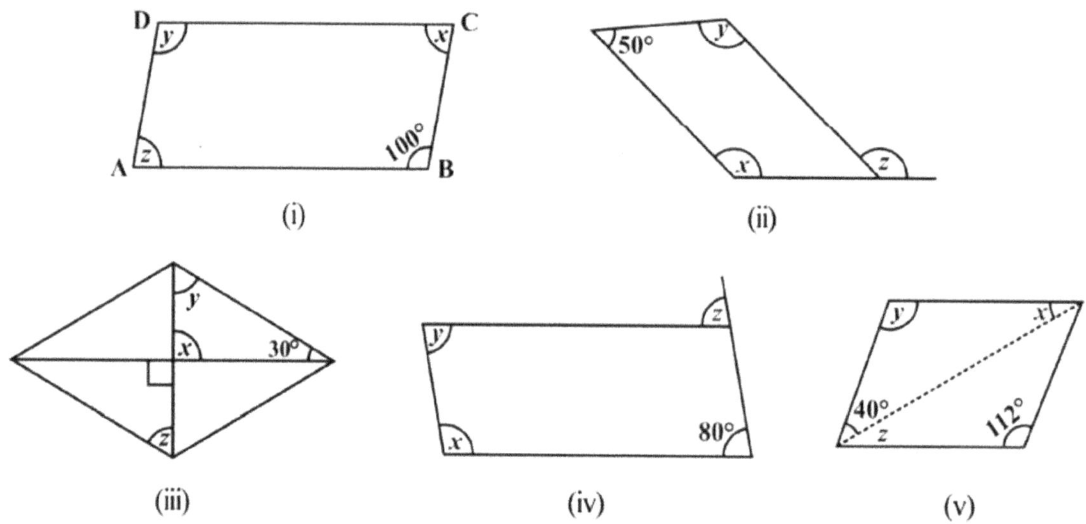

Q 9. Find out area and outer boundary of the following in which side of each of the unit square is 4 cm.

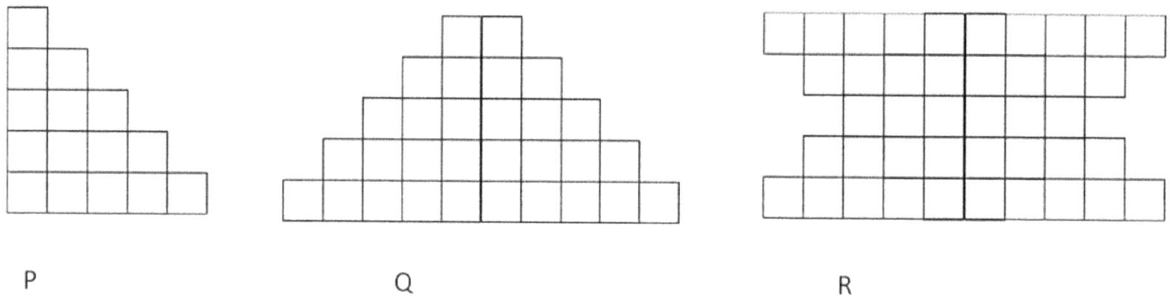

P Q R

Q 10. Identify following variables.

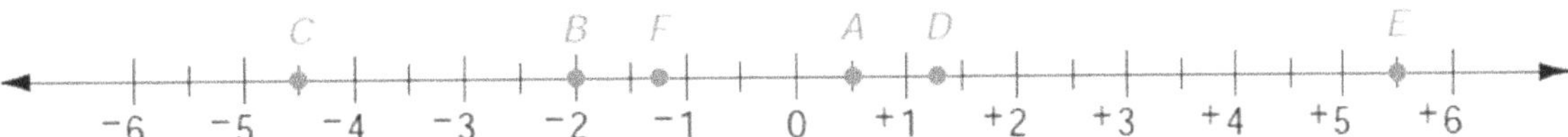

Q 11. Find out sum and difference of P and Q in the following.

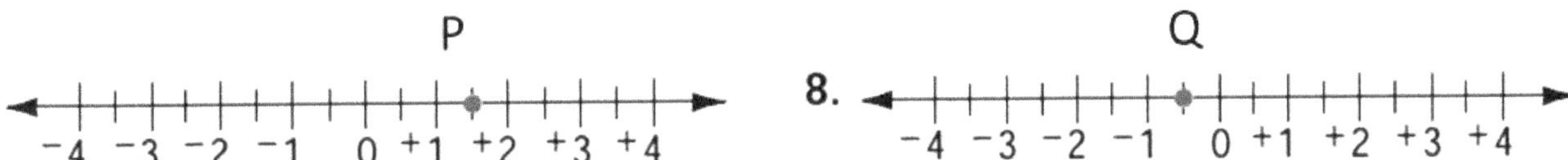

Q 12. Sum of seven consecutive natural numbers is equal to 28 more than seventh multiple of seven digit smallest natural number. Find out the smallest natural number of this number series.

Q 13. 20% of 30% of a natural number is equal to 100,200,302. Find out the number.

Q 14. After selling six cakes a shopkeeper gains an amount equal to selling price of one apple. Find out the gain percentage.

Q 15. A goods train takes 1 m 21 s to cross a light post. That train moves at an average speed of 72 km/h. Calculate total length of that train. That train has to cross a tunnel of length 2 km 34 m. Calculate total time to be taken by that train to cross the tunnel.

Q 16. $(1 + 2 + 3 + \ldots\ldots\ldots\ldots + 50{,}000) \times (50{,}001)^{-1}$ = ...

Q 17. 30% of 50% of 200,300 = ...

Worksheet 34

Divide and check your answer.

1. $\begin{array}{r} 2\,8\,1 \\ 2.3\overline{)6.4\,6\,3} \end{array}$

2. $\begin{array}{r} 0\,9\,2 \\ 0.1\,9\overline{)0.1\,7\,4\,8} \end{array}$

3. $\begin{array}{r} 3\,1\,1 \\ 0.9\,2\overline{)2.8\,6\,1\,2} \end{array}$

4. $\begin{array}{r} 6\,0\,3 \\ 0.8\overline{)4.8\,2\,4} \end{array}$

5. $\begin{array}{r} 8\,5 \\ 0.0\,1\,1\overline{)0.0\,9\,3\,5} \end{array}$

6. $\begin{array}{r} 0\,1\,2 \\ 0.0\,1\,2\overline{)0.0\,0\,1\,4\,4} \end{array}$

7. $\begin{array}{r} 0\,0\,0\,3 \\ 1.5\overline{)0.0\,0\,4\,5} \end{array}$

8. $\begin{array}{r} 0\,2 \\ 0.1\,8\overline{)0.0\,3\,6} \end{array}$

9. $\begin{array}{r} 0\,0\,6 \\ 0.0\,2\,4\overline{)0.0\,0\,1\,4\,4} \end{array}$

10. $0.5\overline{)7.55}$
11. $0.6\overline{)9.66}$
12. $0.4\overline{)0.76}$
13. $0.7\overline{)8.61}$
14. $92.4 \div 0.4$
15. $6.3 \div 0.3$
16. $257.2 \div 0.4$
17. $0.96 \div 0.8$
18. $2.214 \div 0.9$
19. $0.084 \div 0.3$
20. $555.6 \div 0.6$
21. $391.2 \div 0.4$
22. $0.28\overline{)4.396}$
23. $0.75\overline{)0.7725}$
24. $0.07\overline{)3.5028}$
25. $0.08\overline{)1.9216}$
26. $6.9 \div 2.3$
27. $8.93 \div 4.7$
28. $0.78 \div 0.26$
29. $0.014 \div 0.07$

Q 30. What least number should be subtracted from smallest seven digit number to obtain a factor of 9?

Q 31. A cistern takes 45 minutes to fill up half of a water tank, anther cistern takes 30 minutes to fill up quarter of the same water tank. Find out time to be taken by both the cisterns jointly to fill up the same water tank.

Q 32. Simplify:

$$\left(1+\frac{1}{100}\right)\left(1-\frac{1}{1001}\right)\left[2.002-2\,X\,\left(1+\frac{1}{1000}\right)\right]\,X\,34.090823$$

Worksheet 35

Find out products.

1. 10×77 2. 30×40 3. 10×0.5 4. 10×0.0049

5. 100×13 6. 400×125 7. 100×0.7 8. 100×0.1003

9. 20×51 10. 5000×30 11. $10{,}000 \times 0.02$ 12. $20{,}000 \times 0.02$

13. 3000×50.123 14. 4000×22 15. 100×19.41 16. 1000×12.0006

17. a. 10×94 b. 100×930 c. 1000×92

18. a. 100×0.05 b. 10×0.7 c. 1000×0.94

19. a. 1000×0.0062 b. 100×0.005 c. 10×0.042

20. a. 100×0.61 b. 100×0.70 c. 1000×0.0010

Find the missing factor.

21. $b \times 1000 \times 0.0010 \times 10{,}000 \times 0.02 \times 45 = 90000 \times 0.0010$

22. $y \times 96 \times 0.0010 \times 0.0010 \times 0.0010 \times 0.0010 = 9600$

23. $300 \times 100 \times 0.05 \times 100 \times 0.05 \times 100 \times 0.05 \times a = 5100$

Q 24. Rikin went to Kolkata on a day which was Wednesday. His uncle wants to visit the same place 65 days after that day. What will be the day in which uncle planned to visit the place?

Worksheet 36

Observe the numeration chart and write given values in Standard form.

Billions Period			Millions Period			Thousands Period			Ones Period		
hundreds	tens	ones	hundreds	tens	ones	hundreds	tens	ones	hundreds	tens	ones
								8,	6	3	0
							8	6,	3	0	2
						8	6	3,	0	2	0
					8,	6	3	0,	2	0	1
		8,	6	3	0,	2	0	1,	0	0	0

A place that holds a zero may be omitted in expanded form.

(8 × 1000) (6 × 100) (3 × 10) (0 × 1)

(8 × 10,000) (6 × 1000) (3 × 100) (2 × 1)

(8 × 100,000) (6 × 10,000) (3 × 1000) (2 × 10)

(8 × 1,000,000) (6 × 100,000) (3 × 10,000) (2 × 100) (1 × 1)

(8 × 1,000,000,000) (6 × 100,000,000) (3 × 10,000,000) (2 × 100,000) (1 × 1000)

Q 1. 43 million + 43 thousands + 403 hundreds + 324 tens = …………

Q 2. 39 more than 39 million + 3099 thousands = ………………..

Q 3. A wall mount clock spends 4 seconds to ring 4 bells at 4 a.m. Calculate total time to be taken by that clock to strike 10 bells at 10 a.m.

Q 4. Identify the following.

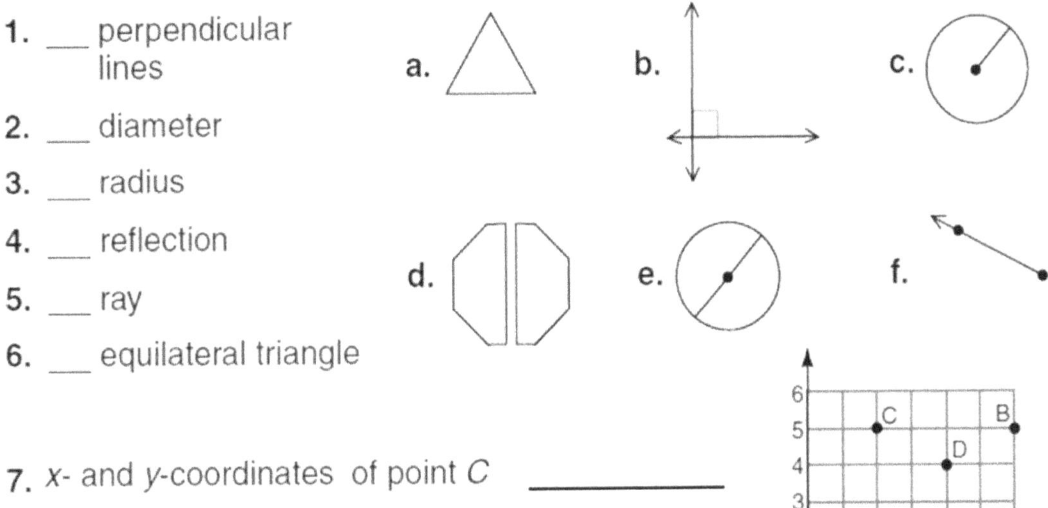

8. ______ is located at (4, 0)?

.

Q 5. Mohanlal wanted to visit a place which is 87 km away from the city drive. He again wants to extend his visit by 23 km to visit another city. His personal car spends 20 seconds to cross near about 189 m of distance. Calculate total time to be taken by his car drive to complete his visits and return back to home after finishing all the visits.

Q 6. A water boat takes 1,5 hours to cross a stream while moving against the flow of water and it can take 30 minutes to cross the same distance while moving along with the flow of water. Find out ratio of the speed of boat and speed of the stream.

Q 7. Sum of two interior angles of a triangle is 121^0 32’ . Find out magnitude of the third angle.

Q 8. Seven seventeenth of a natural number exceeds smallest six digit number by 3. Find out the number.

Worksheet 38

Q 1. Represent shaded portions in the following by using a fraction.

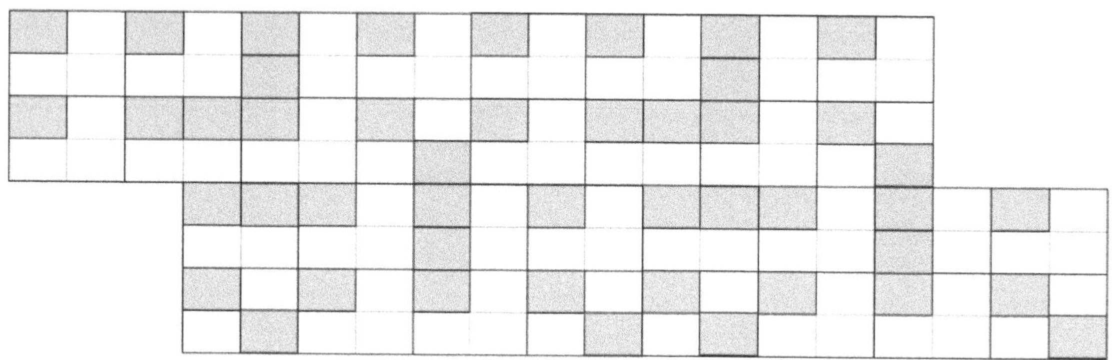

Q 2. Which of the following represents a linear triplet?

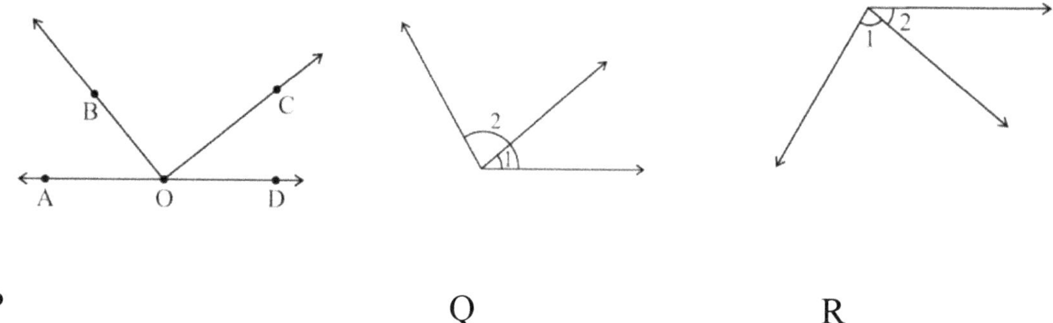

P Q R

Q 3. What fraction of all the numbers starting from 1 to 200 are multiples of 5?

Q 4. A passenger train spends 1m 12 seconds to cross a light post. Average speed of that train was 36 km/h. Calculate total length of that train. While moving on track a train usually covers the distance equal to its own length during crossing a narrow object having negligible thickness.

Q 5. $(1 + 2 + 3 + \ldots\ldots. 21{,}000) \text{ X } (1.001 \text{ X } 10^5 - 100.1) = \ldots\ldots\ldots$

Q 6. Smallest five digit number which can be divisible by 9 leaving a remainder 5 is equal to ……………….

Q 6. Simplify the following.

$$\sqrt{144} = \sqrt{12\,X\,12} = 12\,;\ \sqrt{(a+b)^2} = \sqrt{(a+b)X\,(a+b)} = \cdots.$$

1. $\sqrt{900}$
2. $\sqrt{225}$
3. $\sqrt{20}$
4. $\sqrt{200}$
5. $\sqrt{32}$
6. $\sqrt{4x^2}$
7. $\sqrt{81t^2}$
8. $\sqrt{4(t+2)^2}$
9. $\sqrt{36(j-3)^2}$
10. $\sqrt{64(k+4)^2}$
11. $\sqrt{\frac{16}{4}}$
12. $\sqrt{\frac{25}{9}}$
13. $\sqrt{\frac{125}{16}}$
14. $\sqrt{\frac{50}{4}}$
15. $\sqrt{\frac{x^2}{36}}$
16. $\sqrt{\frac{200}{x^2}}, x \neq 0$
17. $\sqrt{\frac{242}{a^2}}, a \neq 0$
18. $\sqrt{\frac{(d-1)^2}{(f+1)^2}}, f \neq -1$
19. $\sqrt{\frac{(a+b)^2}{(c+d)^2}}, c+d \neq 0$

Q 7. How many bricks are there in each of the following?

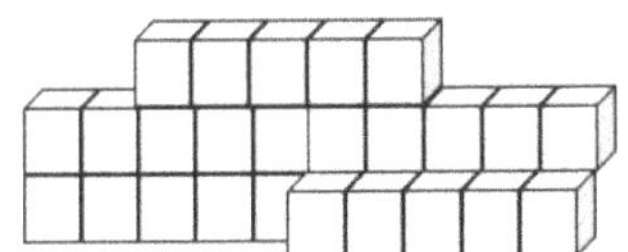

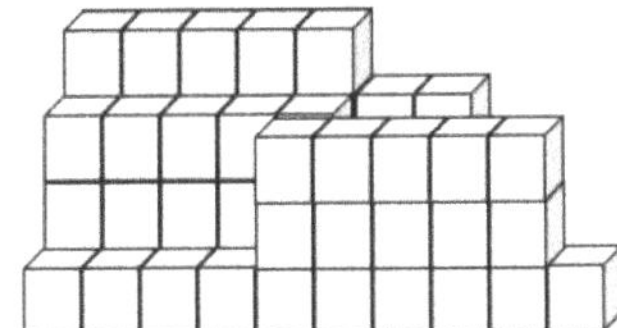

Set A Set B

Q 8. Beat of three counters are repeated at uniform intervals of 5 seconds, 6 seconds and 8 seconds respectively. After what time interval do they beat together? How many times do they beat in a time interval of 2 hours?

Worksheet 39

1: Calculate outer boundary of the following:

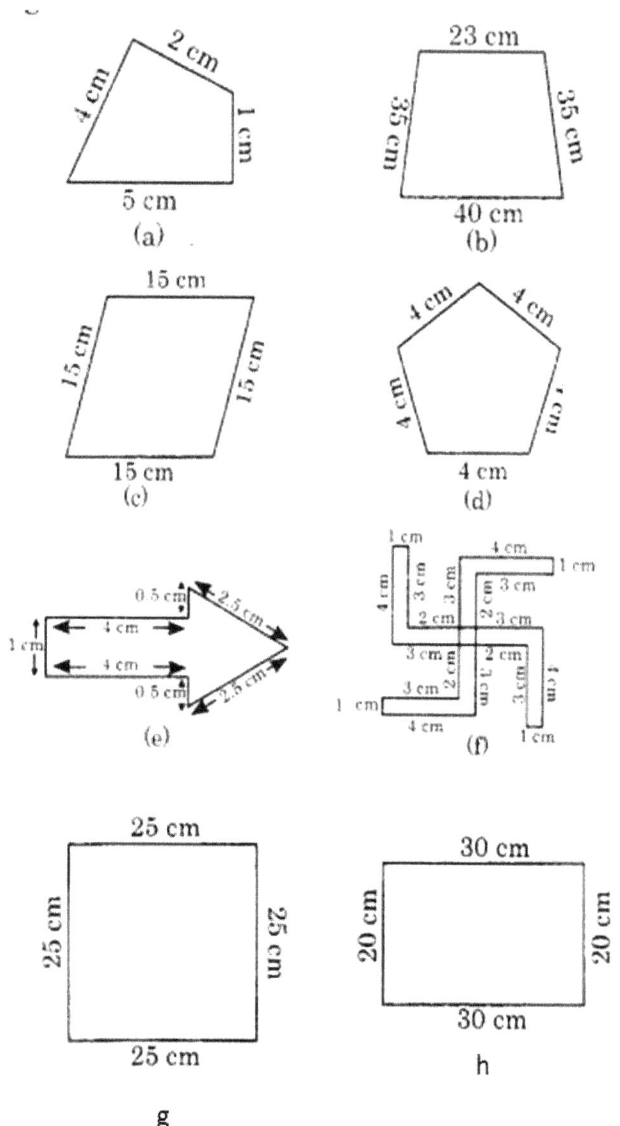

2. We calculate total surface area of a cylinder by using a definite formula.

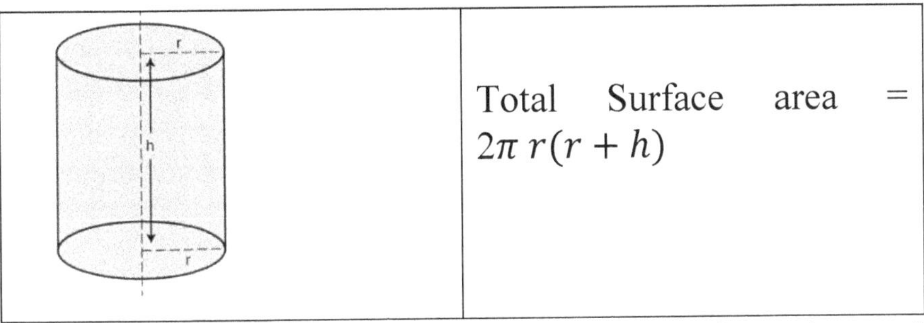	Total Surface area = $2\pi\, r(r + h)$

By using this formula calculate Total Surface Area of the shapes having following specifications.

Sl	Redius of flat face (r)	Height (h)	Total Surface Area (TSA)
1	21	30	
2	35	49	
3	49	58	
4	56	101	

3. The base of a square pyramid has a side length of 27.91 centimeters. The slant height is 25.04 centimeters. Find the surface area.

4. Represent the following in decimal form:

$$154 + \frac{121}{125} + \frac{7}{8} + \frac{39}{40} + \frac{101}{120} + \frac{209}{25}$$

5. How many five digit numbers are there in all ?

6. A passenger train spends 1 m 9 second in crossing a person standing on 2 km 29 m long platform while moving at an average speed of 18 km/h. Calculate total length of the train. Calculate time taken by that train to cross the platform.

Q 7. Compare area of two given triangles in unit square.

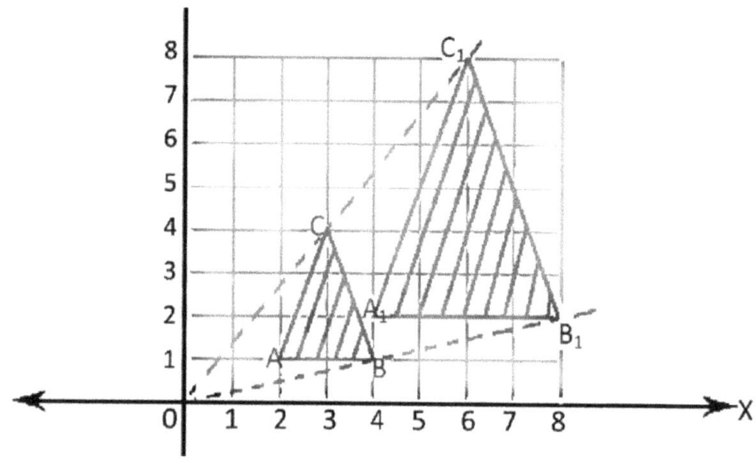

Q 8. 20% 0f 50% of 30,40,500 = ...

Q 9. What least number should be added to the product of greatest five digit number and smallest four digit number to obtain a common multiple of 3 and 9?

Q 10. Is there any pair of natural number having LCM 169 and HCF 11?

Q 11. Sum of seven consecutive natural numbers is equal to 14,028. Find out smallest number of the seven number series.

Q 12. What is the natural number if sum of the number and its reciprocal is equal to 8.125?

Q 13. Sum of five consecutive natural numbers is equal to 15 more than 55,000. Find out the smallest number.

Q 14. Find out unknown angles

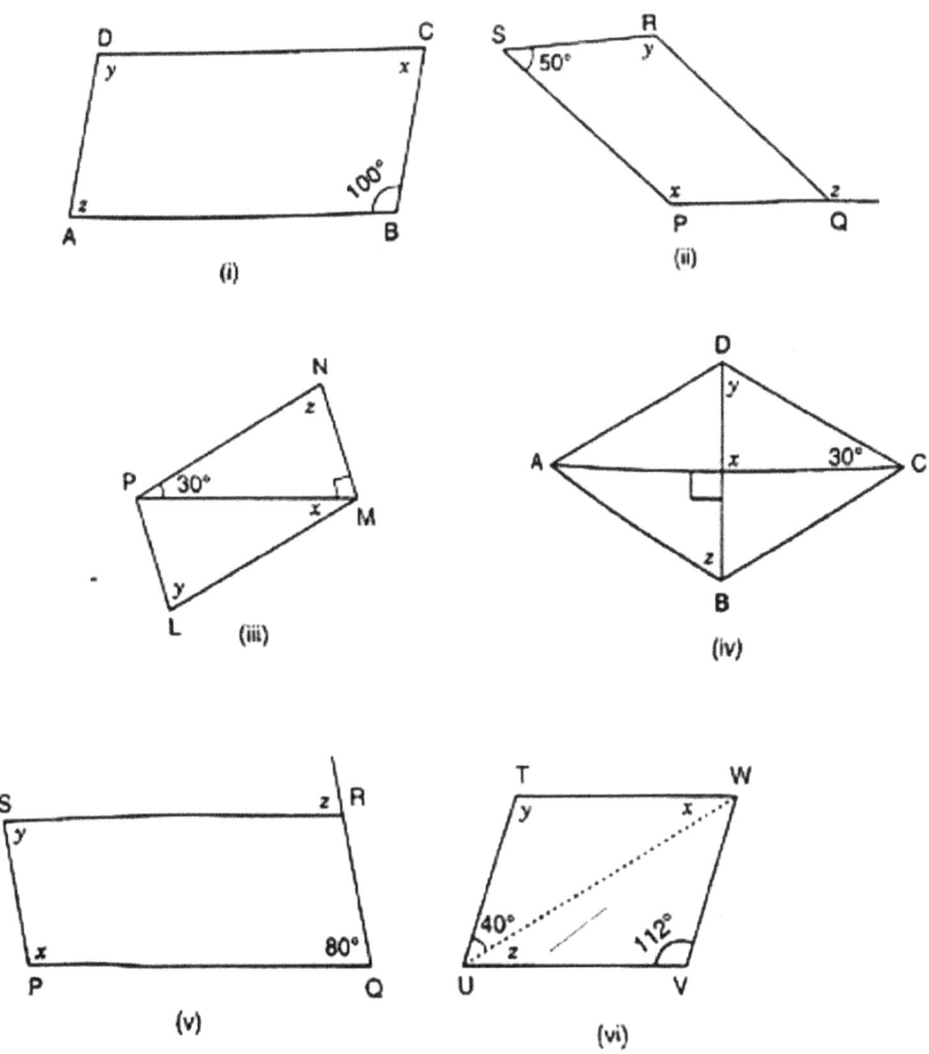

9. Two poles cast shadow on ground up to a definite point. Part of both the shadows superimposed upon each other by part. All lengths displayed in the given figure are on foot. Calculate length of the longer shadow.

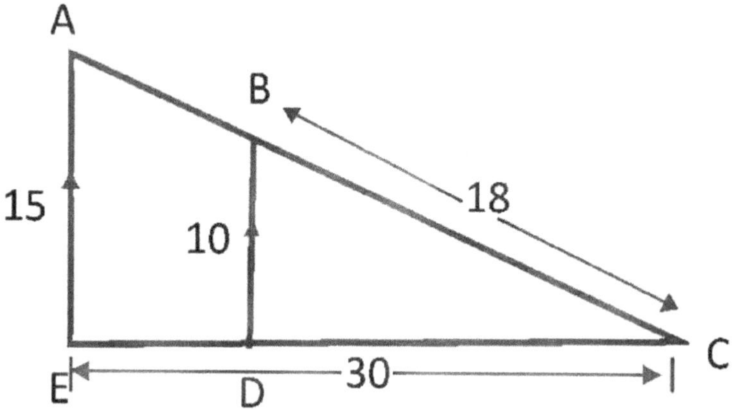

10. Establish relationship in between RW and VB on the basis of the diagram as given.

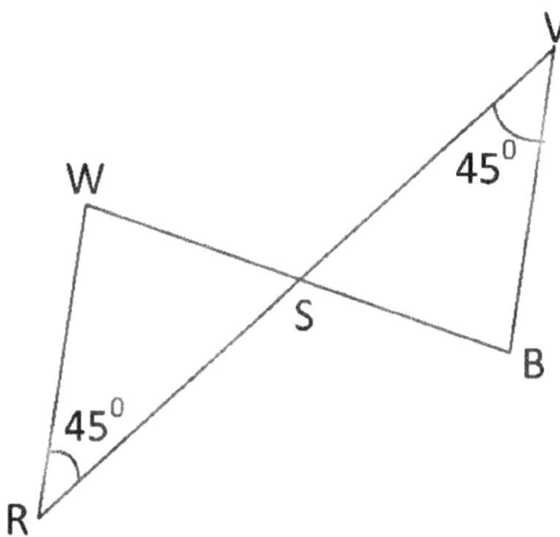

11. Two angles given to construct a triangle are $45^0 45'$ and $39^0\ 39'$. Find out the measure of third angle of that triangle.

12. On the basis of given diagram calculate length of DE.

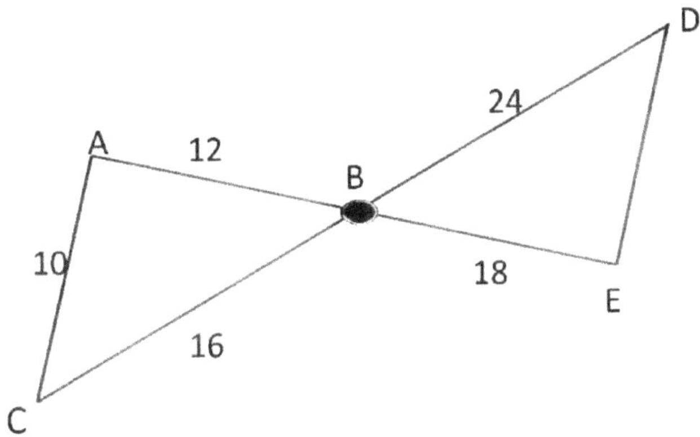

13. BC: EF = …………

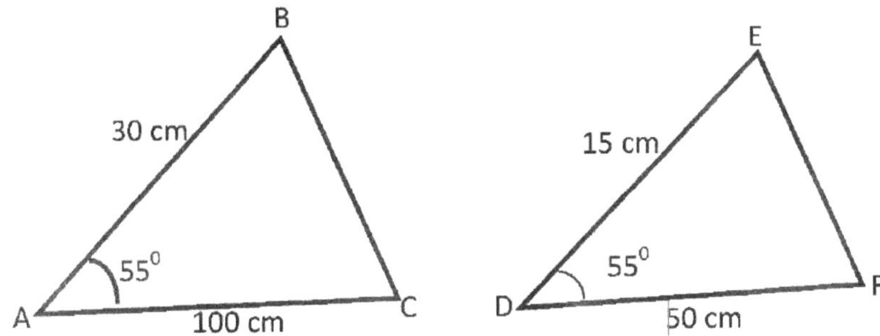

14. After increasing cost of a product by 20% a shopkeeper offered 20% discount on the same product to customers. Find out his total gain or loss percentage.

15. A three digit number prepared in such a way that sum of digits at ones place and hundreds place is equal to digit at tens place. After increasing digit at ones place by 3 it becomes equal to the digit present at hundreds place. Find out the number.

16. The sides of a polygon have lengths 5, 7, 8, 11 and 19 cm. The perimeter of a similar polygon is 150 cm. Find the lengths of the sides of larger polygon.

17. A side of a regular six - sided polygon is 12 cm long. The perimeter of a similar polygon is 90 cm. What is the length of a side of the larger polygon?

18. The ratio of the sides of two similar polygon is 3:2. The area of the smaller polygon is 24cm2. What is the area of the larger polygon?
19. Three trapeziums are similar. The area of first trapeziums is 4 times that of the second and 5 times that of third. Determine the ratios of the perimeters and the corresponding side lengths of all the trapeziums.

19. Rectangle ABCD is similar to rectangle PQRS. Given that AB=14cm, BC=8cm and PQ=21 cm, calculate the length of QR.

20. A football field measures 100 m by 72 m. A school marks a football field similar in shape to a full size football field but only 30 m long. What is its width?

21. A graph is plotted to show relation between weekly growth rate and amount of light received by the plant.

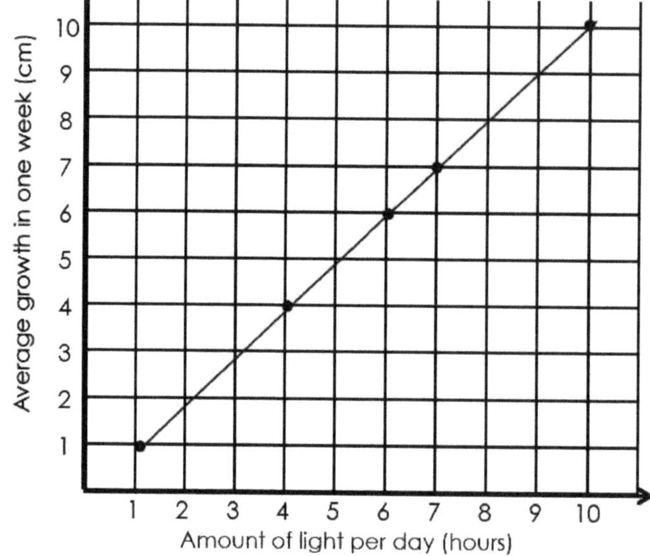

Find out the linear relation in between tow variables on the growth pattern. [Example 4 hours exposure = 4 cm growth per week.]

22. Estimate the part of each of the following grids which is shaded.

a.

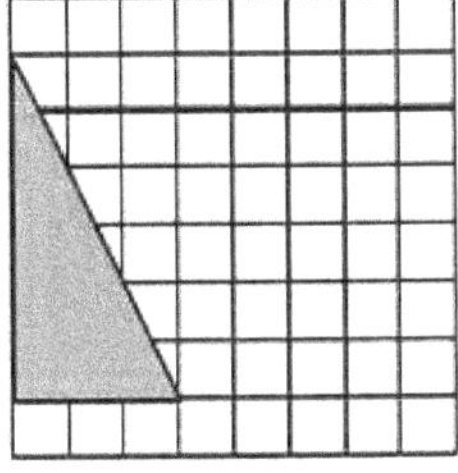

b.

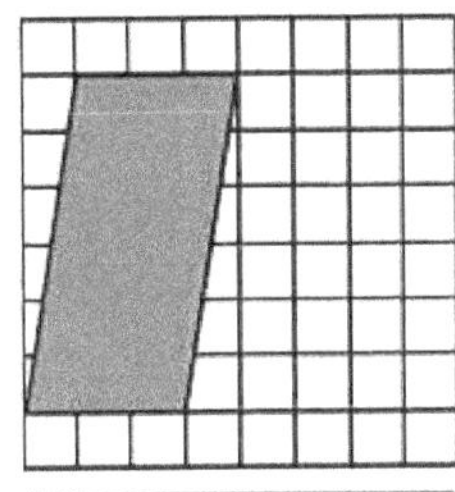

c.

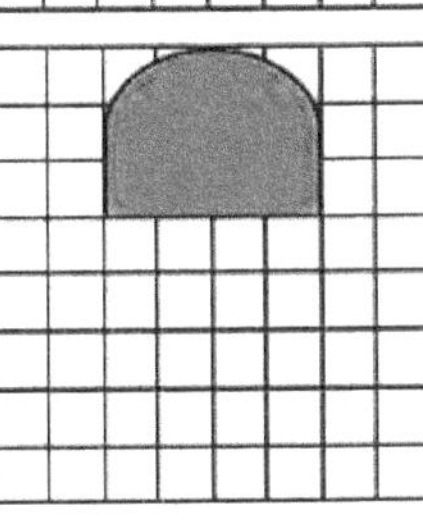

d.

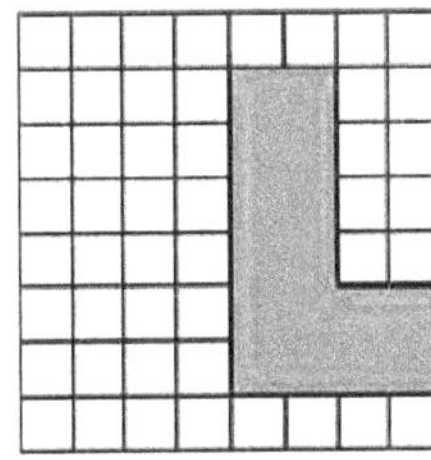

e.

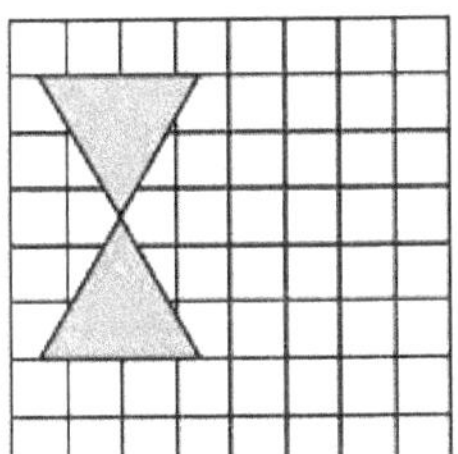

f.

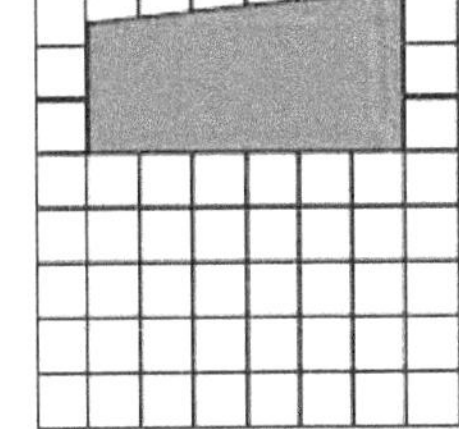

23. Cistern A fills up a water tank in 40 minutes. Cistern B fills up the same water tank in 1 h 20 minutes. If both the cisterns kept open then time taken by both the cisterns to fill up four such water tanks will be ....'

24. Tamanna took 4 days to finish her project works while working 5 hours a day. She can finish six such projects in .... days while working three hours a day.

Worksheet 40

1: The heights of six mountains are 8200 m, 6000 m, 8600 m, 7500 m, 8800 m and 6500 m . Based on this information, What is the approximate average height of the mountains?

2. CE is the angle bisector and Triangle displayed in diagram is an isosceles triangle. Find out all the interior angles of the triangle.

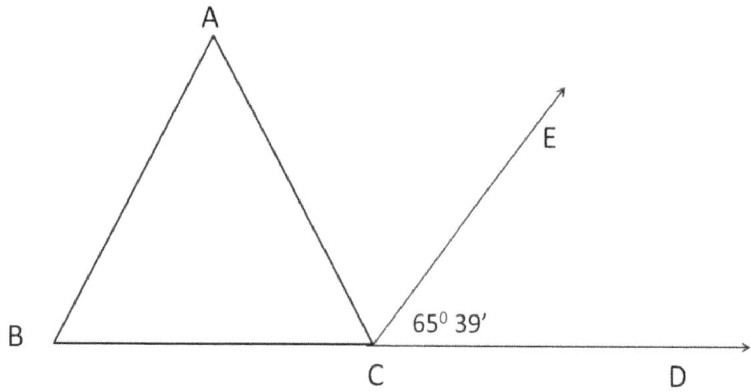

3. $(1 + x + 2x + \ldots\ldots 10{,}000x)(3x - 4) = 0$; then find out simplest value of $\left(9x + \frac{936}{1440}x + \frac{21}{16}x\right)$

4. The heights of 10 students, measured in cm are as follows:

143,132,150, 139,128,135, 151, 146, 141, 149

A: What is the height of the shortest girl?

B: If another student of height 139 cm is included in the group then average height of students will be changed by ……. Cm.

5. What fraction of all the natural numbers starting from 1 to 50 are prime numbers?

6. Write in standard form: $\left(\frac{121}{100} + \frac{121}{1000} + \frac{121}{10000} + \frac{121}{10} + 121\right)$

7. Work out unknown angles.

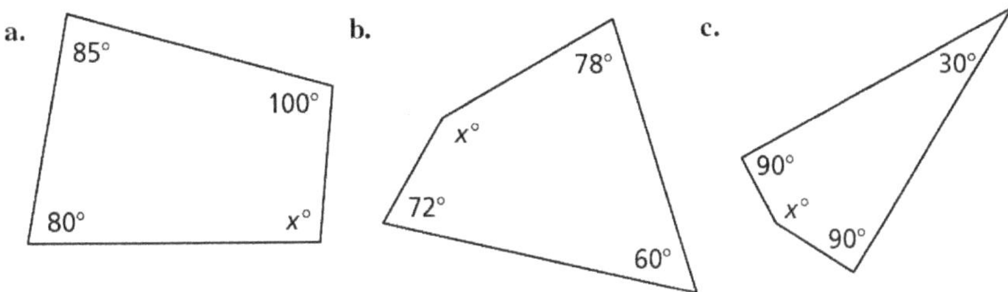

8. Calculate area of shaded portions.

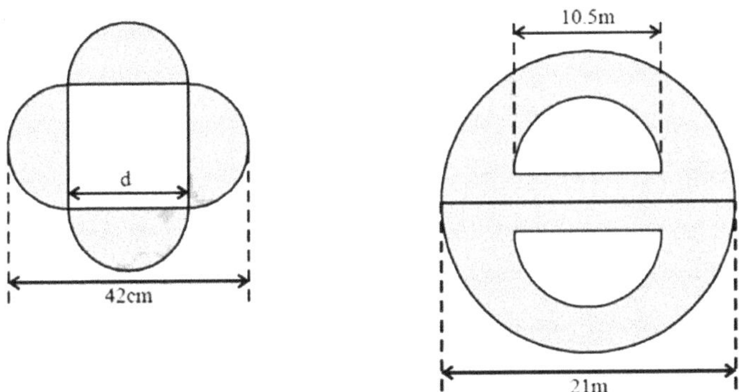

9. If following pattern continues then total number of cubes required for 16th step will be …………………

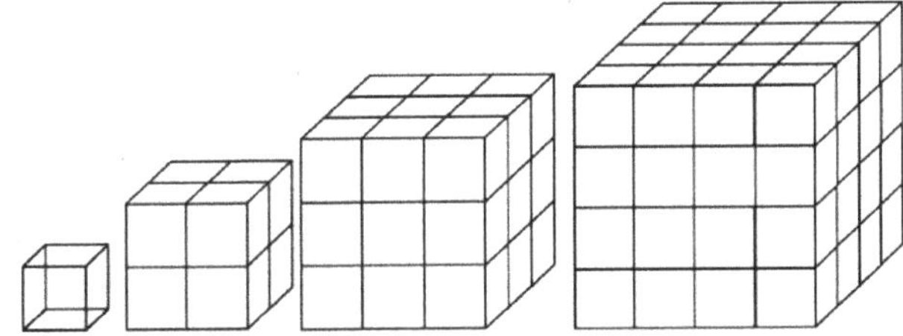

10. Cost of sugar is increased by 20%. A family wants to keep monthly expenditure on sugar unchanged. Consumption of sugar to be curtailed by that family in percentage will be …………

Worksheet 41

1: Find out area of the following:

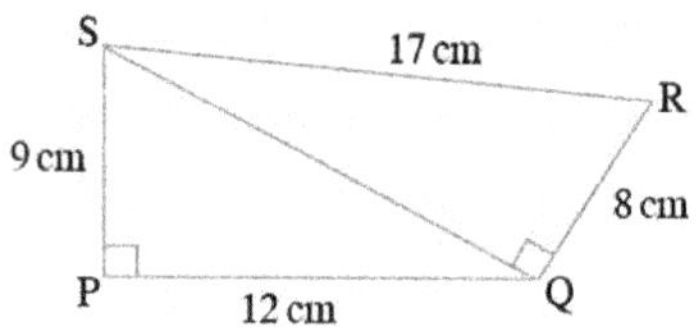

2: ABCD is a parallelogram. AE is perpendicular on DC and CF is perpendicular on AD. If AB = 10 cm, AE = 8 cm and CF = 12 cm. Find AD.

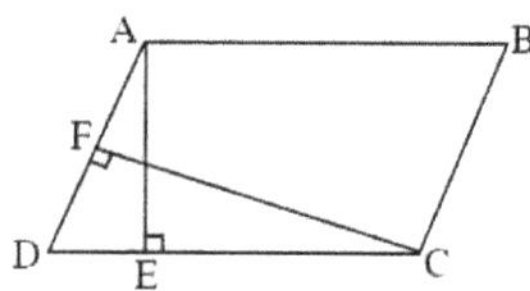

3: A farmer has a field in the form of a parallelogram PQRS as shown in the figure. He took the mid- point A on RS and joined it to points P and Q. In how many parts of field is divided? What are the shapes of these parts? The farmer wants to sow groundnuts which are equal to the sum of pulses and paddy. How should he sow? State reasons?

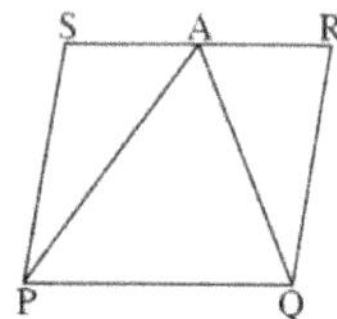

4: State true or false.

i. A circle divides the plane on which it lies into three parts.

ii. The region enclosed by a chord and the minor arc is minor segment.

iii. The region enclosed by a chord and the major arc is major segment.

iv. A diameter divides the circle into two unequal parts.

v. A sector is the area enclosed by two radii and a chord

vi. The longest of all chords of a circle is called a diameter.

vii. The mid point of any diameter of a circle is the centre.

viii. A triangle can have two obtuse angles as interior angles.

ix. A quadrilateral can have two reflex angles as interior angles.

x. Sum of all the interior angles of a quadrilateral is equal to 360^0.

6: How many solid bricks each of dimension 10 cm X 200 cm X 30 cm can be casted off by melting a solid metal brick of volume 1331 cubic cm?

7: In the given figure, point O is the centre of the circle. Find the length of CD, if AB = 5 cm.

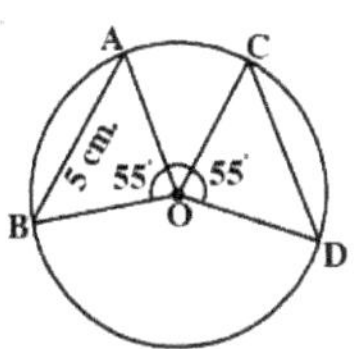

8: What digit will be there at the tens place of the product of 125, 40, 25 and 8?

9: How many four digit numbers are there in all?

10. If we multiply 129 by 125 and the product is further multiplied with 40, then digit at hundreds place will be ....

Worksheet 42

1: Find out area of the shaded portions in the following.

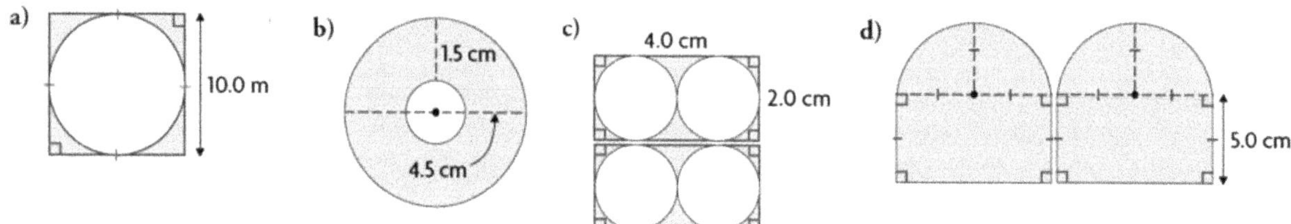

2: Calculate area of each of the following;

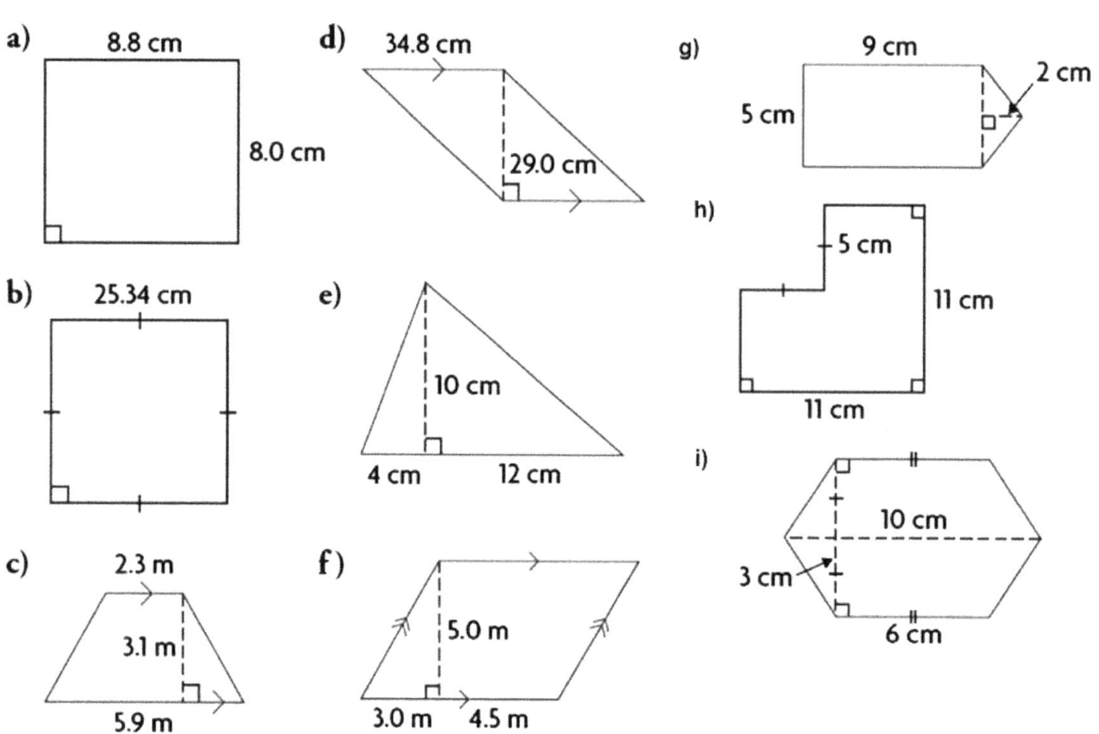

3: Find out missing angles.

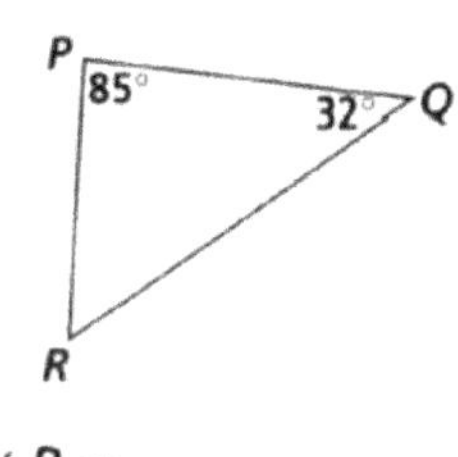

$\angle R =$ ______

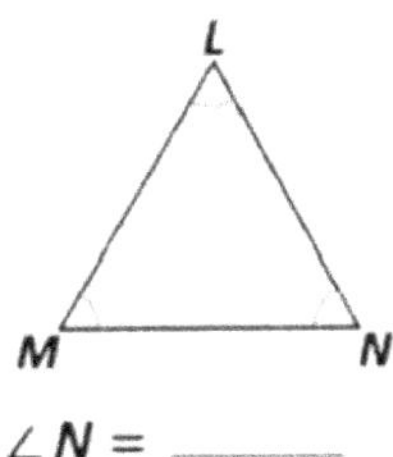

$\angle N =$ ______

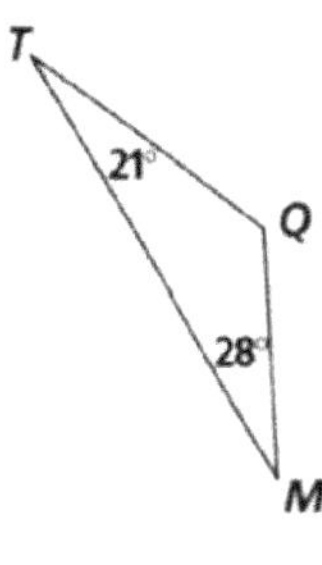

$\angle Q =$ ______

4: Find out values of x and y in the following.

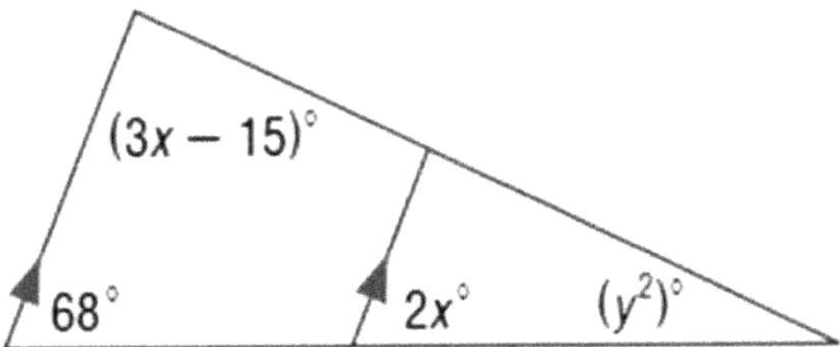

5: Find out missing angles by using angle sum property of triangle.

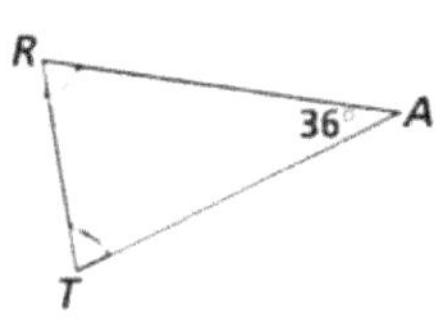

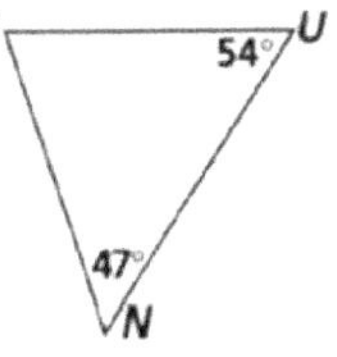

$\angle F =$ ______

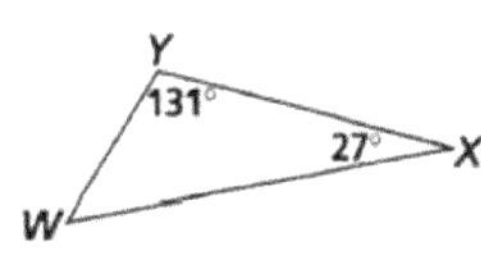

$\angle W =$ ______

6: Find out magnitude of angle 1.

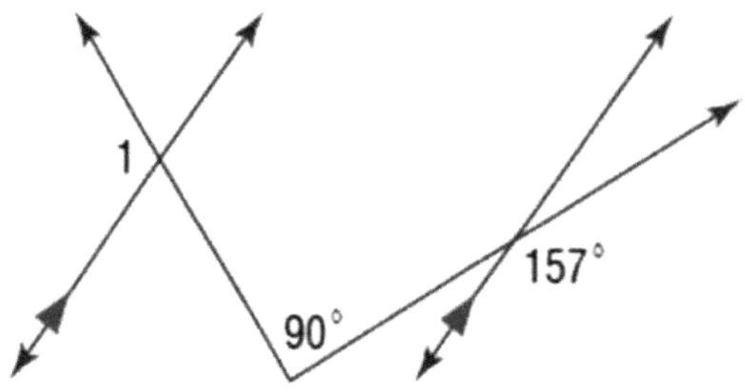

7: Find magnitude of angle 1 in the following.

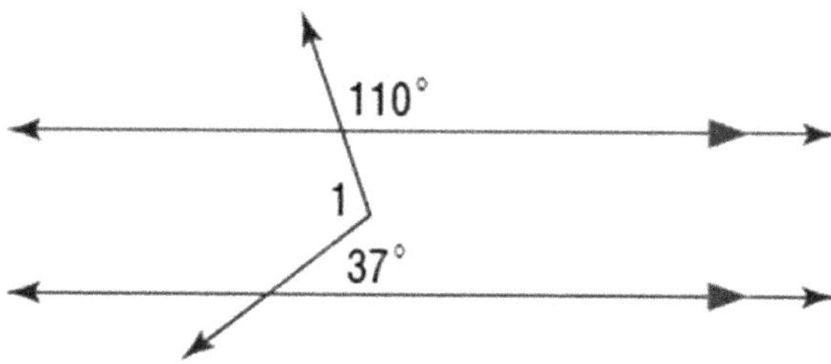

.

8: Find out area of shaded portions:

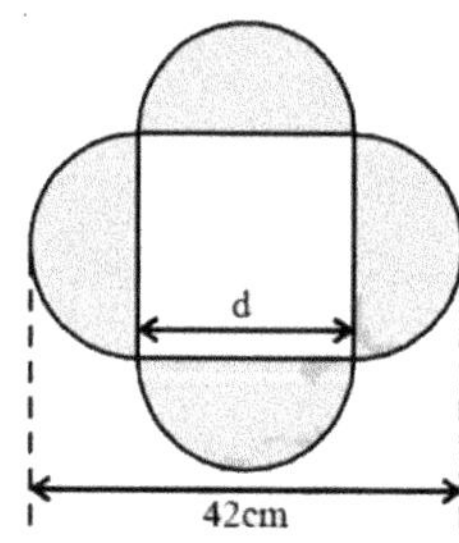

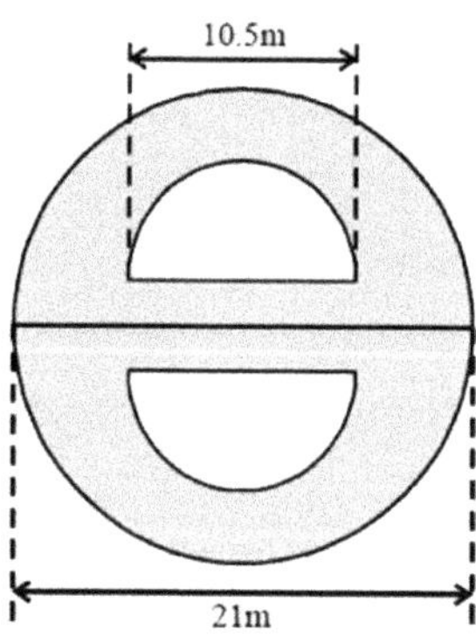

9: How many cubes are there in each of the following?

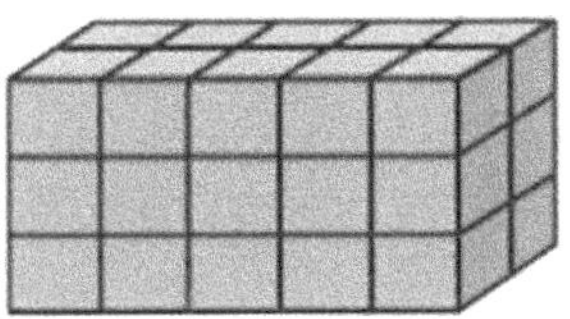

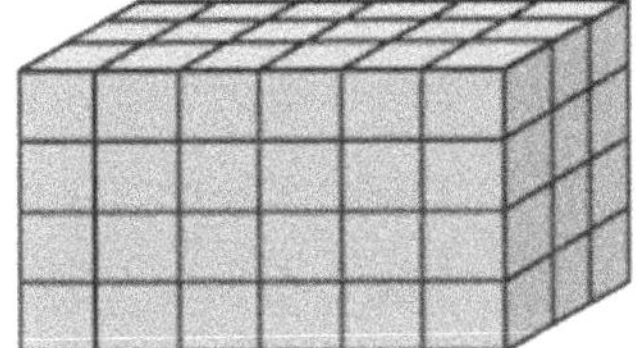

10: A large box of cakes contains same number of cakes as 12 small boxes. Each of the small boxes contains equal number of cakes. A large box contains 168 cakes. Find out total number of cakes that a large box and three small boxes contain.

11. Find out difference of digits which could be there in tens place and units place of the product of greatest six digit odd number and smallest six digit number.

12. P = (10,000 – 1); Q = (1,001 – 2); R = P X Q; The digit at ones place in standard form of R will be ....

13. Find out the missing number in the following:

683216; ....; 713216; 728216; 743216

14: 21st multiple of 100,100,203 = ...

15: Calculate area of the shaded portion.

16: Minoti had 2 m long ribbon. She used half of it and rest of the part is divided equally into 8 equal parts. Calculate length of each of the smaller parts duly obtained.

17: There were 3/5 as many girl students as boy students in a school. There were 48 fewer boy students than girl students in the school. How many students are there in all?

18: What fraction of all the numbers from 1 to 1000 are multiples of 125?

19: Evaluate the following using suitable identities.

(i) $(99)^3$ (ii) $(102)^3$ (iii) $(1003)^3$ (iV) $(599)^3$

20: Which of the following statement is not true?

a) Only one line can pass through a given point.

b) All right angles are equal to each other.

c) Circles with same radii are equal to each other in terms of area.

d) A line segment can be extended on its both sides endlessly to get a straight line.

21: How many lines can be drawn by using ay two out of three non-collinear points?

22. What least number should be subtracted from 32,089 to get a multiple of 4?

23. Three interior angles are in the ratio of 4: 5: 9. Find out the greatest angle of this triangle.

24. A shopkeeper sold six apples and made a profit equal to selling price of one apple. By using this information to calculate percentage profit gained by the shopkeeper.

25. Arya observed that train A started crossing Train B after 3 minutes. Intermediate gap in between both the train was 1 km 80 m. Average seed of train B was 36 km/h. Find out Average speed of train A.

Worksheet 43

1: Angle A + B + C + D + E + F = ……

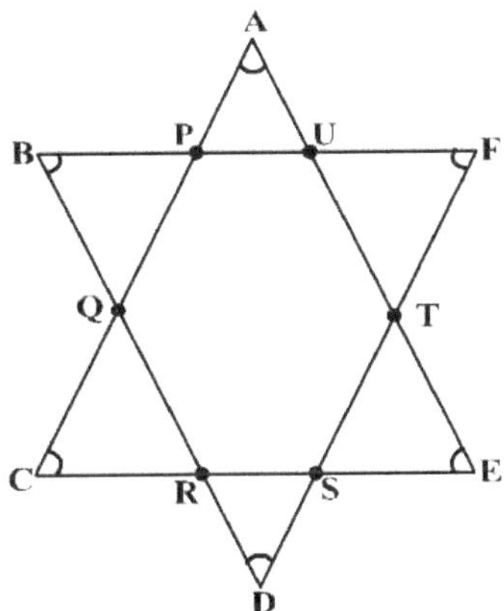

2: If the measure of an angle is 62° 32', what is the measure of its complementary angle?

3: Find value of x in the following.

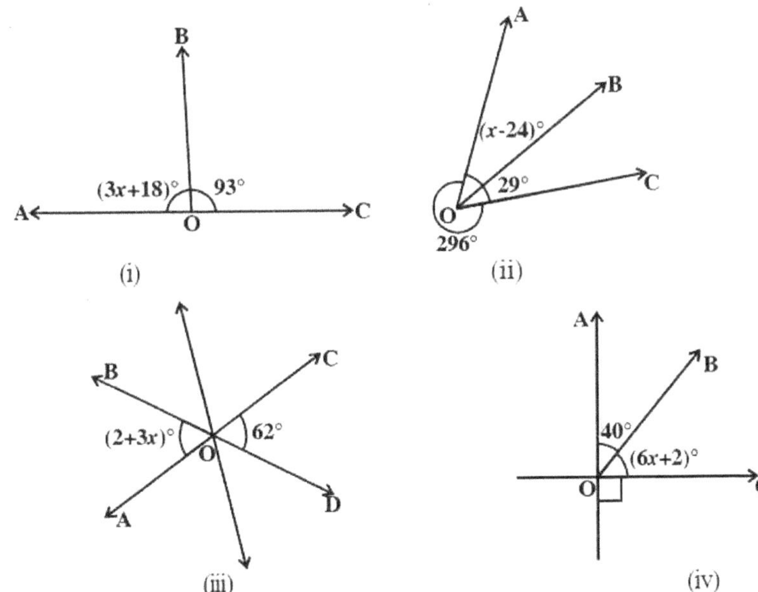

4: Two complementary angles are in the ratio 4:5. Find the angles.

5: Find out unknown angles in the following in which $l \| m$.

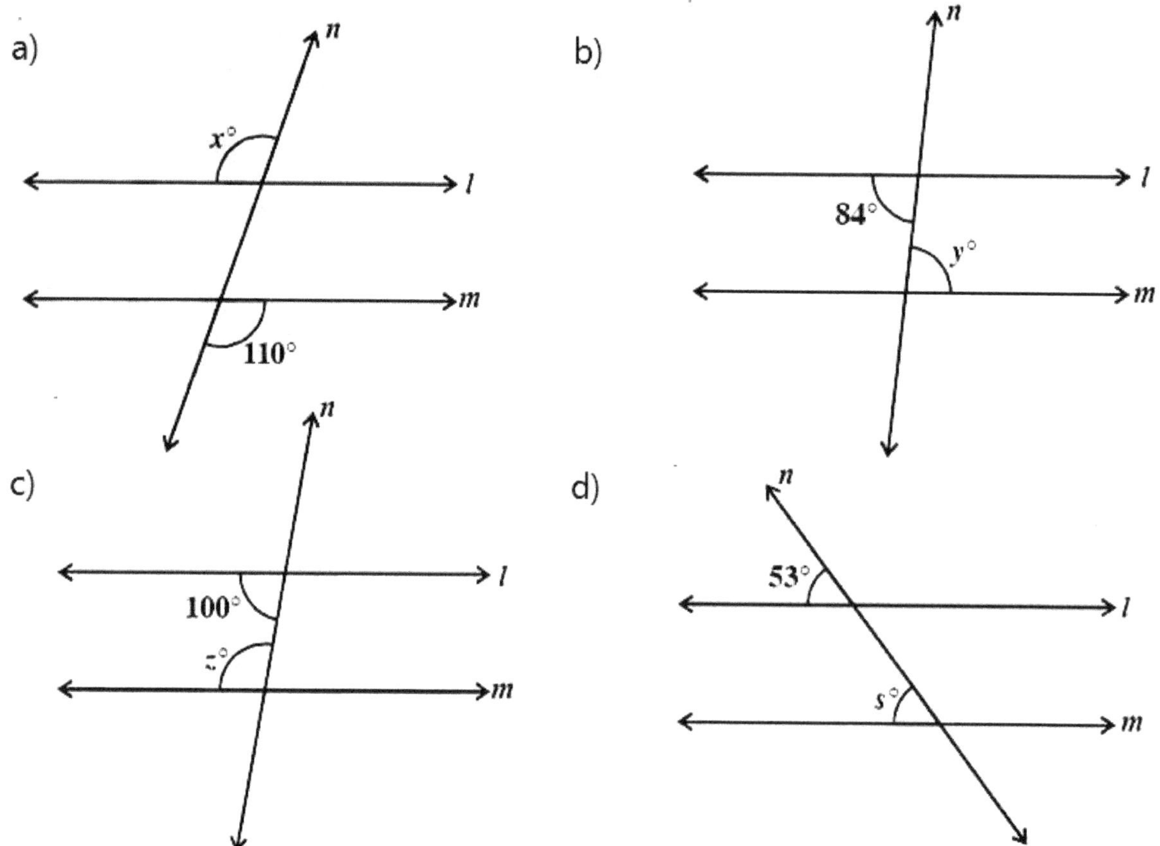

6: What fraction of all the numbers from 1 to 50 are prime numbers?

7: There are ………… diagonals in a pentagon.

8: Each of the interior angles of a regular hexagon will be equal to ……

9. We can draw a triangle by taking at least ……. Obtuse angle or at least ….. right angle.

10. There are .... Right angles in a rectangle.

11. In each of the following figures AB||CD. Find values of x.

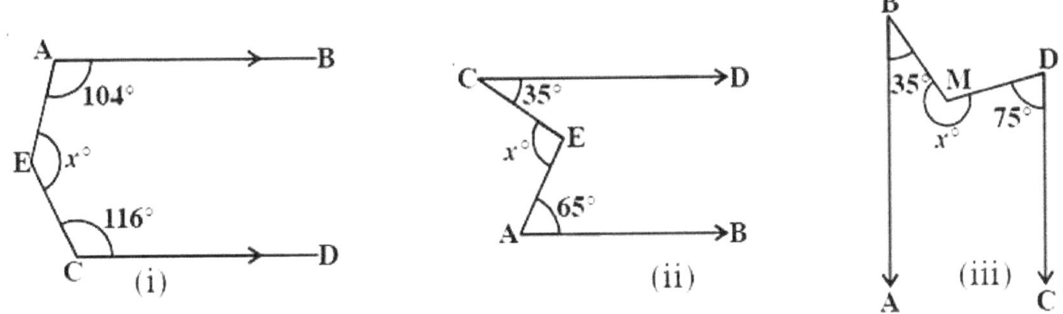

12: Find out values of x. y and z in the following.

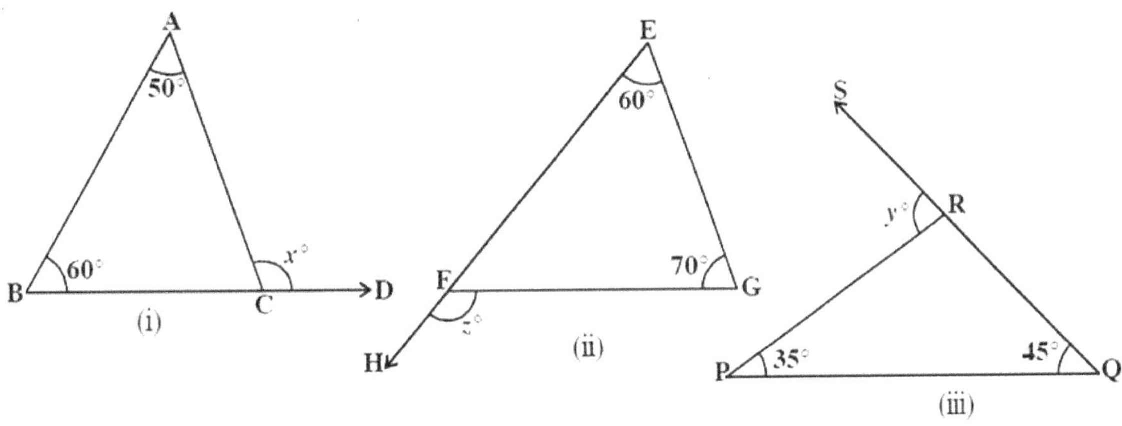

13: A metal cuboid of dimension 22 cm. × 15 cm. × 7.5 cm. was melted and cast into a cylinder of height 14 cm. What is its radius?

14: An overhead water tanker is in the shape of a cylinder has capacity of 61.6 cu.mts. The diameter of the tank is 5.6 m. Find the height of the tank.

15. A metal pipe is 77 cm. long. The inner diameter of a cross section is 4 cm., the outer diameter being 4.4 cm. Find its

(i) inner and (ii) outer curved surface area (iii) Total surface area.

16: A cylindrical pillar has a diameter of 56 cm and is of 35 m high. There are 16 pillars around the building. Find the cost of painting the curved surface area of all the pillars at the rate of Rs. 5.50 per 1 m^2.

17: The diameter of a roller is 84 cm and its length is 120 cm. It takes 500 complete revolutions to roll once over the playground to level. Find the area of the playground in m^2.

18: The base area of a cone is 38.5 cm^2. Its volume is 77 cm^3. Find its height.

19. The volume of a cone is 462 m^3. Its base radius is 7 m. Find its height.

20. Curved surface area of a cone is 308 cm2 and its slant height is 14 cm Find. (i) radius of the base (ii) Total surface area of the cone.

21. The cost of painting the total surface area of a cone at Rs 1.25 per cm^2 is Rs. 625. Find out volume of the cone, if its slant height is 25 cm.

22. From a circle of radius 15 cm., a sector with angle 216° is cut out and its bounding radii are bent so as to form a cone. Find its volume.

23. The height of a tent is 9 m. Its base diameter is 24 m. What is its slant height? Find the cost of canvas cloth required if it costs Rs 7 per sq.m.

24. What length of tarpaulin 3 m wide will be required to make a conical tent of height 8m and base radius 6m ? Assume that extra length of material that will be required for stitching margins and wastage in cutting is approximately 20 cm (use $\pi = 3.14$)

25. Water is pouring into a conical vessel of diameter 5.2m and slant height 6.8m (as shown in the adjoining figure), at the rate of Rs 3.6 cu. m. per minute. How long will it take to fill the vessel?

Worksheet 44

1. Temperature of a city increased by 5 ^{0}C last week. If a corresponding increase of temperature in ^{0}F is 1.8 times more than that of the value in ^{0}C, then find the value of such increase of temperature in ^{0}F

   A: 18^0 F B: 9^0 F C: 8.9^0 F D: 6 ^{0}F
2. A racing car covers 100 km in 2 hours and another 400 km 4 hours. The speed of the car during second time is ____ times more than that of the first time.

   A: 1 B: 2 C: 3 D: 4
3. The product of the place values of 5 in the following number is ______________

   32,435

   A: 9,000 B: 90,000 C: 9,00,000 D: 900

4. What must be added to 10932 to make it exactly divisible by 9?

5. $\frac{3}{6}, \frac{7}{6}, \frac{1}{6}, \frac{5}{6}, \frac{11}{6}$

   If we arrange these fractions in ascending order, then denominator of the product of 2nd and 3rd fraction in simplest form will be __________

   A: 12 B: 24 C: 36 D: 48
6. Half of one sixth of 72 is the _______ multiple of three.
7. A wire of a square sized shape of side 32 cm is reshaped to form a circle. Find the circumference of that circle. [Circumference of a circle is the outer boundary of a circle].
8. A solid cylinder has ____ flat faces and ____ curved faces.
9. The product of all the factors of 121 is _______ less than its greatest factor.

   A: 1 B: 11 C: 1,452 D: 1331

10. Two bells toll at an interval of 6 seconds and 8 seconds respectively. They toll together at 11:55 a.m. When do they toll together again for the second time?
    A: 12:19 pm B: 12:19 am C: 12: 24 pm
11. Ruchika observed that a 300 m long goods train is taking 45 seconds to cross a light-post. Find the average speed of that train. Also find the time taken by that train to cross a 1500 m long railway platform.
12. Compare the place value of 5 in 235,934 and 54,435. Find difference of both the place values.
13. A milk-dairy produces 25,545 liters of milk every day. It supplies 15,625 liters of milk to a milk-depot and the rest to the market. How much milk is supplied to the market?
14. The sum of two numbers is 94506. One of the numbers is 49605. Find the other number.
15. The sum of two numbers is 45650. One of the numbers is 22587. Find the other number. Which part of the sum is the given number?

16. There are 35,278 students in Class III, 32,184 students in Class IV and 25,375 students in Class V in the schools of a city. Find the total number of students reading in Classes III, IV and V. Among these students 60,324 are girls. Find the number of students who are boys.
17. A person had \$ 197,865. He gave \$ 50,753 to his wife and \$ 75,928 to his son. The rest of the money he gave to his daughter. How much did the daughter get?
18. What should be added to the sum of 3,46,068 and 3,24,263 to get the sum of 8,05,400?
19. There are 4021 students in a school. Each section can accommodate a maximum number of 25 students. There are equal number of students in each section, find

their number in each section. Is there any section having less than 25 students? How many such sections are there?

20. Write in standard form:

33 tens + 54 hundreds + 121 ones + 1001 ten thousandths = _________.

21. Points located on same line are called ______________ points.

22. A line has no __________________ but a line segment has ___ such ______ ____________.

23. A ______ can be extended endlessly in both the directions.

24. 32 hundreds + 302 hundredths + 1008 thousandths = _______.

25. Instead of writing 321 thousands Rita has written 3 lakhs 12 thousands. Find the difference between the original and the derived answer.

26. Total cost of 5 pens and 6 pencils is Rs. 145. Total cost of 6 pens and 5 pencils is Rs. 251. Find individual cost of a pen and a pencil. Also find the total cost of 5 pens and 3 pencils.

27. 5 km 5 m + 102 km 102 m + 32 km 32 m = ________________ m

28. Sam has a collection of 963 comic books. What are the five different ways Sam could divide his comic books into equal groups?

29. A study table is 3 m long and 1.5 m wide. Another large table is thrice as long and twice as wide as the study table. What is the area of both the table?

30. Cost of fencing a square shaped garden at the rate of Rs. 120.00 per m was Rs. 48,000.00. Find the length of a side of that garden.

31. At the end of the party, the kids broke open the gift packs. When they assembled all the candy, Bill got 9 pieces. Sara got 3 times as many pieces as Bill. Nitin got one third of the number of candies gathered by Bill. Which of the statements depicted below are true?

I. They have collected total number of candies which is also equal to third multiple of 3.

II: Sara got 4 times more than Nitin.

III: Share of Nitin and Bill was 15 less than that of Sara.

IV: Sara got 9 times more candy than that of Nitin.

32. A wall mount clock takes 2 seconds to toll 2 bells at 2 a.m. Find the time by that clock to toll 11 bells at 11 a.m.
33. Simplify:

$$\left(1+\frac{1}{9}\right)\left(1+\frac{1}{10}\right)\left(1+\frac{1}{11}\right)\ldots\left(1+\frac{1}{1{,}007}\right)\left(1+\frac{1}{1{,}008}\right)=$$

34. How many five digit numbers are there in all?
35. What least number should be subtracted from five digit greatest number to obtain a common multiple of 2, 4, 6 and 8?
36. Product of 9099, 1089, 203899 and 10879 is represented in standard form. The digit at ones lace in that product will be ….
37. Mohan wants to distribute 129 sweets and 321 almonds amongst his 63 friends equally. Calculate the number of sweets and almonds that remain to Mohan after the distribution.
38. The product of two numbers is 41310. If one of them is 270, find the other.
39. In certain division algorithm the quotient is 57, the divisor is 45 and the remainder is 29, find the dividend.
40. The annual income of Sam is Rs. 98,364. What is his monthly income if he earns an equal amount every month?
41. A number was divided by 97; the quotient was 3806 and the remainder 76. Find the number.
42. When 650 is multiplied by a number, the product is 5590. Find the number.
43. 49,000 fruits were distributed among 1,000 clubs equally. How many fruits did each club get?

44. There are 2,983 boys and 2,175 girls in a school. Find the total enrolment of the school. Find also the number of more boys than girls on the rolls of the school.

]

45. What least number must be added to make the six digit smallest number a multiple of 11?

46. What should be added to 79,415 to make it the greatest five-digit number?

47. By how much is 89283 is greater than 79382?

48. What should be subtracted from 98989 to get 88888?

49. There are ____ vertices, ____ faces and _____ edges in a cuboid.

50. Two cubical block of edge 30 cm each joined side by side to form a cuboidal block. Find the surface area of the top and bottom part of that cuboid.

51. Malavika prepared a 25 m long rope by joining different segments of 200 cm each. Find the number of segments she used for making that rope.

52. ______ is the predecessor of smallest four digit multiple of 9.

53. How many times do 7 appear if we write all the natural numbers from 1 to 100?

[Ans: 1]

54. How many natural numbers from 50 to 100 are prime numbers?

55. What least number should be subtracted from sum of smallest number of six digits and greatest number of five digits to obtain a common multiple of 6 and 9?

56. 30% of 12% of 20,40,800 = ...

57. Three angles of a triangle are in the ratio of 5: 6: 7. Find out angles.

Worksheet 45

1: Find out area of PQRS.

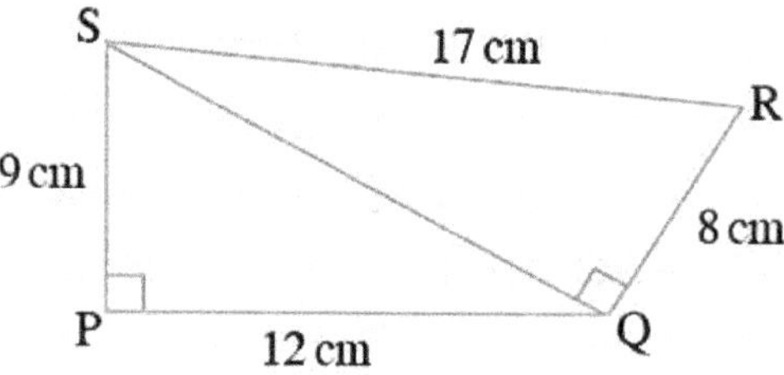

2: ABCD is a parallelogram. AE is perpendicular on DC and CF is perpendicular on AD. If AB = 10 cm, AE = 8 cm and CF = 12 cm. Find AD.

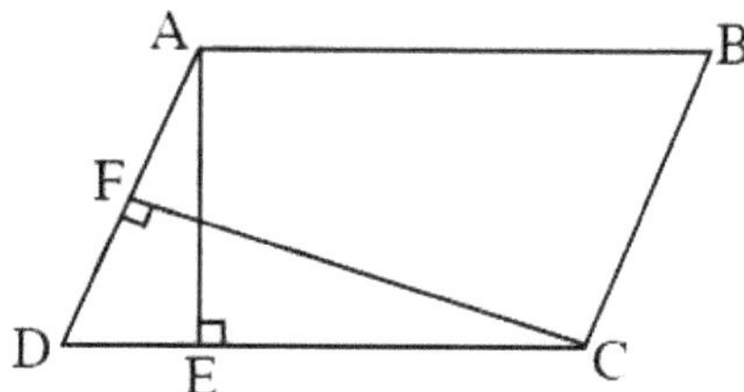

3: A farmer has a field in the form of a parallelogram PQRS as shown in the figure. He took the mid- point A on RS and joined it to points P and Q. In how many parts of field is divided? What are the shapes of these parts? The farmer wants to sow groundnuts which are equal to the sum of pulses and paddy. How should he sow? State reasons?

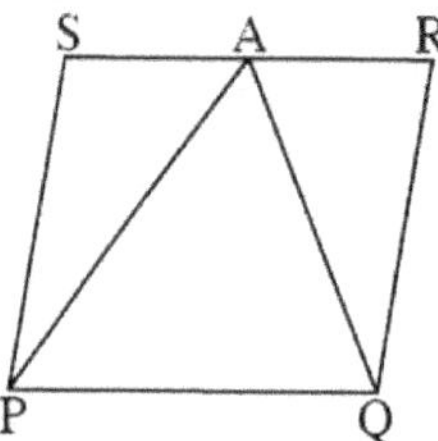

4: State true or false.

i. A circle divides the plane on which it lies into three parts.

ii. The region enclosed by a chord and the minor arc is minor segment.

iii. The region enclosed by a chord and the major arc is major segment.

iv. A diameter divides the circle into two unequal parts.

v. A sector is the area enclosed by two radii and a chord

vi. The longest of all chords of a circle is called a diameter.

vii. The mid point of any diameter of a circle is the centre.

viii. A triangle can have two obtuse angles as interior angles.

ix. A quadrilateral can have two reflex angles as interior angles.

x. Sum of all the interior angles of a quadrilateral is equal to 360^0.

5: In the given figure, point O is the centre of the circle. Find the length of CD, if AB = 5 cm.

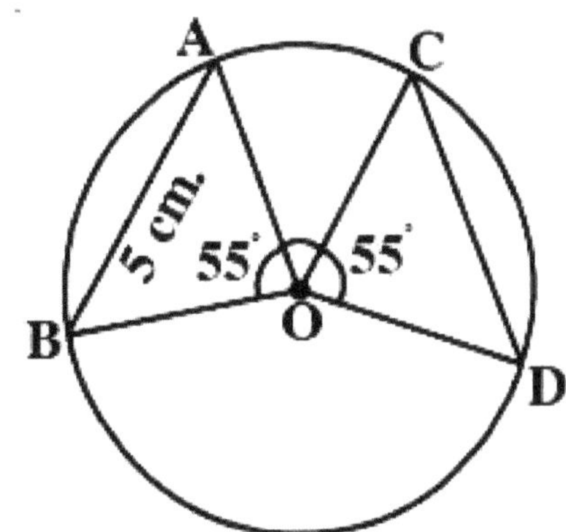

Worksheet 46

1: Find out missing angles.

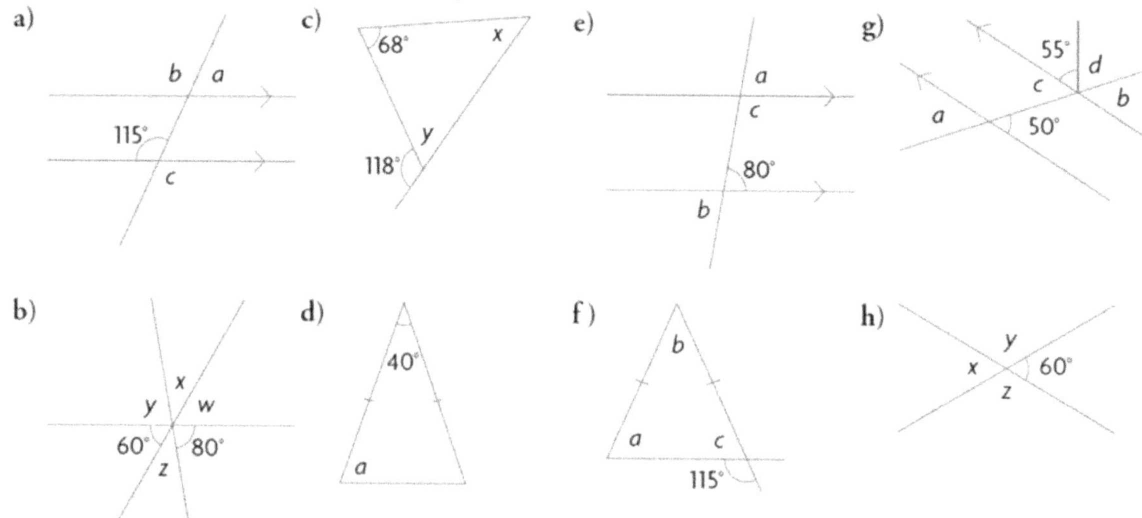

2. Find out unknown angles.

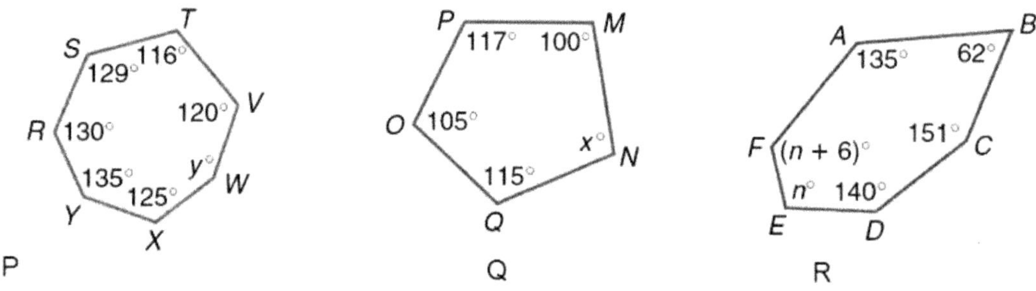

3. Mr. Jordon prepares to put fencing around his rectangular kitchen garden of width 95 m and the length 105 m. How long fencing wires does he need?

A: 190 m B: 200 m C: 210 m D: 400 m

4. A half filled oil container is used to store residue oil of capacity 125 litters. After filling the residue three eighth of the container remained empty. Find the capacity of the container.

5. One tenth of a container is equal to 16 cans of capacity 8 litters each. The entire container can hold __________ litters of oil.

6: What least number must be subtracted from 219.376 to make the result exactly divisible by 219? [Ans: 0.157]

7: A train, moving at the speed of 15 m per second, is taking 20 seconds to cross a telephone post. This train can take _______ seconds to cross a 1.5 km long platform.
[Ans : 2 minutes]

8. Veena rides her bike to the park for 18 minutes at an average speed of 9 m per second to meet a friend. Veena arrives at the park at 11:00 a.m. and stays there for 58 minutes. Her friend will arrive there at 12:15 p.m. they had a meeting for 32 minutes.

Try to answer the following questions.

A. What is the distance between the park and Veena's house?

B. How long could Veena have to wait for her friend?

C. How long does Veena stay at the park?

D. When will Veena leave to go home?

9. Write a number greater than 1, 50,000 by using digits 5, 4 and 2.

10. 324 thousands = ________________ tens.

11. 32 crore = __________ thousands.

12. __________ crore is 400 greater than 99,99,600.

13. Write a number smaller than 39 lakhs by using digits 4, 3 and 8. Digits can be repeated.

14. Write the predecessor of 7 digit greatest even number.

15. Calculate the sum total of place values of 3 in the following numbers

34,55,67,505, 30,56,05,506 and 35,05,04,050

16. Difference of the place value and face value of 8 in 65,76,80,653, 78,806 and 48,65,678 = ____________.

17. Numbers divisible by 2 are also called _________ numbers.

18. All prime numbers have only _____ factors. ____ and the number itself.

19. Sum total of 2 eve numbers is always an _______ number.

20. A prime number between 95 and 100 = _________.

21. All the multiples of 8 are also multiples of 2 and ______.

22. All the multiples of ____ and 4 may or may not be a multiple of 8.

23. All the multiples of ___ and ____ are not necessarily multiples of 10.

24. All multiples of 10 are also multiples of _____ and _____.

25. There are ______ flat faces and ___ curved faces in a cuboid.

26. What least number should be subtracted from the six digit greatest number to make the value divisible by 3, 6, 9 and 18 independently leaving remainder 2 in each case?

27. 59 square shaped tiles each of 20 sq. cm. are used for flooring a room. Find the area of that room.

28. Renuka prepared a bar graph that shows the number of kg of food eaten each day by each animal. What information goes on the horizontal axis? What information can be placed on the vertical axis?

29. Tim lives in New Delhi. He prepares a line graph that shows the amount of LPG used in his home kitchen for a year. Will the line graph show any change throughout the year?

30. Martin wants to represent the data related to pets owned by his classmates. He makes a bar graph that shows the number of dogs owned by members of his class. If the smallest number is 1 and the largest number is 4, what interval should Jon use for representing the data scale in the graph?

31. Find the value: $\frac{11}{144} X \frac{12}{121} X \frac{12}{49} X \frac{11}{169} X \frac{7}{10} X \frac{7}{100} =$

32. The town newspaper is published every alternate day. One copy has 12 pages. Every alternate day 21,980 copies are printed. How many total pages are printed for all copies every month? [Consider one month equal to 30 days]

33. Simplify:

$x^2 + 5y^2 + 3xy + 6x - 7y + 8 - [\ 12x^2 - \{\ 14x^2 - 9y^2 + 4xy + 3x + 9\ \}\ ]$

34. The quotient of x by y added to product of x and y. Write the expression which is obtained.

35. What least number should be subtracted from six digit greatest common multiple of 3, 6, 9 and 18 to make the value a common multiple of 5 and 10?

36. Sum total of reciprocal of a number and half of the given number is equal to 5.1. Find sum total of 10th and 15th multiple of that number.

37. Calculate outer boundary and area of the following.

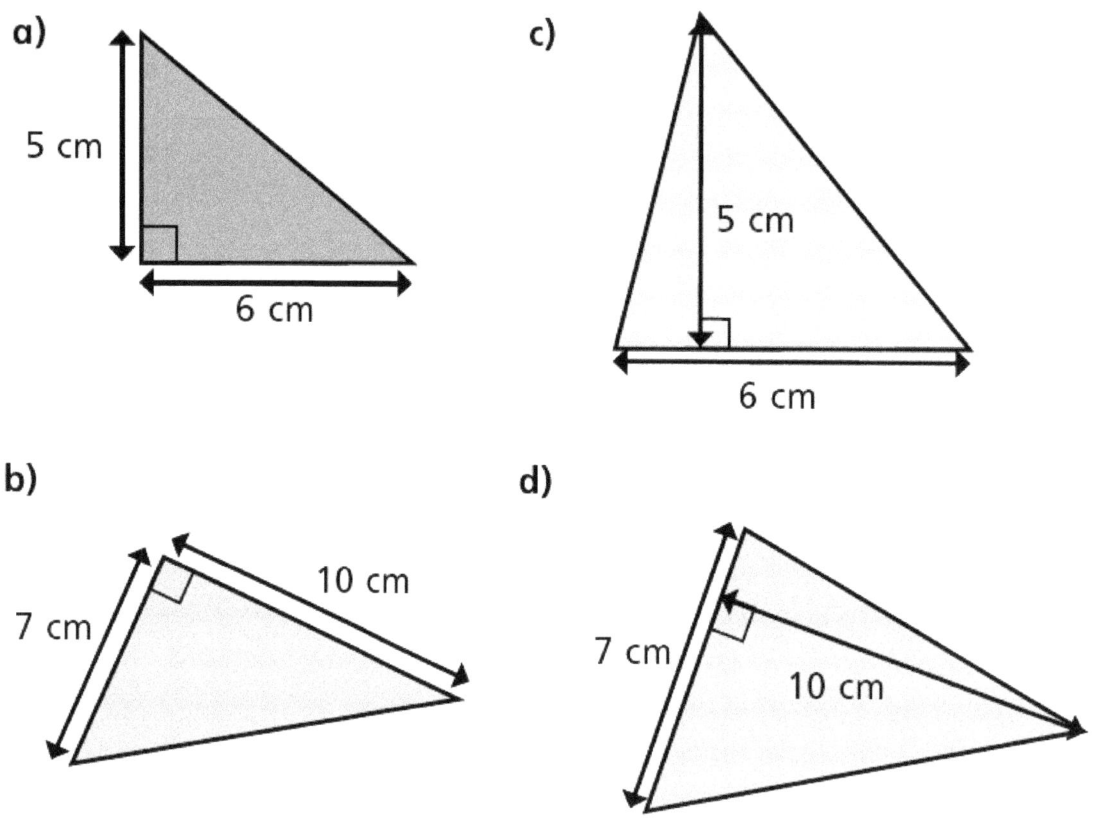

38: What least number should be subtracted from greatest number of seven digits to get a multiple of 3 and 9?

39: $(1 + 2 + 3 + \ldots\ldots\ldots\ldots\ldots\ldots + 10{,}000) \text{ X } (10{,}001)^{-1} \text{ X } 5{,}000 = 25 \text{ X } \ldots\ldots\ldots\ldots$

40: Calculate area and outer boundary of the following.

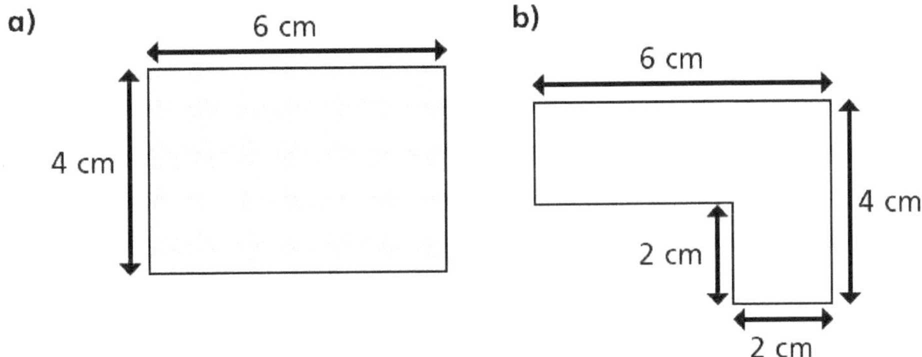

41: How many non-overlapping triangles can be accommodated inside a pentagon?

42: Find out area of the following.

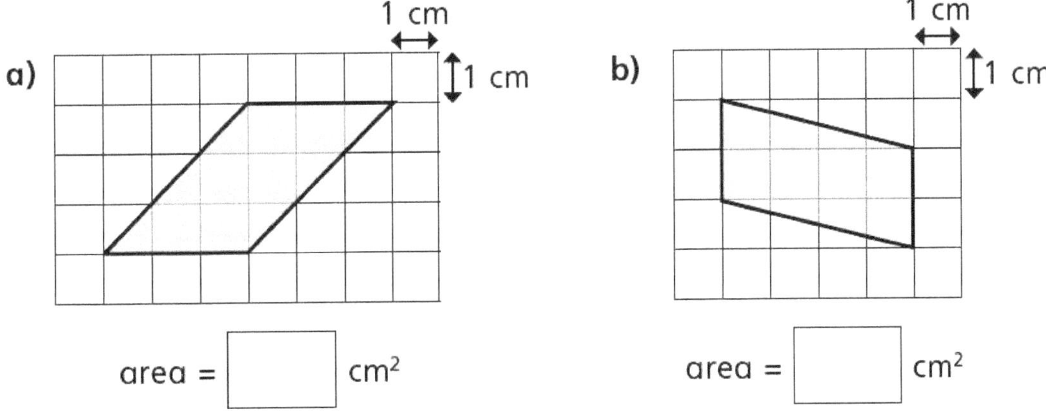

43: Calculate area and outer boundary of the following grid.

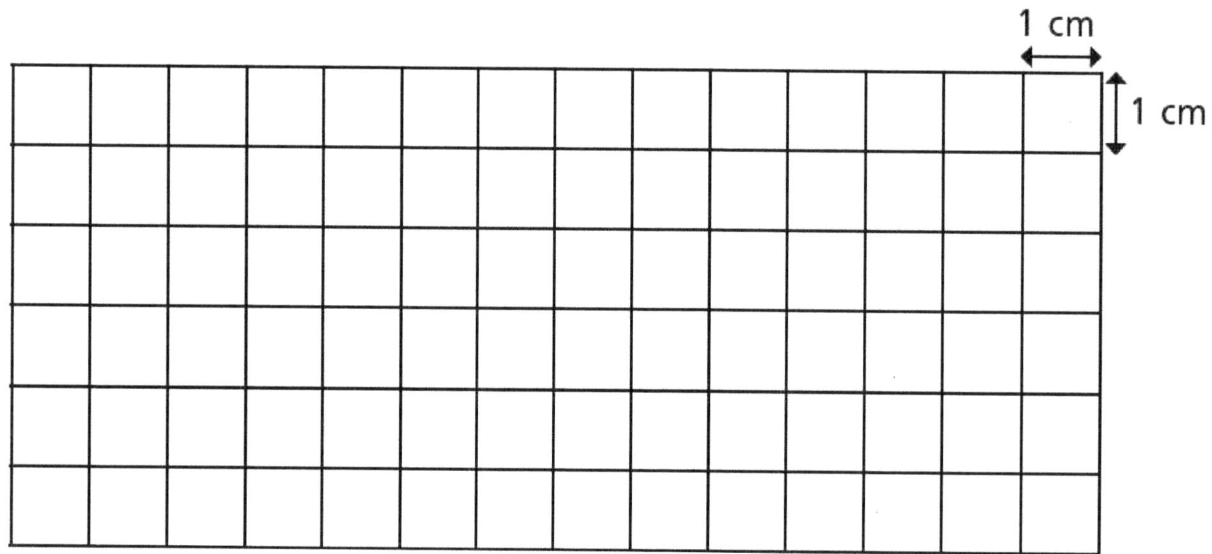

44: The area of each triangle is 12 cm^2. Find the missing lengths.

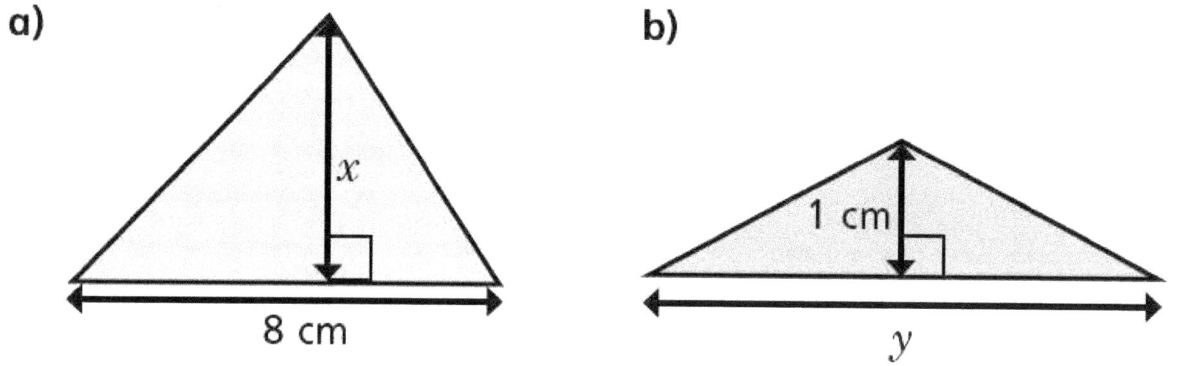

Worksheet 47

1. 776 is the ______________ multiple of 97.

   A: 4th B: 8th C: 5th D: 9th

2. Romanika counted a bundle of sheets, excluding that of top 15 ones, as 132. She has placed 21 sheets in to the printer. How many sheets were there in all?
3. Monika calculated 15th multiple of 5 added to 5th multiple of 15. Find the digit that she might have in the one's place of the product.
4. There are _______ flat faces and ___ curved faces in a cuboid.
5. Find the difference of place values of 5 in 22,543 and 54,432.
6. What least number must be added to make 12,543 divisible by 9?
7. What least number must be added to the hundreds place of 12,424 to make it divisible by 3?
8. A 3 m 60 cm thread is used for bordering a square shaped poster throughout edges. Find the length of each side of that poster.
9. 59 square shaped tiles each of 20 sq. cm. are used for flooring a room. Find the area of that room.
10. Renuka prepared a bar graph that shows the number of kg of food eaten each day by each animal. What information goes on the horizontal axis? What information can be placed on the vertical axis?
11. Tim lives in New Delhi. He prepares a line graph that shows the amount of LPG used in his home kitchen for a year. Will the line graph show any change throughout the year?
12. Martin wants to represent the data related to pets owned by his classmates. He makes a bar graph that shows the number of dogs owned by members of his class. If the smallest number is 1 and the largest number is 4, what interval should Jon use for representing the data scale in the graph?

13. Kim gathered information about the population of individual states of her country. If she prepares a bar graph of this data, what information will be displayed on the vertical axis? What information will be displayed on the horizontal axis?
14. 15th multiple of 5 is also a ________ multiple of 25.
15. ______________ is the smallest three digit even number.
16. 32 hundreds + 21 tens = ____________ .
17. What least number should be subtracted from five digit greatest number to make the value a common multiple of 4, 6, 8 and 12?
18. Find out a smallest five digit number which can be divided by 7, 8 and 9 leaving remainder 5 in each case.
19. Simplify:

    $1/11^{th}$ of 11,011 + $1/12^{th}$ of 12,012 + $1/13^{th}$ of 13,013 + $1/15^{th}$ of 15,015 = ...

20. Two bells toll at an interval of 4 seconds and 7 seconds respectively. How many times do these bells toll together in the time interval of 9 minutes 20 seconds?
21. What least number should be subtracted from the greatest number of five digits to obtain a common multiple of 3, 4, 8 and 16?
22. Find a smallest five digit number which can be divided by 2, 3, 5, 7 and 9 leaving remainder 1 in each case.
23. What least number should be subtracted from the product of 400, 3001 and 200 to obtain a common multiple of 3 and 9?
24. Supplementary angle of 121 54' = ...

Worksheet 48

1: Complete the following.

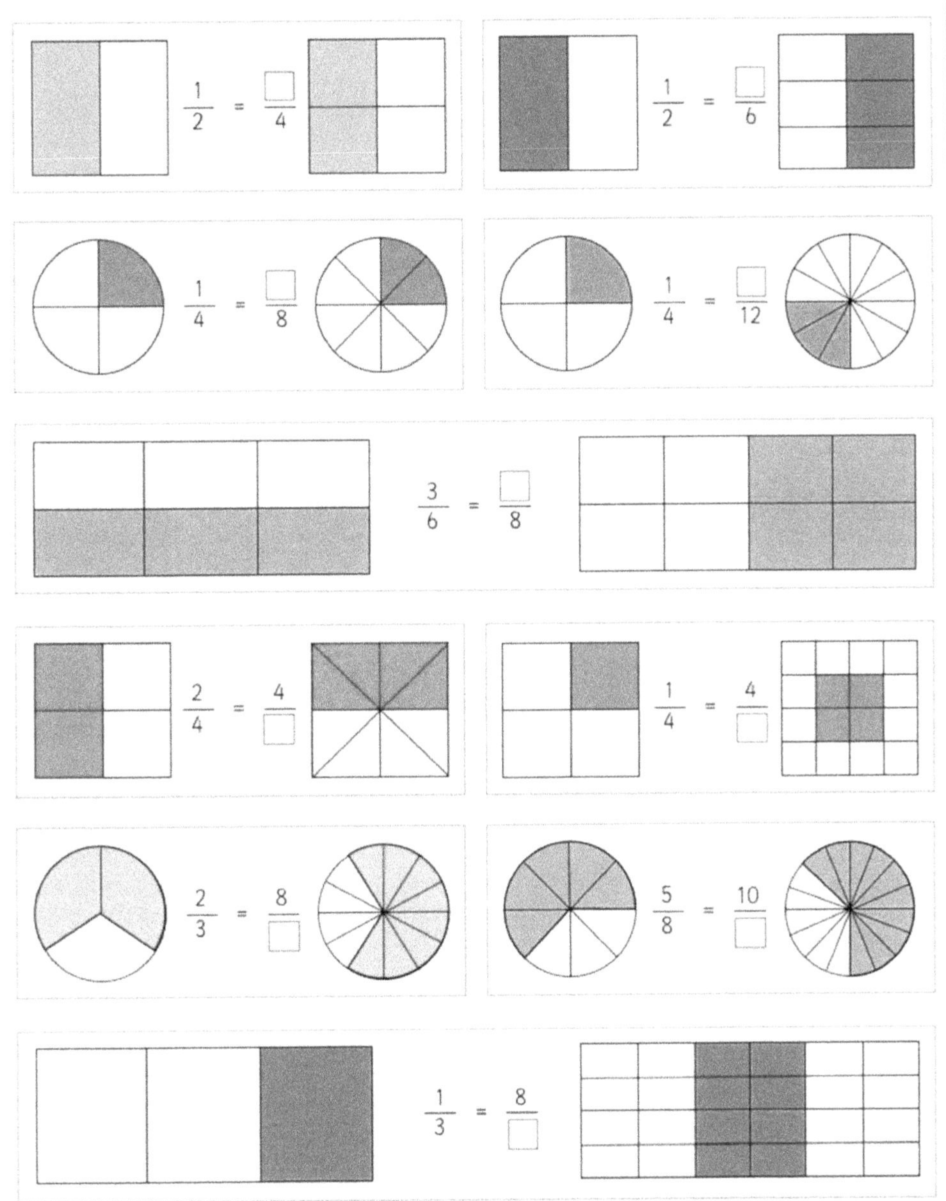

2: How many non-overlapping triangles can be accommodated inside a hexagon?

3: Each of the interior angle of a regular pentagon will be equal to ……

4: Complete the expanded form:

a: 21 thousands + 201 hundreds + 2001 tens + 20,001 = …………..

b: 21 million X 1,000 + 20 million X 11 + 1,201 = ……………………..

c: $\left[\frac{1}{1,003}+\frac{1}{1,003}+\cdots \ldots 1,000\ times\right] X \left(1+\frac{3}{1000}\right) X\ 101,101-\frac{101}{1000}=\ldots$

d. 605 thousands + 1,004 X 1,000 + 204 X 100 + 2,004 X 10 + 121 = …

e. (1 + 2 + 3 + ….. + 1,000) X 0.001 – 1.0001 = ……………..

f: (1.006 + 1.006 …+ 2,000 times) X $\left(1+\frac{6}{1,000}\right) X\ 300,300 = \ldots$

g: $\frac{11}{12} X \frac{12}{13} X \ldots \ldots \ldots . \left(1+\frac{1}{10,000}\right) X\ 121,121\ X \frac{5}{121}$ = …………

h: (1.001 + 11.01 + 121.003 + 1001.203) X 0.001 = ……………..

i. (121.0121 ÷ 11) + (242.0242 ÷ 22) = ……………………

5: What percentage of all the even numbers from 1 to 400 are multiples of 40?

6: (1,004 + 1,004 + ….. 3,000 times) ÷ 30,000 = ……………………..

7: Is there any pair of number having a common multiple 1210 and a common factor 97?

8: (203 tens + 203 hundreds + 203 thousandths) ÷ 1,000 = ………..

Worksheet 49

1: Calculate outer boundary of the following grid if area of each of the unit square is equal to 1.21 sq. cm.

2: Calculate area of the rhombus which is embedded inside the rectangle.

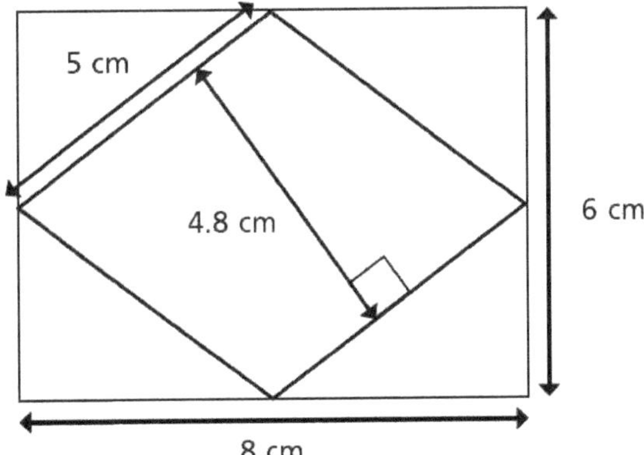

3: Calculate decrease of sale from April to May.

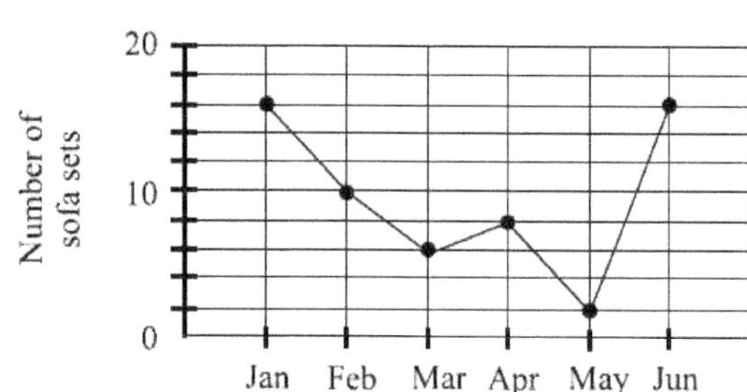

4: In 189485 place value of 8 in ten thousands place in ……. more than the place value of 8 in tens place.

5. Find out statement which is not true.

a) Number 4 have exactly three factors.

b) If a number is divisible by 21 then it must be divisible by 3 and 7 as well.

c) 78776 is divisible by 6

d) There are only 2 pairs of twin prime numbers between 10 and 20.

e) If a number is divisible only by 13 and 169 then that number is divisible by the only prime factor 13.

6. Which of the following is a convex polygon?

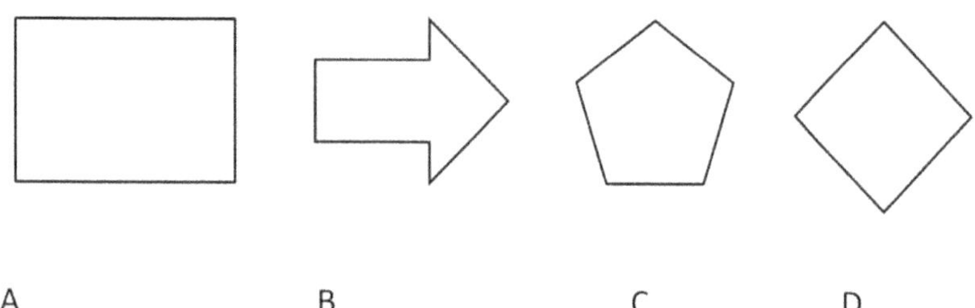

A B C D

7: Namrata can finish her project work in 20 days while working 8 hours a day. Pinki can finish similar type of project work in 30 days while working 6 hours a day. They jointly wanted three such projects while working 5 hours a day. In how many days do they finish three such kinds of project works?

8: How many digits will be there in the product of 100, 200, 300, 2000 and 99?

9: Is there any pair of natural number having HCF 121 and LCM 1690?

10. 4/7th of 14,56,084 + 5/9th of 81,72,054 = ...

11: Find out missing angles.

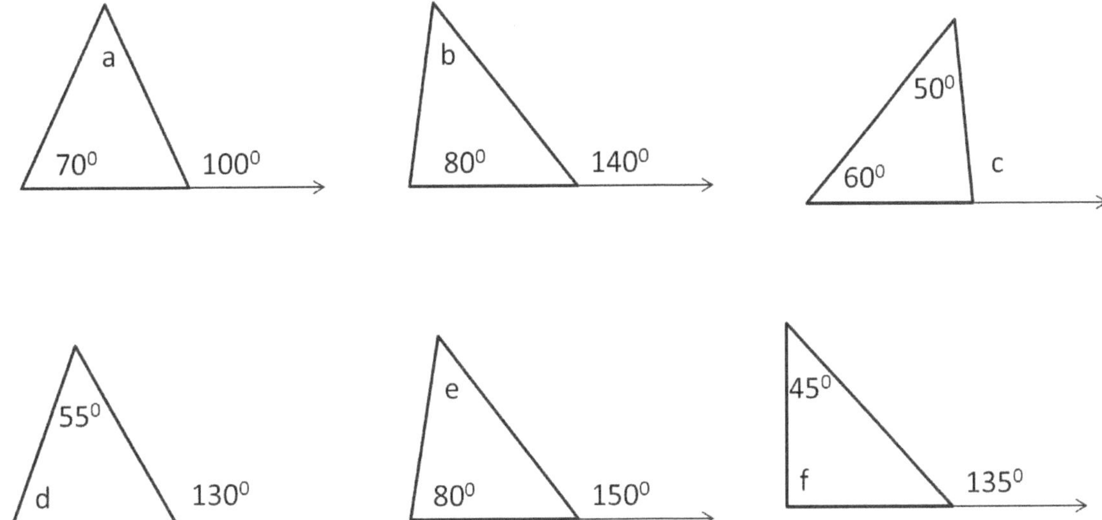

12. The area of a rectangular field is 35 times the sum of its length and breadth. If the breadth of that field is 40 metres, then what is the length of that field?

13. Snehal's uncle is 5 times as old as her age. After 15 years, her uncle will be 2 times as old as her age. Snehal is _____ years old and her uncle is __ years old.

Worksheet 50

1. What percent of all the numbers starting from 1 to 25,000 are multiples of 250?

2. Write greatest and smallest numbers of four digits by using following digits 4, 9 , 3 and 0. Also write sum total of both the numbers.

3. $(x^3 - y^3) \div (x - y) =$ ……………………; Evaluate this value for $x = 6$ and $y = 5$.

4. Three equilateral triangles are arranged side by side to form a polygon. Find the number of sides of that polygon. Also find sum total of all the interior angles of that polygon.

5. How many diagonals are there in a pentagon?

6. Supplementary angle of complementary angle of a definite angle is 133^0 . Find measure of the given angle.

7. Two equal sides of a triangle are of 5 cm each. Base of that triangle is equal to 6 cm. Find area of that triangle.

8. Product of three consecutive multiple of 5 is equal to 750. Find sum total of all the three multiples of 5.

9. Mohanlal painted a wall in 20 days while working 6 hours a day. He can paint two such walls in …….. days while working 8 hours a day.

10. 33. $\left(\frac{1}{\sqrt{6001}} + \frac{2}{\sqrt{6001}} + \frac{3}{\sqrt{6001}} \ldots \ldots\ldots.. + \frac{6,000}{\sqrt{6001}}\right) X \frac{1}{\sqrt{6001}} \div \frac{1}{3,000} = 3^p\ X\ 10^q$; Find value of $\left(\frac{p+q}{p-Q}\right)$

11. A shopkeeper gains an amount equal to cost price of 5 cakes by selling 25 cakes. Find out the gain percentage.

12. $\left(\frac{1}{a} + \frac{1}{b} + \frac{1}{c}\right) = 9; find\ \ the\ value\ of\ 3(ab + bc + ac) - 27\ abc.$

13. It is observed that sum total of a natural number and two times its reciprocal is equal to 8.25. Find sum total of square and cube root of that number.

14. A passenger train crosses a person standing on 1.5 km long platform in 45 seconds while moving at an average speed of 36 km/h. This train will cross the platform in …….m …….s while moving with same average speed of 36 km/h.

15. A wall mount clock strikes 6 bells at 6 O'Clock in 12 seconds. Find the time taken by this clock to strike 11 bells at 11 a.m.

16. (1 + 2 + ……. + 10,000) ÷ 10,001 X 25,000 = 5^X 10^y; find the value of $\left(\frac{x+y}{x-y}\right) - 4xy$

.

17. What fraction of all the numbers starting from 1 to 1000 are multiples of 121?

18. Mohanlal planted saplings at a uniform interval of 20 m alongside a stretch of 2 km 40 m long road. Find the number of saplings used by Mohanlal for this purpose.

19. Sum total of three consecutive number is equal to 3,0003. Find all the numbers.

20. Speed of a boat while moving against river stream is 2 m/s. That boat moves along stream at an average speed of 18 m/s. Speed of stream is less than the stream of the boat. Calculate the actual seed of that boat.

21. Is there any pair of number having LCM 1331 and HCF 169?

22. How many five digit numbers are there in all/

23. What least number should be subtracted from five digit greatest number to obtain a multiple of 8?

Worksheet 51

1: Find out fraction of the following which is shaded.

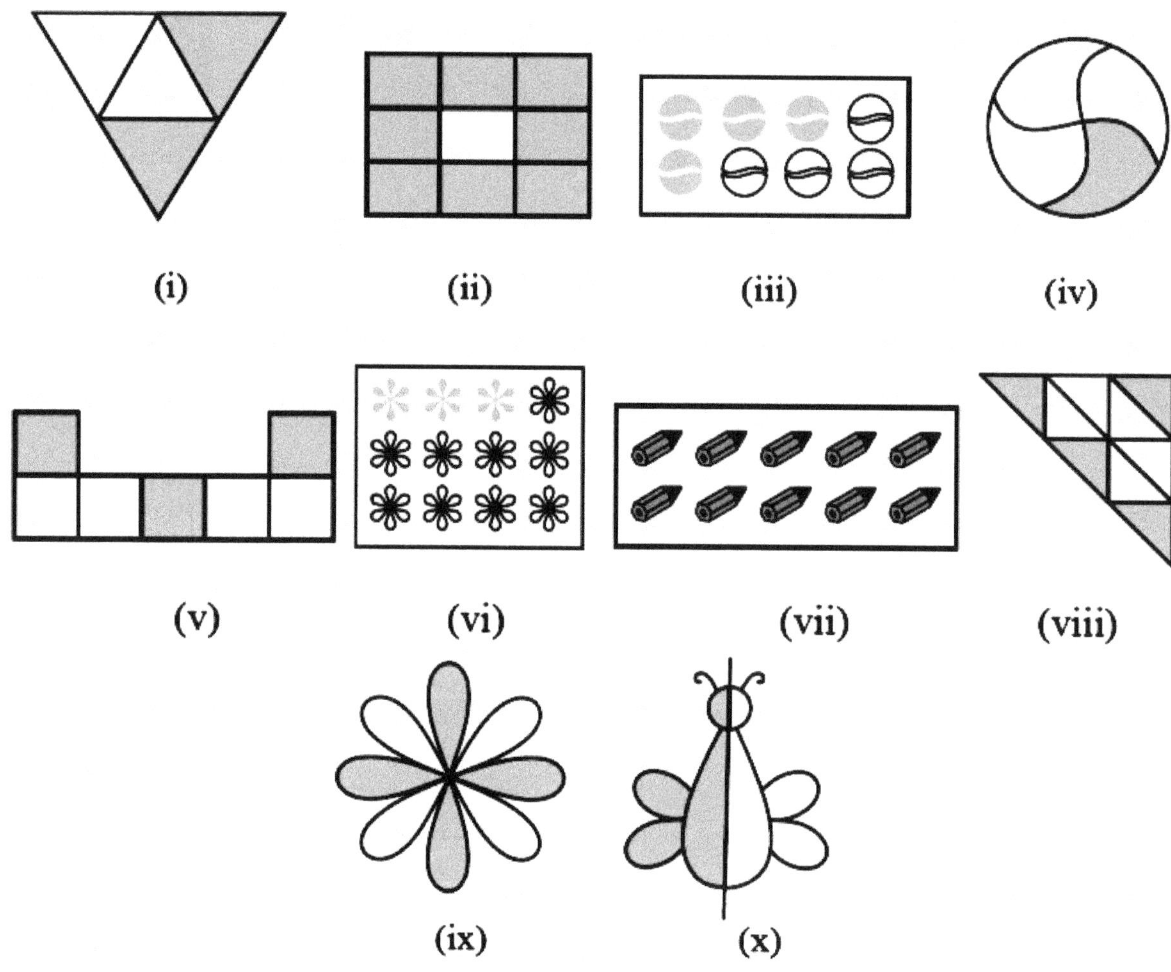

2: Find values of x in each of the following.

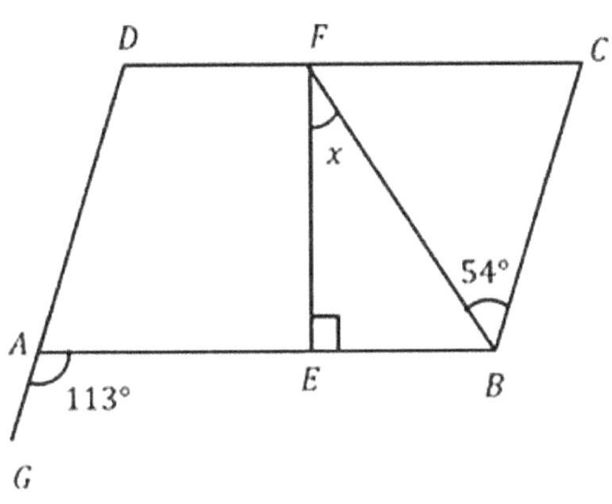

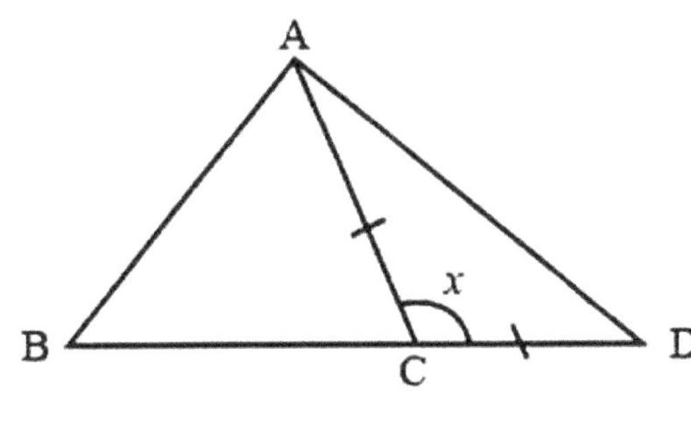

____________________ ____________________

3. A frog jumps 3 steps at a time starting from 0. Count the jumps he takes to reach 27. So, he has taken 27÷ 3 = ______ jumps. He has taken _________ jumps, if he is at 36. If he is at 42, he has taken _______ jumps.

4. Pandelonia wants 1850 sacks of cement for making a house. A truck carries the maximum load of 250 sacks at a time. How many trips will the truck make for carrying all the sacs of cement? The fellow driver charges ` Rs 900 for a trip. How much will Pandelonia pay the driver for all the trips?

5: Meera made 204 candles to sell in the market. She makes packets of 6. How many packets will she make? If she packs them in packets of 12, then how many packets will she make?

6: Tamanna used a box having capacity of holding 16 sweets for packing all the 3280 sweets. She needs _____ boxes of such types for packing all the sweets.

Worksheet 52

1: Area of each of the unit square is 36 sq. cm. Compare outer boundary of the following grids.

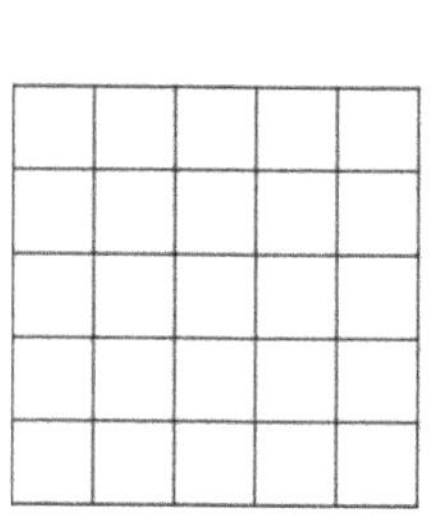

Shape P

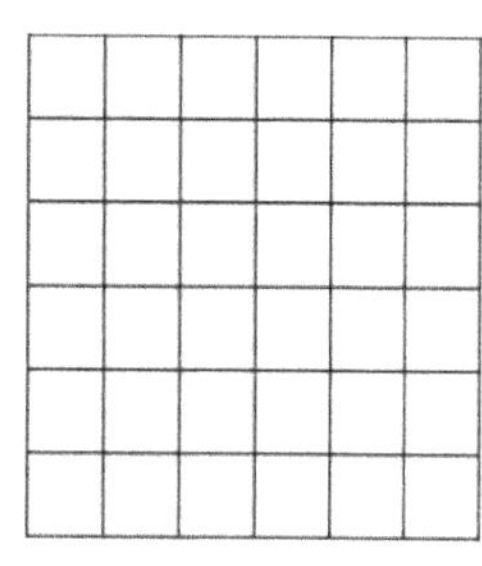

Shape Q

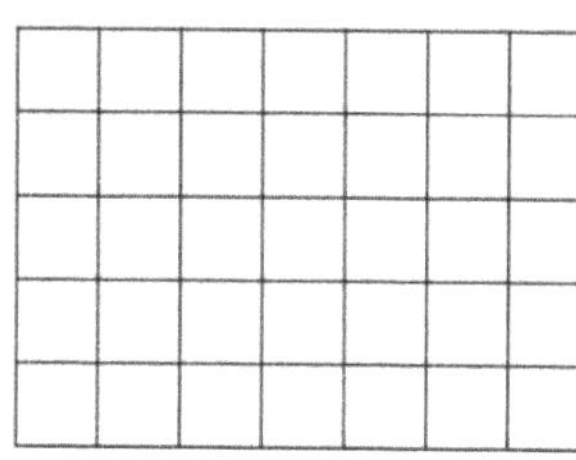

Shape R

2: Rijuana painted a wall in six days. Somalia can paint the same wall in four days. If they work jointly then the painting of a wall can be finished in .... days.

3: 3/4th of Snehal's money is equal to 4,800. Snehal and Nikita has equal amount of money. What will be 2/5th of Nikita's Money?

4: Solve the following:

$\frac{2}{3} X \frac{3}{4} X \ldots.\left(1+\frac{1}{10{,}000}\right) X\ 11{,}055\ X\ 0.5 =$ ....

5: Find the smallest number which can be subtracted from the greatest number of six digits to make the value divisible by 4.

6: Is there any pair of number having a common multiple 55 and a common factor 9?

7: Write in standard form: $\frac{11}{100}+\frac{101}{1000}+\frac{1001}{10000}+121+\frac{7}{10}=$ ....

8: What fraction of all the numbers starting from 1 to 1200 are multiples of 120?

9. Square root of 144 + cube root 125 + 10^8 = ...

10. Find the difference of greatest and smallest numbers formed by using different digits without repeating any of the digits.

11. A bell rings at an interval of 2 seconds. Another bell rings at a uniform interval of 3 seconds. Both the bells toll together at a uniform interval of ……….. seconds.

12. What fraction of the following grid is shaded?

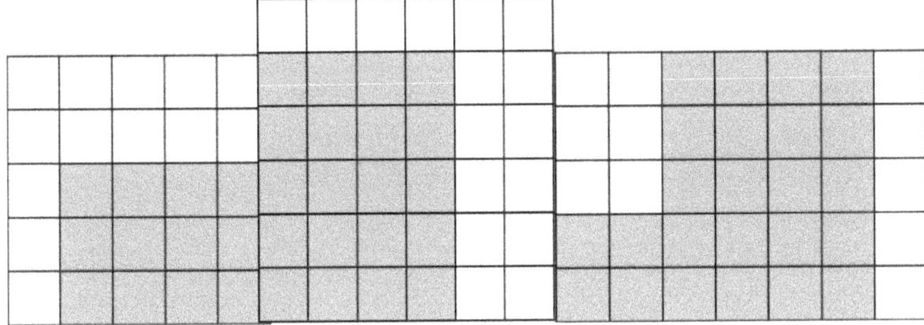

13. Sum total of three consecutive even numbers is equal to 66. Find the numbers.

14. After increasing 20% price of a product is further reduced by 20%. Calculate total increase or decrease of the price.

15: Sum total of two digits of a two digit number is 9. After altering digits another number is formed which exceeds the original number by 63. Sum total of both the number is 99. Find the original number.

16: What fraction of all the numbers starting from 1 to 500 are multiples of 25?

17: Total cost of 4 pens and 3 pencil is equal to Rs 167. Total cost of 3 pens and 4 pencils is equal to Rs 63. Find total cost 14 pens and 14 pencils.

18: 4/13th of 39,065 + 5/11th of 33,055 = ……… X 3,005

19. Somalwar works 8 hours a day to finish a project work in 14 days. He preferred working 7 hours a day. Calculate additional days needed to finish his project works.

20. What fraction of each of the following is shaded?

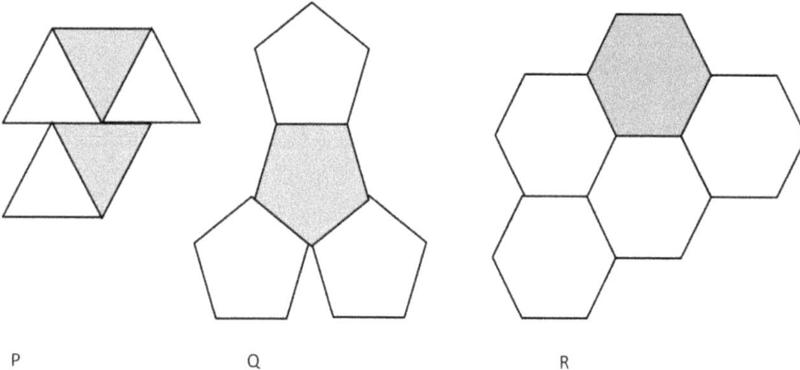

21. $\frac{11}{12} X \frac{12}{13} X \frac{13}{14}\ X \ldots \ldots \left(1 + \frac{1}{20{,}000}\right)\ X \frac{19}{209}\ X\ 40{,}080 =$ ……

22: The greatest and the smallest numbers of four digits are formed by using digits 4,3, 8 and 9. Find difference of both the numbers.

23. It was 11:20 p.m. when Jobelina reached home after spending 1hr 25 minutes of journey. When did she board the vehicle?

24. An apple costs 1/3rd of a papaya. Somanthika took three apples and a papaya by paying Rs 72. Find total cost of 5 apples and 3 papaya.

25. $\frac{1}{13}$ *of* 26,091 + $\frac{2}{15}$ *of* 30,105 + $\frac{1}{7}$ *of* 14,049 = ...

26. What fraction of all the numbers starting from 100 to 200 are multiples of 20?

27. Greatest and smallest numbers of five digits are formed by using digits 9, 3, 8. 5 and 2. Find the difference of both the numbers.

28. two hands of a clock form right angle with respect to each other at 3:35 p.m. After what time interval do they form right angle with respect to each other? How many times in an hour do they form right angle with respect to each other?

29. Length of a rectangle exceeds its breadth by 29 cm. If outer boundary of that shape is equal to 258 then find area of that rectangle.

30. 0.1 + 0.101 + 1.001 + 11.001 + 101.101 = ...

31. $\left(1+\frac{1}{10}\right) X \left(1+\frac{1}{11}\right) X \ldots.\left(1+\frac{1}{9999}\right) X \frac{1001}{10,000}$ =........................

32: Rijuana finishes a project work in 40 days. Smitha alone can finish it in 60 days. Both of them jointly can finish the same project in .... Days.

33. 11/13th of 65,078 + 12/19th of 95,114 = ... X 5,006

34. (1 + 2 + ... + 10) = 11 X ....

35. Represent shaded portions by using decimals and fractions.

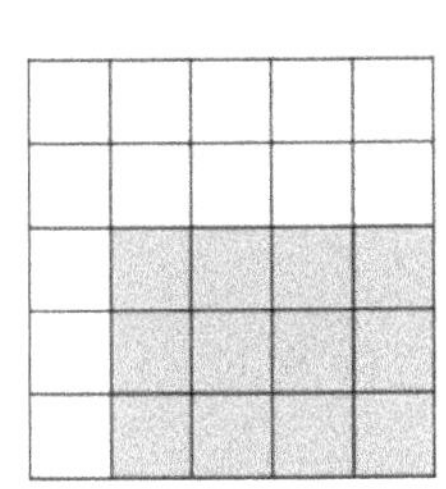

Shape P

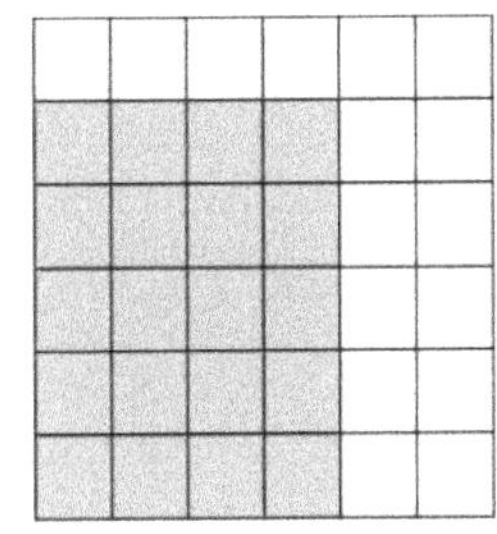

Shape Q

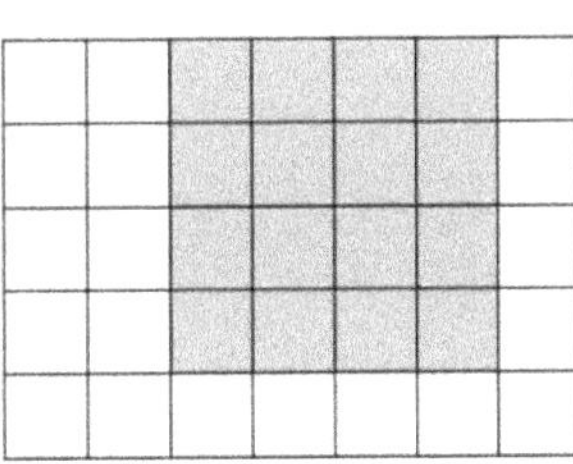

Shape R

36. Rijuana finished a project activity in 14 days while working 8 hours a day. She can finish the same project work in .... days while working 7 hours a day.

37. 11/17th of 34,051 + 12/19th of 38,057 = ... X 2,003.

Worksheet 53

1: If the following pattern continues then number of cubes used to represent tenth pattern will be ……………

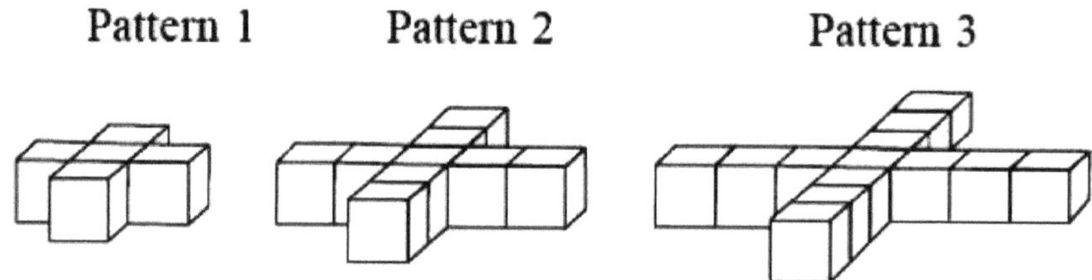

2. Find out value of variables in each of the following.

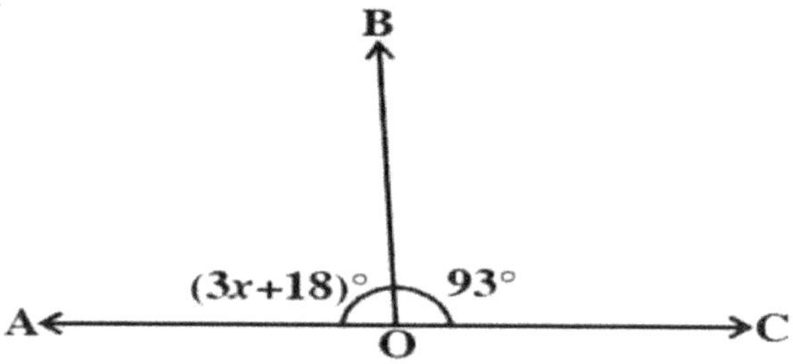

B, A, C, O, $(3x+18)^\circ$, 93°

(i)

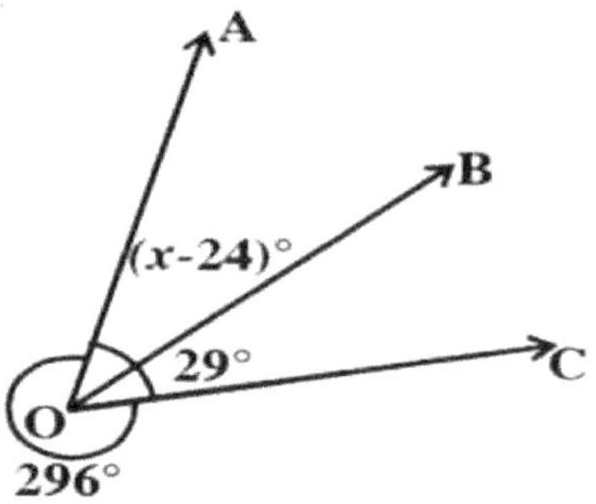

A, B, C, O, $(x-24)^\circ$, 29°, 296°

(ii)

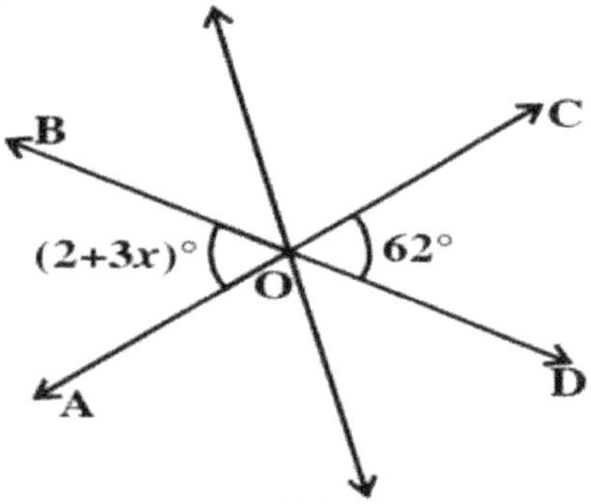

B, C, A, D, O, $(2+3x)^\circ$, 62°

(iii)

A, B, C, O, 40°, $(6x+2)^\circ$

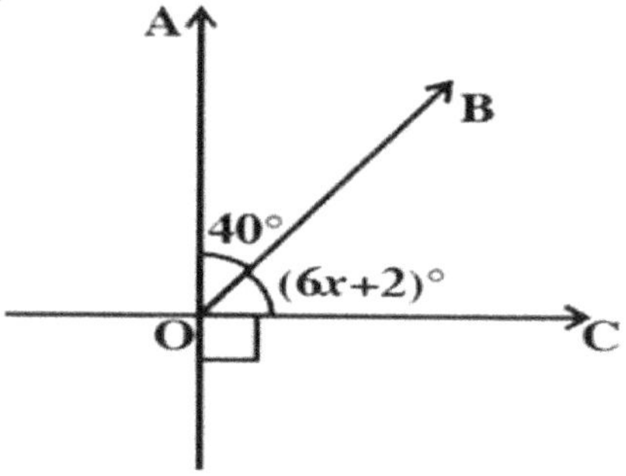

(iv)

3. A passenger train spends 1 m 32 seconds to cross a passenger standing on a platform and spends 8 m 48 seconds to cross 4 km 360 m long tunnel. Calculate average speed and length of the train.

[Ans: length = 932 m; speed 36 km/h.]

4. Half of a quarter of a natural number exceeds five digit smallest number by 1001. Find out the number.

5. Find out x, y and z in the following.

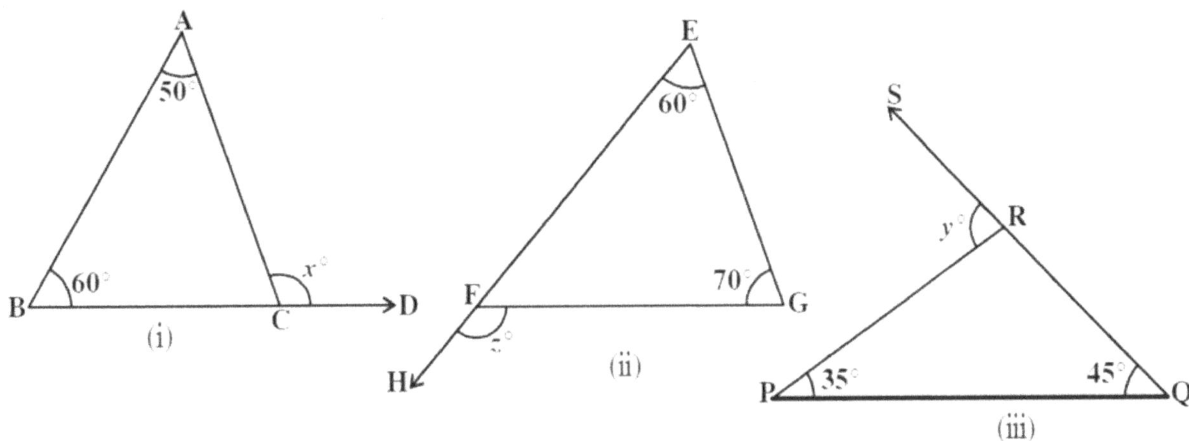

6. Half of a natural number exceeds sixth multiple of smallest six digit number by sixteen thousand six. Find out fourth multiple of that number.

7. Three interior angles of a triangle are in the ratio of 2: 3:4. Find out supplement of the greatest number.

8. Three sides measuring 3 cm, 4 cm and 9 cm were provided to construct a triangle. Find out greatest possible length of the greatest side and smallest possible length of the smallest side for ensuring construction of a triangle.

9. What least number should be added to sum of greatest five digit number and smallest six digit number to obtain a common multiple of 3 and 9.

10. Find out volume.

1.

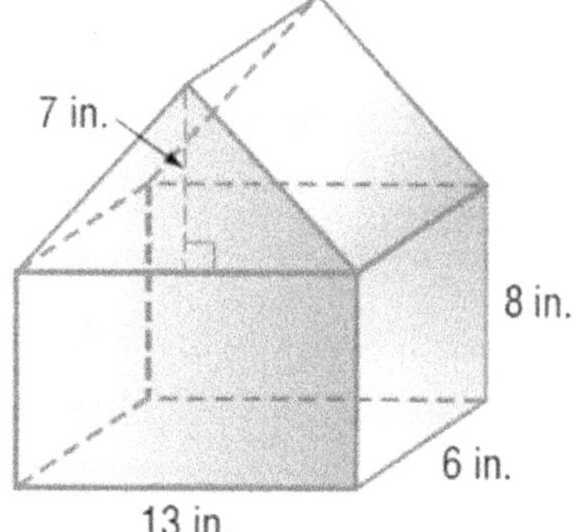

2.

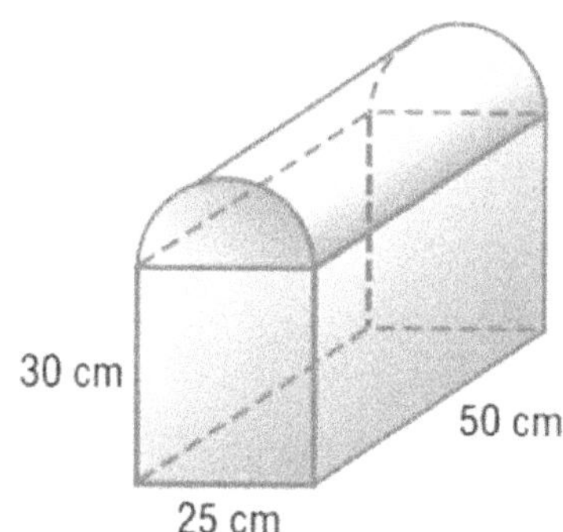

3.

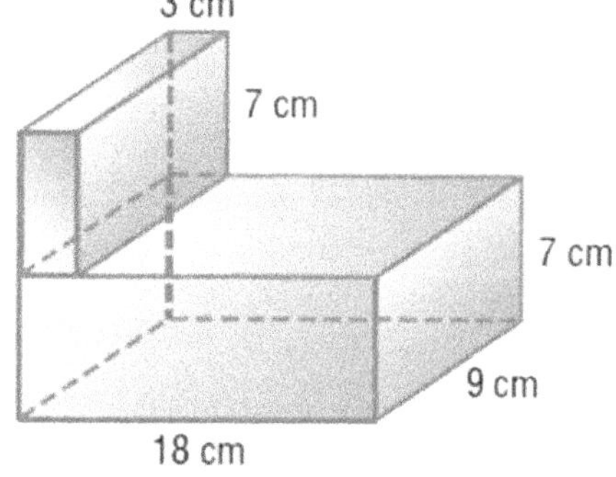

4.

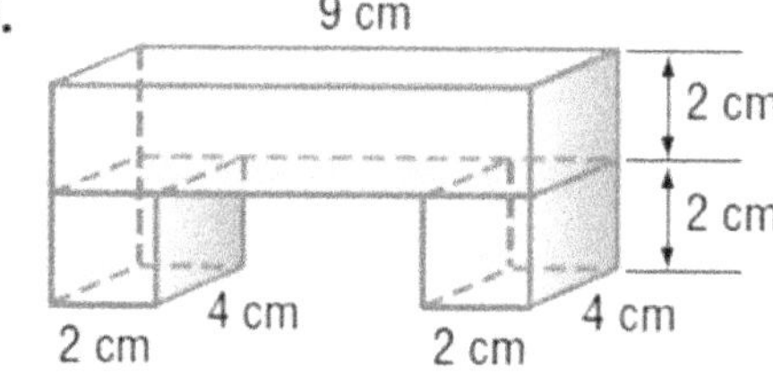

11. How any three digit numbers can be made by using digits 2, 6 ans9 only once for each number?

12. How many three digit numbers are there in all?

13. How many times do 7 occur if we write all the numbers starting from 1 to 100?

14. Four interior angles of a quadrilateral are in the ratio of 3: 4: 5: 6. Find out supplementary angle of the greatest interior angle.

15. Reciprocal of three variables x, y and z are in the ratio of 4: 5: 6. Find out simplest ratio of $(x^2 + y^2 + z^2)$ and $(xy + yz + zx)$.

16. What fraction of all the natural numbers starting from 1 to 1000 are multiples of 125?

17. Is there any pair of number having HCF 19 and LCM 12321?

18. If 125 X 8 = 1,000 and 25 X 40 = 1,000 ; then find the value of 121X 125 X 40 X 8 X 25

19. If 11 X 11 = 121 and 111 X 111 = 12321 then find the product of 1,111,111X 1,111,111

20. Cistern A can fill up a water tank in 40 minutes. Cistern B can fill it up in 60 minutes. Find the time taken by both the cisterns to fill up the water tank if they work jointly.

21. Mohanlal can paint a piece of poster in 6 days while working 2 hours a day. He preferred working 3 hours a day for finishing three such paintings. Find the number of days taken by Mohanlal to finish the work.

22. Mrs Jenna travelled half of the distance while moving back from the countryside by bus, half of the remaining distance was covered by her along with other friends in by car. She travelled half of the remaining distance by auto. She covered last portion of 1.5 km simply by walking. Find out the distance of her farm house in km.

23. Chintawar can solve 49 mathematical problems while doing self-study for 1h 4 minutes. How many problems can be solved by Chintawar while doing self-study for 56 minutes? In such a way how many problems can be made by him in a fortnight?

24. A car driver increases the average speed of a car by 10% to save 40 minutes while moving through a highway of 120 km. What was the original speed of that car?

25. Consider p as a natural number. $(p^0 + p^1 + p^2 + \ldots\ldots p^{10,000}) = 10,000$; What is the value of p?

26. Mathematics teacher of a school took her 9th standard students to show Red fort. It was a part of their Educational trip. The teacher had interest in history as well. She narrated the facts of Red fort to students. Then the teacher said in this monument one can find combination of solid figures. There are 2 pillars which are cylindrical in shape. There are two domes at the corners which are hemispherical. There are 7 smaller domes at the centre. Flag hoisting ceremony on Independence Day takes place near these domes.

I: Find lateral surface area of 2 pillars having height 7 m and base 1.4 m.

II: Volume of hemisphere having radius of base equal to 3.5 m.

27. Sum total of three consecutive numbers is equal to 306. All the numbers are greater than smallest three digit numbers. Find the numbers.

28 . $\frac{3x}{4a} = \frac{5y}{7b} = \frac{9z}{11c}$; .calculate simplest value of $\frac{(3x)^3 + (5y)^3 + (9z)^3}{604\,abc}$.

29. Quarter of a natural number exceeds ix digit smallest number by 1004. Find out sum of predecessor and successor of that number.

30. Half of a quarter of number is equal to 16,096. Find the fifth multiple of that number.

31 A shopkeeper gained an amount equal to selling price of one cake after selling six cakes. Find out his gain percentage.

32: What least number should be subtracted from six digit smallest multiple of 9 to obtain a common multiple of 2, 4 and 8?

33. $(169 - 13x + x^2)(1 + x^2 + x^3 + \ldots. + x^{1009}) = 0$. Calculate value of x.

34. One sixth of a natural number exceeds smallest seven digit number by 10,001. Find out the number.

35. The measures of the angles of a triangle are in the ratio 4 : 5 : 9. Identify the type of triangle.

Worksheet 54

1: Represent the following grid in the form of fraction, decimal and percentage.

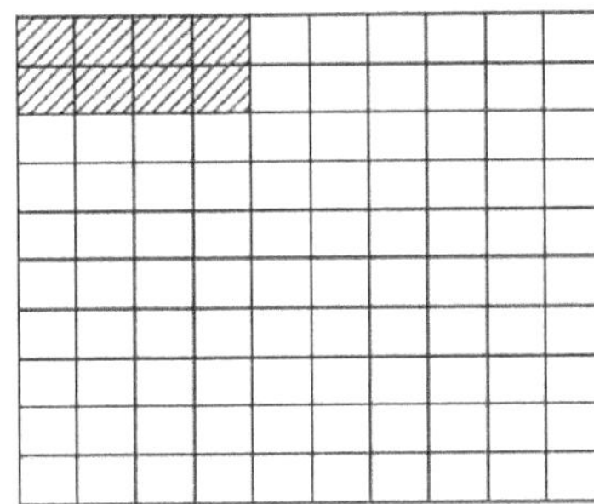

2: Complete the following statement.

All positive numbers are represented on the right side of zero and all negative numbers are represented on the left side of the zero on the…………….. …………….. Let us say 2 is represented on the right side of zero and 2 units away from zero.

3: The LCM and the HCF of two numbers are 96 and 12, respectively. If one of the numbers is 24, then find the other number.

4. Find the least positive integer that should be multiplied to 720 so that the product obtained is a perfect square.

5. Monika covers a certain distance in 250 min. He covers half of the distance in 4/18 of the time. Find the time taken to cover the remaining distance.

6. A family requires 4.2 L of milk every day. Find the total quantity of milk required in a month of 31 days.

7. Simplify: 44.4444… − 27.2727… + 3.333….

8. $P = \sqrt{6 - \sqrt{6 - \sqrt{6 \ldots . \propto}}}$ $\quad Q = \sqrt{20 - \sqrt{20 - \sqrt{20 \ldots . \propto}}}$

Calculate the value of ((P+Q) (P – Q)

9. Find the greatest number that exactly divides 81, 144 and 162.

10. If $p = (-1)^{205}$ and $q = (-1)^{202}$, then $(p + q)(p - q) + 4pq$ is ....

11. A has to travel a certain distance. If he travels three fifth of the distance on a day and the rest the next day, then what part of the distance has he travelled on the second day?

(a) 3/5 (b) 2/5 (c) 1/5 (d) 4/5

12. X is the smallest four-digit number formed by all the digits 0, 7, 8, and 9. Y is the greatest four-digit number formed by all the digits 0, 7, 8 and 9. Find Y − X.

13. Calculate outer boundary of the following if area of unit squares is 16 sq. cm.

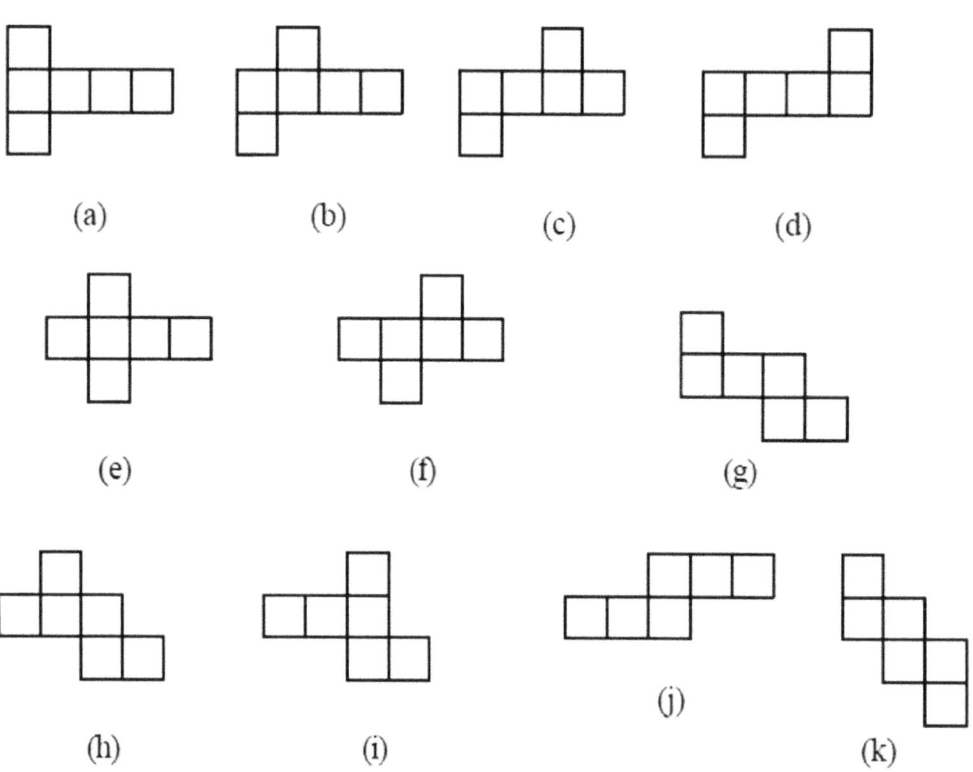

14. Find out missing angles in each of the following.

a.

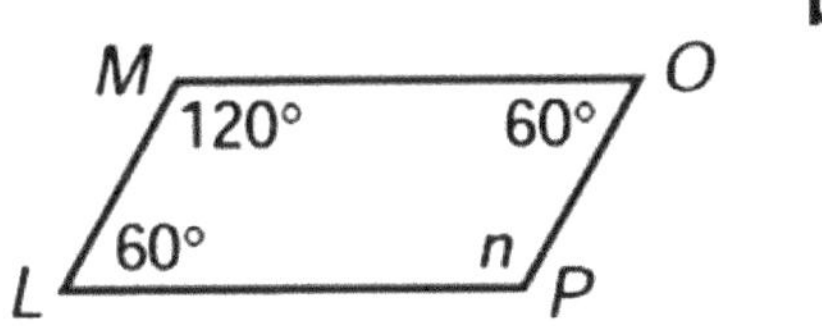

b.

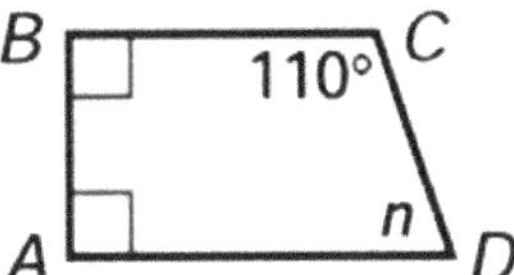

c.

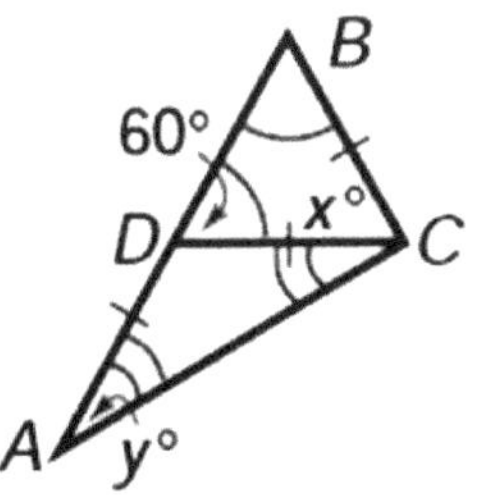

d.

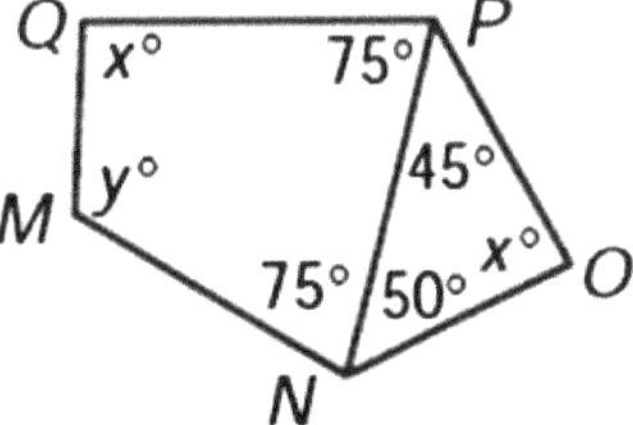

e.

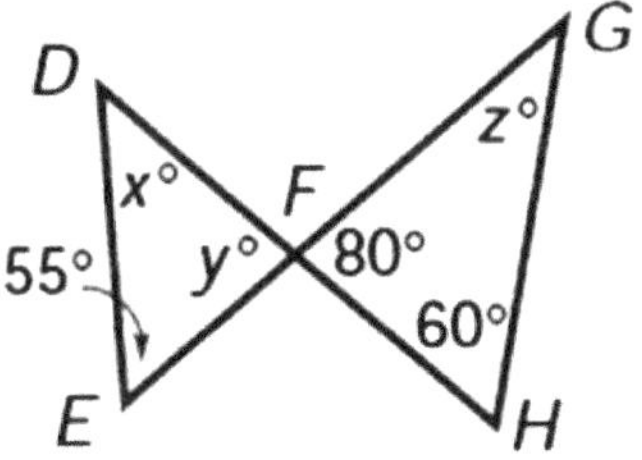

f.

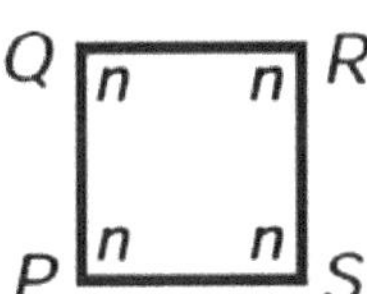

15. Calculate area of shaded portions in A and B and Outer boundary in the composite shape C..

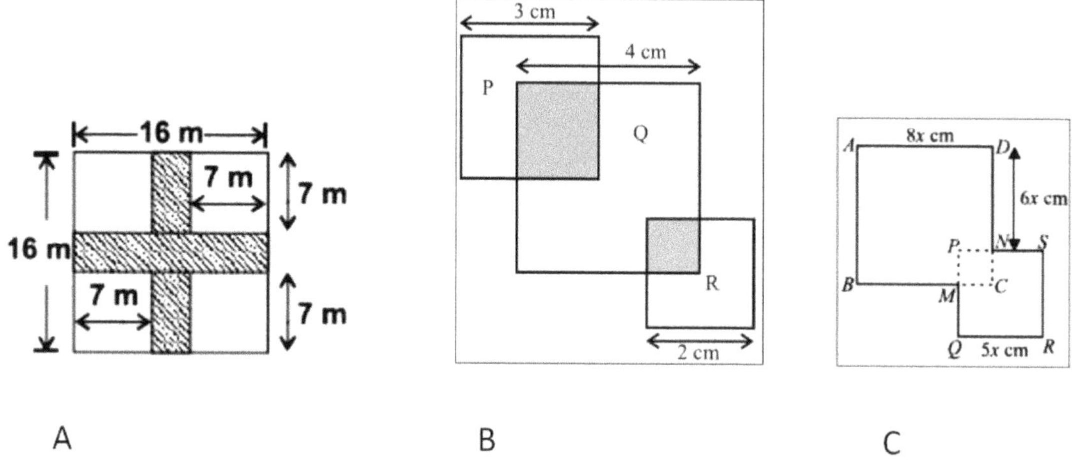

16. Snehal prepared a five digit greatest and six digit smallest number without repeating any digits. Find sum of these two numbers.

17. 1/9th of 81,81,081 + 1/7th of 63,63,063 = ...

18. Mathematics teacher of a school took her 9th standard students to show Gol Gumbaz. It was a part of their Educational trip. The teacher had interest in history as well. She narrated the facts of Gol Gumbaz to students. Gol Gumbaz is the tomb of king Muhammad Adil Shah, Adil Shah Dynasty. Construction of the tomb, located in Vijayapura , Karnataka, India, was started in 1626 and completed in 1656. It reaches up to 51 meters in height while the giant dome has an external diameter of 44 meters, making it one of the largest domes ever built. At each of the four corners of the cube is a dome shaped octagonal tower seven stories high with a staircase inside.

(a) What is the total surface area of a cuboid? (i) lb + bh + hl (ii) 2(lb + bh + hl) (iii) 2(lb + bh) (iv) $l^2 + b^2 + h^2$

(b) What is the curved surface area of hemispherical dome ?

(c) What is the height of the cuboidal part ?

(d) Circumference of the base of the dome = ………………

19. Identify and select suitable names for the following.

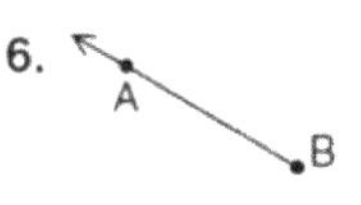

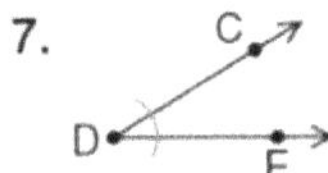

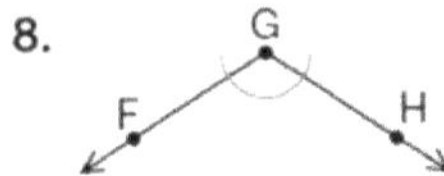

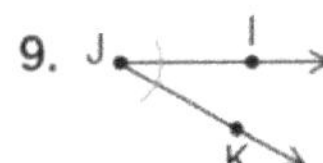

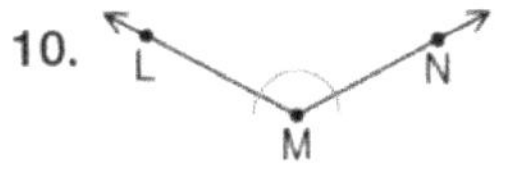

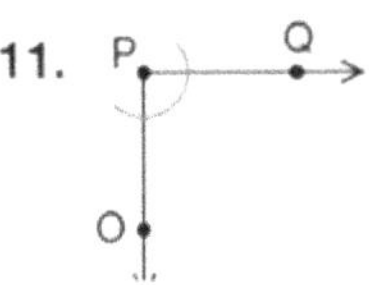

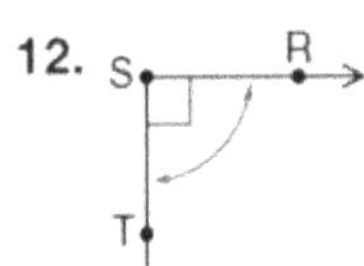

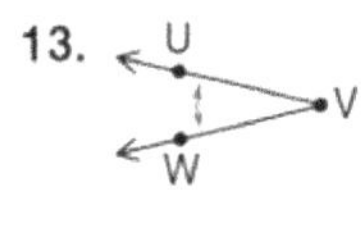

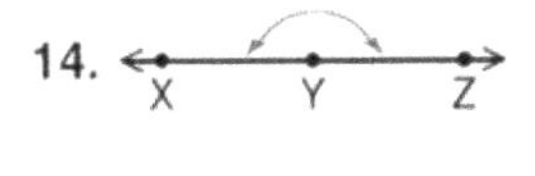

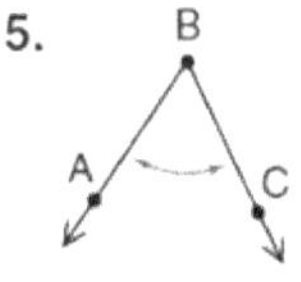

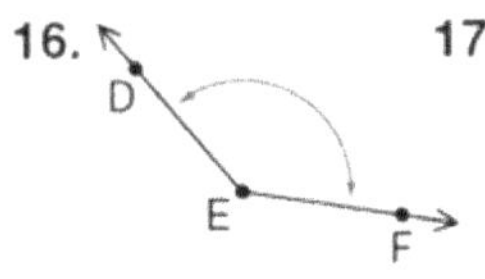

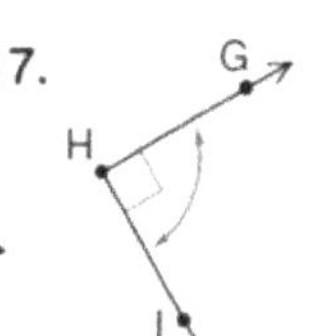

18. J K L

22. (5.555… + 4.444….) – 8.888… = ………………

23. $A = \sqrt{72 - \sqrt{72 - \sqrt{72 - \sqrt{72 \ldots \propto}}}}$ Calculate simplest value of the expression $(A^2 + A - 72)(A^{81} - 9^{72})(A^{31} - 81)$

24. Calculate area of the following:

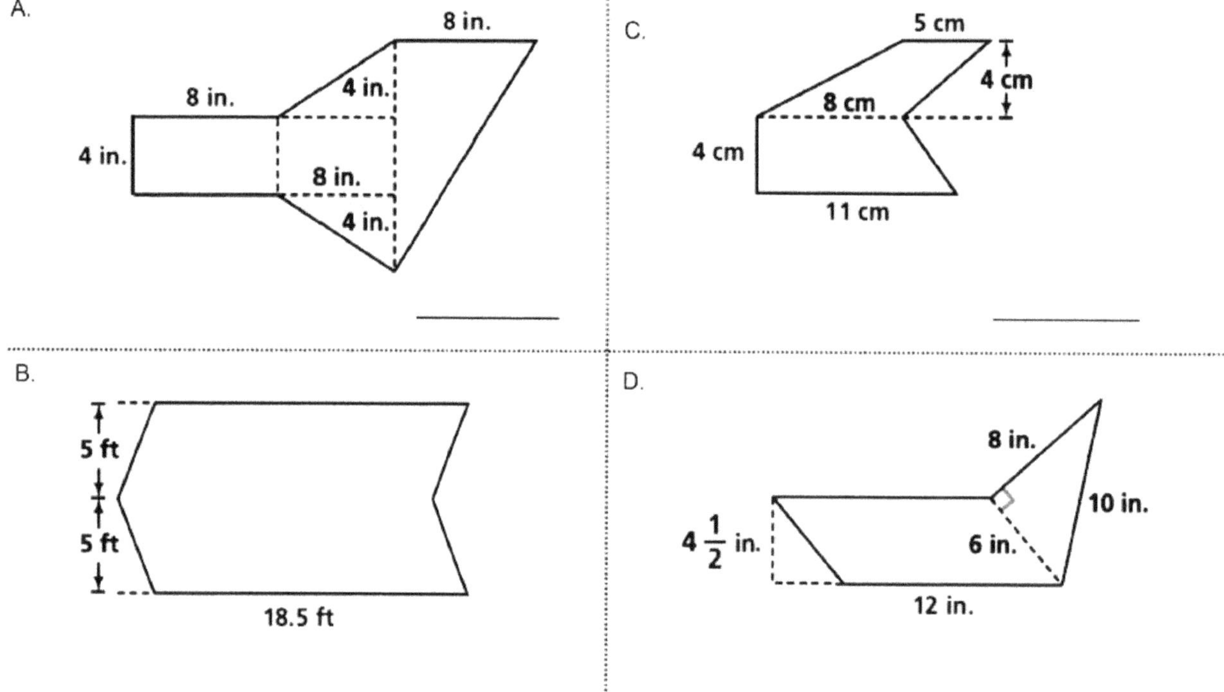

25: 10% of 40% of a number is equal to 2,009. Find sum total of one fifth and 20% of that number.

26: 21 tens + 2201 thousandths + 101 tenths = ... (Standard form)

27. What number and its reciprocal returns a sum of 8. 125?

28: Supplementary angle of 9^0 54’ = ...

Worksheet 55

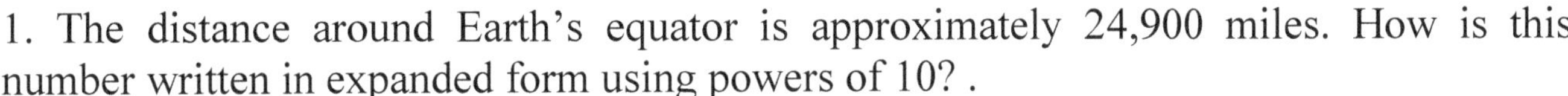

1. The distance around Earth's equator is approximately 24,900 miles. How is this number written in expanded form using powers of 10? .

2. Write each in expanded form using exponents.

a. 3 millionths b. 6 hundredths c. 9 thousandths d. 4 hundred thousandths

3. What fraction of a year is equal to 2 fortnights?

4. What smallest number should be subtracted from 5 digit greatest number to make the value divisible by 11?

5. Nandanwar can cover a distance of 60 m in 6 seconds and Sangitika runs at an average speed of 36 km per hour. If they start running together then who will finish the race of 200 m first ?

6. 20 tens + 20 hundredths + 20 thousands = ________________.

7. 20% of 30% of one sixth of 1,100 = _____________.

8. 30% of 50% of 2,008 = ……………………

9. Nine students gave oral reports for their science project. Of those reports, three were each 18 minutes 7 seconds long and the rest were each 5 minutes 15 seconds long. How long did it take for all the reports to be given?

10. What least number should be subtracted from 21,021,092 to obtain a multiple of 5?

11. Three tenth + 21 hundredths + 302 thousandths = ………………

12. 1/5th of 15% of 10,20,300 = ……………..

Worksheet 56

1: What fraction of the given grid is shaded?

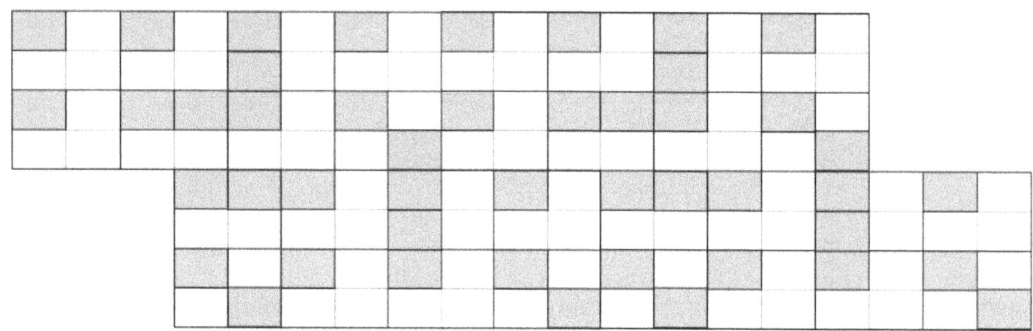

2. Represent shaded portion by using a suitable fraction.

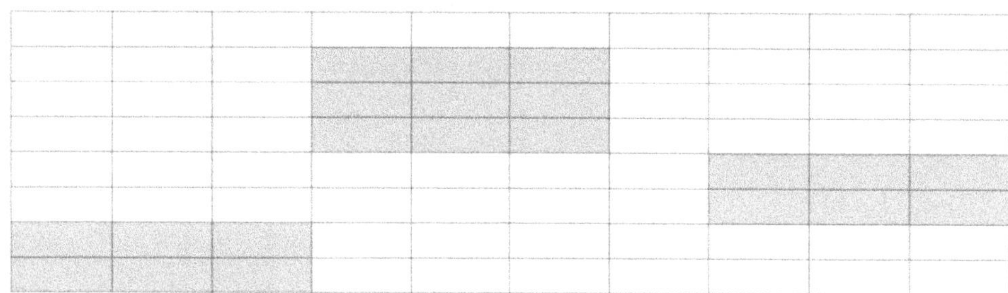

3. $P = \sqrt{6 + \sqrt{6 + \sqrt{6 + \cdots .\propto}}}$; $Q = \sqrt{24 + \sqrt{24 + \sqrt{24 + \cdots .\propto}}}$;

Calculate the simplest value $(P + Q)(P - Q - 1)$

4. Factorise $x^4 + x^3 - x^2 - x$.

5. $A = (3p - 7)$ and $B = (9p^2 + 21p + 49)$. Calculate simplest value of the expression: $(AB - 27p^3 + 49)$.

6. $3x = 4y = 5z$; calculate simplest value of $(x^3 + y^3 + z^3) \div 180\ xyz$.

7. Four interior angles of a quadrilateral are in the ratio of 1:2:3:4. Find out supplementary angle of the greatest interior angle.

8. $(x^{32} - 121)(x^{16} - 169)(x^2 - 25x + 625) = 0$; $(x^3 - 2x^2 + 50x + 139) = ..$

9. 1/12th of 144 + 1/13th of 169 + 1/15th of 225 + 1/20th of 400 = ...

10: Which of the following is labelled incorrectly?

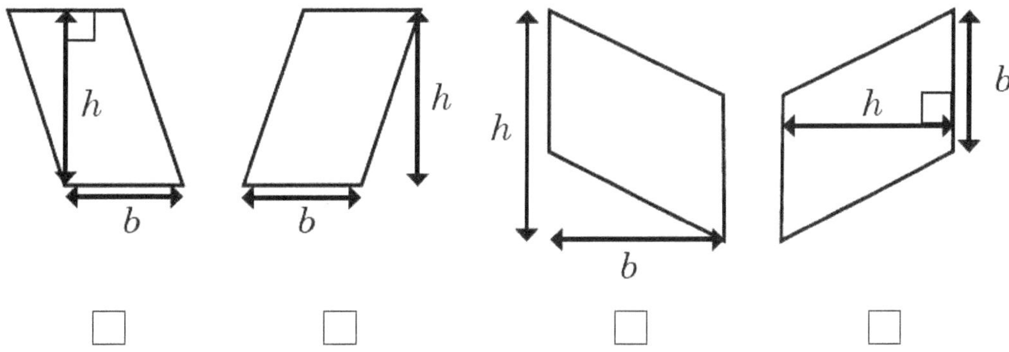

☐ ☐ ☐ ☐

11. After selling 11 cakes a shopkeeper gains an amount equal to selling price of 1 cake. Find out his gain percentage.

12: Roshanlal can paint a wall in 3 days while working 10 hours a day. He preferred working 5 hours a day to finish painting 4 such walls. Calculate total number of days needed to finish painting walls.

13. Sum of a number and its reciprocal is 4.25. Find out 7th multiple of that number.

14: four triangles placed side by side to make a polygon. How many sides are there?

15: Calculate area.

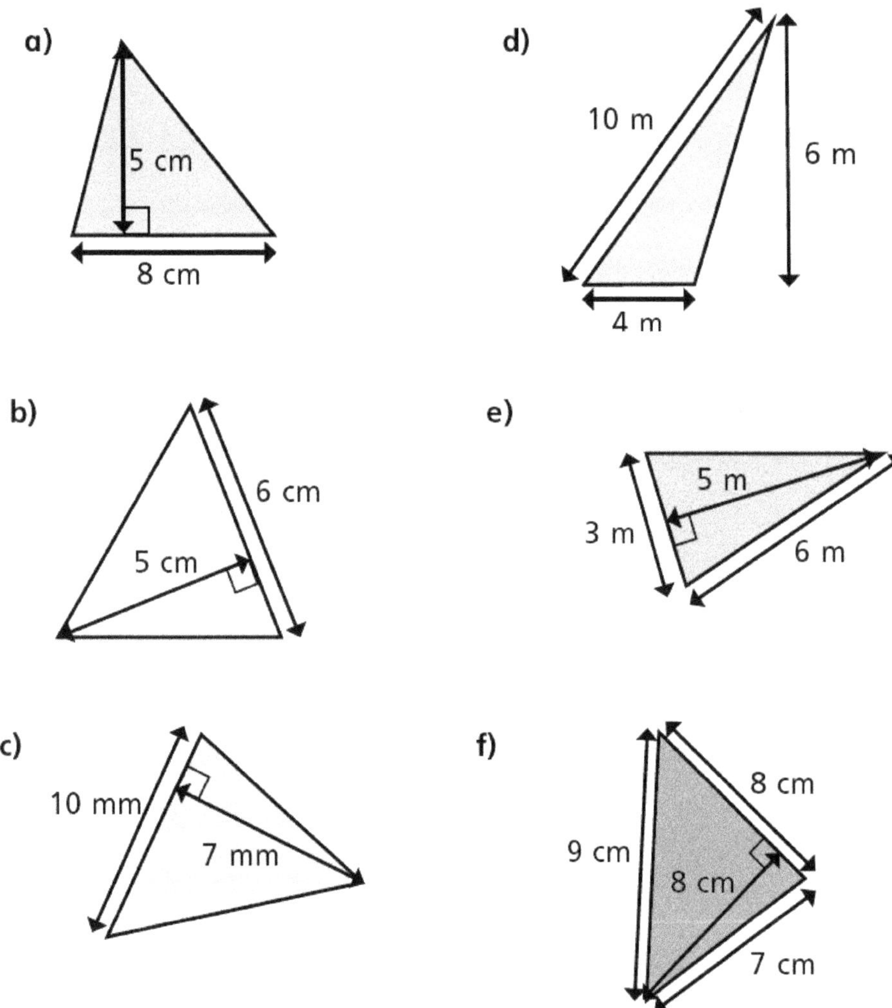

***.

www.ingramcontent.com/pod-product-compliance
Ingram Content Group UK Ltd.
Pitfield, Milton Keynes, MK11 3LW, UK
UKHW062003290726
14090UKWH00022B/1359

9 798889 595083